We Live Forever

The Story of the 'Woman with X-ray Eyes'

ANNE OWEN was born in London, an only child; her parents curiously enough moved shortly afterwards to Chislehurst in Kent, where her husband Peter was born. She says of this, 'We seemed to just not connect with each other, as my first job as a trainee professional photographer was only a short distance away from Peter, where he commenced his engineering training. We often went to the same musical concerts and coffee bars in London's West End without ever quite getting together. Some years later I applied for a post with a publishing company within 500 yards of where Peter was living at the time in Kent; in fact we kept just not meeting each other all our lives – until our dramatic first encounter, since when we have never looked back.' Living between France and England, and mother of two now grown-up children, in her spare time Anne shares her love of flying with Peter, while continuing to enjoy working with people to improve the quality of their lives using her very special abilities.

We Live Forever
The Story of the 'Woman with X-ray Eyes'

Anne Owen
and
Peter Valentine

ATHENA PRESS
LONDON

We Live Forever
The Story of the 'Woman with X-ray Eyes'

Copyright © Anne Owen and Peter Valentine 2008
All Rights Reserved

No part of this book may be reproduced in any form
by photocopying or by any electronic or mechanical means,
including information storage or retrieval systems,
without permission in writing from both the copyright
owner and the publisher of this book.

Every effort has been made to trace the copyright holders of works quoted within this book and obtain permission. The publisher apologises for any omission and is happy to make necessary changes in subsequent print runs.

ISBN: 978 0 7552 1332 0

First published 2008 by Athena Press.

This edition published 2011 by
Bright Pen
19 The Cinques
Gamlingay
Sandy
Bedfordshire
SG19 3NU

www.authorsonline.co.uk

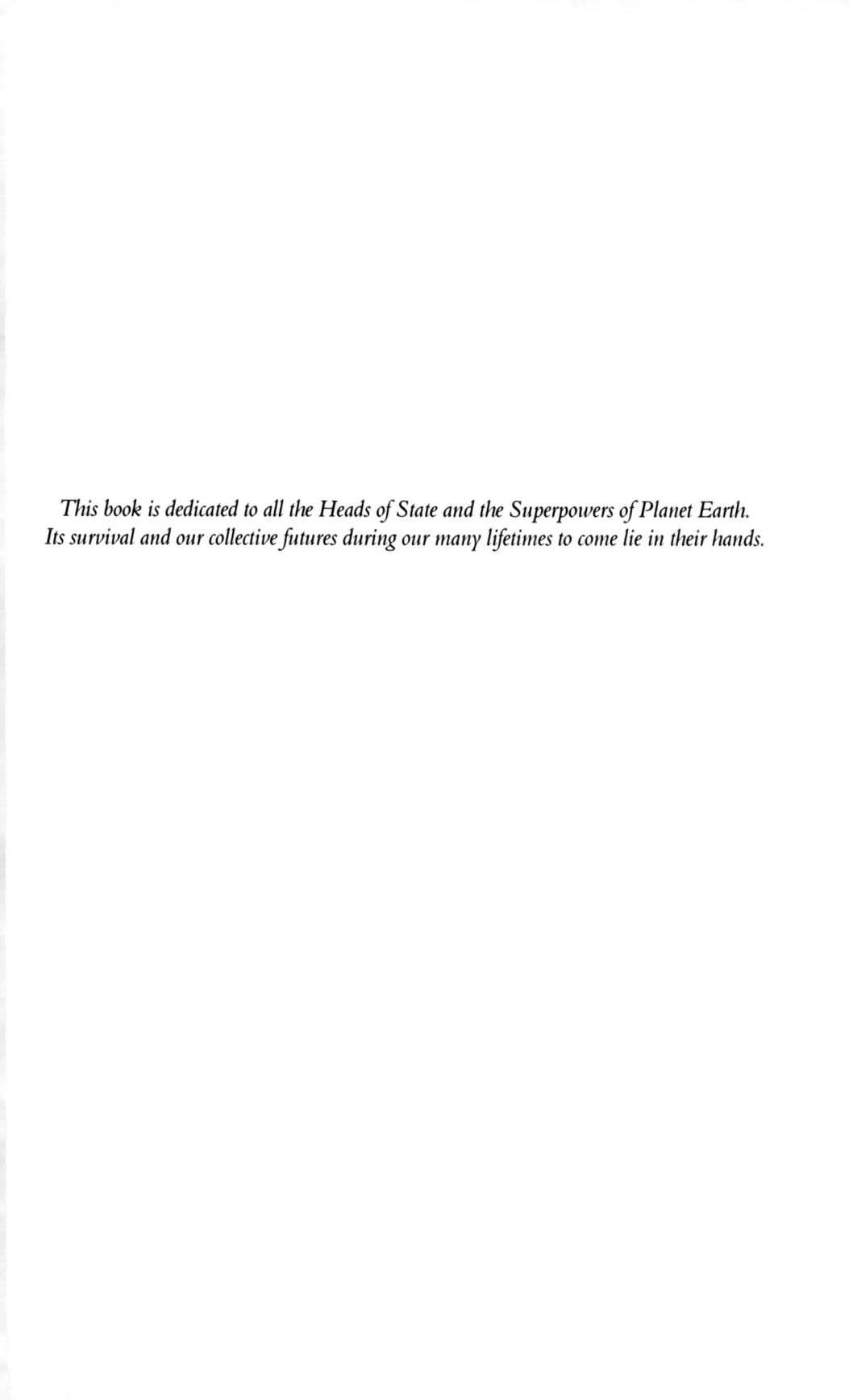

This book is dedicated to all the Heads of State and the Superpowers of Planet Earth. Its survival and our collective futures during our many lifetimes to come lie in their hands.

Acknowledgements

With special acknowledgements to Grahame Payne, Annie Watsham and Michael Wright, whose help and support in the writing of this book have been invaluable.

Out of the Stillness of Vibrant Being
An Island slowed to Understanding
A Jewel in a Sea of Time –
A pause, no more, to grow and learn
And then return from whence thou came
And know that thou hast been.

                                                                   Anon

Anne as her clients know her

Contents

Chapter 1:	My Eyes the X-ray	13
Chapter 2:	The Wheel that Almost Came Off	21
Chapter 3:	Everyone in their True Colours	28
Chapter 4:	Of Little Green Men, UFOs and Strange Lights at Night	39
Chapter 5:	Former Lives – A Deeper Perception	46
Chapter 6:	I Meet Peter	54
Chapter 7:	A Tale of Self-discovery	60
Chapter 8:	Past Lives – Our Heritage	74
Chapter 9:	A Cosmic Crash and the Man in Black	88
Chapter 10:	More on UFOs – I Meet an Abductee	98
Chapter 11:	Time, Ladies and Gentlemen	112
Chapter 12:	Between Two Worlds	119
Chapter 13:	I Can See Through You	129
Chapter 14:	The Party Circuit	139
Chapter 15:	Death on the Party Circuit	150
Chapter 16:	Psychic Detectives	158
Chapter 17:	Zeebrugge – Night of Terror	169
Chapter 18:	Days in the Life of…	181
Chapter 19:	A Clairvoyant Overview	192

List of Illustrations

Anne as her clients know her	Frontispiece
The Chinese artist Tao Chi	70
The eyes that followed Peter everywhere	73
Aftermath	90
ET – *Communion* book cover	110
Plaster cast of the stolen bronze statue by Antonio Sciortino	161
Death by spontaneous human combustion	168
A few samples of press cuttings from some hundreds worldwide	178–180
A note received from Ronnie Kray	186

Chapter 1
My Eyes the X-ray

The lamb lay on its side, eyes glazed, panting. The early June sun warmed the air from a deep azure sky; nearby the drone of a large bumblebee lulled the senses into tranquillity. Above me in the distance the mountains towered; while over the rising pine forests a buzzard soared majestically, its wings unmoving as it rode the upcurrents of the slope.

I turned to look at the lamb again, its distress only too apparent. The Inner Eye with which I had been gifted since childhood showed me, much as an X-ray scanner would, that its neck and shoulder were dislocated. A mental picture in colour appeared in my mind's eye of the displaced neck vertebrae and shoulder tendons. Instinctively I reached down and took its head in my hands. A wrench, and then a click told me I had been successful; now I rolled it over onto its back. To get its shoulder in I had to kneel and straddle the animal; unfortunately, it was weakened by having been caught up in some fencing, which made my task easier. A pull this time; a twist, and with a sigh of relief I felt it go in. I could 'see' that the vertebrae and tendons had returned to where they belonged; however it would take time for the inflamed areas to settle, and for the animal to recover from its weakened condition, a result of not having been able to feed properly.

With a sudden motion it rolled onto its knees, then stiffly stretched its forelegs to stand erect. Without further ado, it commenced to feed.

Kath and Huw stood looking on, amazement and disbelief marching hand in hand across their features. Welsh hill farmers both, of an older generation born and bred to the rigours of the rugged uplands of Snowdonia in North Wales, to them sheep in the condition they had seen didn't normally recover. I found it difficult to explain how I could 'see' what had been wrong; communication was often a problem with these delightful and charming people. They habitually spoke in their native Welsh tongue, but conversed with us in beautifully lilting English, sometimes with difficulty regarding common concepts.

I felt embarrassed as the seeming perpetrator of a miracle. In vain I struggled to explain the working of my 'Inner Eye', to be met with knowing smiles and the occasional averted gaze. It was easier for Peter, my husband, and myself to give up; to accept our hosts' wonderful Welsh hospitality and descend the hill to the charming little old Welsh farmhouse with its great waterwheel reflecting the sunlight, relic of the days before 'the Electric' had reached the hills. Here we could be sure of boundless hospitality: tea from the seemingly limitless pot, impossibly thin slices of buttered Welsh bread with home-made jam; and currant cakes that tasted as only they could to appetites honed razor-sharp by exercise in the keen mountain air.

Nowadays, when people come from all over the world and from all walks of life to see me for readings about everything ranging from enormous business deals to domestic intrigues, I look back with deep affection to those wonderful people of the Snowdonian uplands and valleys, whose hospitality and generosity helped us through those early and difficult days.

We had gone there, Peter and I, to start a new life brought about by the fuel crisis of 1973. My husband's business had suffered a great deal from the depression of those times, and clients were prone to keep their purse strings tightly drawn in the mood of the period. Rumours were rife regarding the drying up of the world's fuel reserves and food supplies. Why not therefore, we asked ourselves, sell up our home in the South, as many others were thinking of doing at the time, and retreat to an entirely different lifestyle, where the pace was slower and overheads reduced? The simple rural life made its appeal in the face of current pressures; but where to go?

Finally a pin decided for us. Reading a national weekly advertising paper, we turned to the property page, where properties were listed by county. More as a joke than anything else, I picked a pin from my workbox, which was conveniently near at the time, looked away and – presto! Under 'Wales', about halfway down… 'Remote cottage for conversion with two acres in Snowdonia; overlooking Conway Valley. Tel…' We telephoned; the price seemed very reasonable. We then discovered that the vendor lived north of Birmingham, and during the conversation were given to understand that a number of other people were interested. After a brief discussion between us, Peter and I decided we must have it – sight unseen! A mad impulse seized us in its grip: perhaps even now others were wending their way, clutching cheques for an outright purchase. We telephoned back confirming we would buy, and that a ten per cent deposit would be delivered the following morning.

As I was unable to go the next day, Peter set off on his own in our little four-seater Dellow sports car. He told me later that the transaction was completed, the property still unseen, after a drive in some of the worst conditions he had ever encountered. Rain apparently lashed down continuously, and the car was buffeted from side to side by gales that swept the country; an apparent omen of things to come.

It was a month before we could view our purchase. On a cold November day with lowering clouds, we reached North Wales and the Conway Valley. Carefully following the map the vendor had sketched for us, we commenced a long climb, the final stages of which consisted of one-in-three gradients with hairpin bends between quaint dry stone walls enclosing magnificent pine forests on either hand. These gradually gave way to vistas of the typical Snowdonian uplands; towering grey crags with snow on the higher tops, and hill pastures of coarse, flattened grasses interspersed with patches of scrub and rocky outcrop where the hardy Welsh mountain sheep grazed.

We turned right through a succession of cattle gates. The narrow track ran parallel to the top of the ridge above us, while to our right below ran a steep pine-covered slope. Suddenly we emerged onto an open, windswept plateau. The track meandered on ahead of us, but our sketch showed a footpath running off to the right. We looked carefully, but could see nothing but a low stone wall in the distance. We followed the directions, and as we approached the wall at an angle, a gateway slowly appeared. Arriving at the opening, a breathtaking panoramic vista spread itself before us of the Conway Valley 1000 feet below. Dense pine forests fell away to the valley floor; on the far side, soft rolling hills, under chequerboard cultivation, disappeared into a misty horizon. Behind us, the landscape changed abruptly, with mountains towering in succession to what we later discovered to be Carnedd Llywelyn – at 3,485 feet the second highest mountain in Snowdonia. Its summit was then wreathed in mists which caught the rays of the setting sun, and the scene presented one of the most dramatic landscapes we had seen anywhere.

Just below us to our right was a delightfully picturesque Welsh cottage, sadly, however, in need of much repair. An air of dereliction surrounded it; the slate roof had collapsed in several places, and where the windows had once withstood the fierce autumn and winter gales were now undistinguished apertures in the stonework, free for bird and beast to enter as they pleased.

Blaen-y-Wern. Romantically named in this way, and meaning 'Hollow-in-the-Hill-by-the-Spring', according to local lore, the mellowed ruin held a mute appeal, as if almost saying, 'Save me and I will warm and shelter you.'

We fell in love with it there and then, Peter and I. We wandered through the rooms, admiring the ancient beams and rafters and the big wide open hearth that must have seen many a warming of hands, raw from working in the harsh winter elements. Outside, from our sketch, with much difficulty, we found our water supply some distance from the house. Almost covered in reeds, which when parted revealed slate slabs surrounding a pool of clear water, the spring completed the picturesque name of our new-found home-to-be.

We left entranced, to return in early summer. We brought with us a caravan behind our Land Rover (no mean feat up those tracks) and settled in to start renovation in earnest. The wonderful friendliness of the Welsh hill people soon manifested itself. Bryn Williams and his son, Will 'Post', who brought our mail to us in all weathers to this remote spot, the gold letters *Post Brenhinoll* – 'Royal Mail' – on the little red van always standing out; a welcome sight in the distance. Then, half a mile away behind some trees, Mrs Griffiths, a wonderful old lady of advancing years who preferred the isolation of the mountains in which to live alone, and who insisted on walking three miles down to the valley and back again just to do her weekly shopping. In vain came offers of assistance from her family, cosily nestling in a centrally heated bungalow in the valley. Born and bred to the hills, nothing could separate her from the rugged uplands of her childhood. Her charm and hospitality were overwhelming; a knock at her door on our part in passing to ask if she wanted any shopping would be met with a stern insistence to enter for tea and a boiled egg, with bread, butter and jam to follow.

The incident of the lamb followed shortly after. Kath and Huw Hughes, local hill farmers, had begun to drop by, taking a keen interest in our progress. The usual warm hospitality of those parts followed. We became seemingly drawn in as part of their family; their charming farmhouse threw a mantle of affection over us that the passing of many years can never diminish.

On our way by one day, Huw mentioned he had found one of his lambs trapped by the neck in some fencing. Due to the prolonged entanglement (some hours), and the animal's struggles to free itself, the dislocation mentioned earlier had occurred. However it seemed to us that their gratitude at the time, well meant though it was, was out of all proportion to what for me was the use of an ability I'd had since an early age.

I can remember when I was sixteen or so and in my first job as a photographer's assistant. A lady client had come in complaining of a headache. Almost before I could stop myself I found I had seated her in a chair, taken hold of her head and gently stretched her neck, turning it at the same time. There was a slight click, and she got up looking surprised, rubbing her hand over the affected area. 'I don't believe it – it's gone!' she said in amazement. 'I've had headaches on and off for nearly five years now, and nothing has ever been able to get rid of them.' Still shaking her head in surprise, she left.

At the time, the significance of the incident never occurred to me. It seemed so natural, without thought almost, that what had taken place was hardly cause for comment. However, word of 'the girl at the photographer's' soon got around, and during the remaining months that I was there, a gradually increasing number of people would call, ostensibly for photographic enquiries. At some point they would complain of a headache, and I was called upon to do my party piece. My boss was very good about this, and even better when he found his business was increasing because of it!

I can remember mental flashes of things like displaced tendons and vertebrae as I was manipulating from time to time. I tended to dismiss these as fantasy, until one day I happened to see a medical illustration of the same part of the human body that exactly coincided with one of the mental impressions I had received earlier that day. I suddenly associated the two, and found that when I worked from that point on with people I could 'see' the medical problem or problems associated with that person. However, sadly I found no one with whom I could discuss these experiences. At that time, in the early fifties, there was far more ridicule of and resistance to psychic matters generally. These things were thought to be anything from 'not quite nice' to downright wicked, so I found it better to keep my own counsel. Much later, I managed to meet many people who were not only sympathetic, but gifted in their own right; but in those days I learned to keep a low profile.

As on that far-off day at the photographers, word soon got around the Welsh community. I had mentioned to Huw after manipulating the lamb that I was far more used to working with people than animals. *'Diew,'* Huw said with an inscrutable twinkle in his eye, 'you'll have to be looking at our Davydd then, won't you?'

The following day, Peter and I were seated at the tea table with the Hughes, indulging in another of those never-to-be-forgotten teas. It was a cold day outside with a high wind; through the window I could see the tops of the pines bending well over, with a backdrop of lowering clouds scudding across the late afternoon sky. A car arrived with the first flurry of rain, pulling up in front of the farm. 'You'll be meeting Davydd now,' said Kath with her endearing lilt. 'You'll remember what Huw told you yesterday.'

Davydd came in. He was a short, stocky pleasant individual, but obviously in some discomfort as he carried his head slightly to one side. He had a pronounced limp, and lines of strain showed around his eyes. His wife Vi fussed around him; obviously a very anxious and caring person. I could see at a glance that he had some form of spinal displacement; my inner vision was also telling me that that it had been in this condition for some time, probably due to ill-advised lifting of something heavy. After the usual pleasantries had been exchanged, he confirmed what I had diagnosed. In his capacity as foreman at a local garage, he had slipped while helping to lift an engine. 'Never been right since, mind,' he said. 'On my back I was for three months, and never free from pain from that day.'

I concealed my concern as best I could. Looking mentally at the displaced vertebrae, I noticed that one of the segments was worn away at the edge, where it was out of alignment. I felt that this could be tricky, inasmuch as damage had occurred due to this abrasion, and although I would be able to manipulate the displacement over the course of a few visits, it could be that the problem would not entirely disappear because of this. However I felt that relief, of course, would be infinitely preferable to having to put up with continuing pain. 'I'll have to have you face down on the carpet,' I commanded. 'Jacket off and shirt up.'

I got down beside him on my knees, my fingers following my mind as I sought out the displacements and strained ligaments. I had to manipulate and knead the area adjacent to the problem for some time, to limber up muscles that had become set in a manner foreign to their natural function. However, I was able to relax these, and soon afterwards, using the technique that has always come naturally to me, I managed to move the section of vertebra back where it belonged. Unfortunately, owing to the wear and tear of the bone trying to work in the wrong position, I was very concerned that it might slip back.

'Davydd, you'll have to come and see me a few more times,' I said. 'It's possible your back may move out of alignment again and I want to keep an eye on it.'

As Davydd started to get up, a look of surprise and pleasure crossed his features. 'My, that's better! I can't believe it.' He stood up and straightened; started to move about. Incredulously, he shook his head.

'Now remember to come and see me this time next week,' I said. 'Be careful how you move, and try to lie as flat as you can on something when you sleep tonight.'

Davydd now seemed quite speechless, and Vi had the beginnings of tears in her eyes as she gathered their things to leave.

'Goodbye and thank you,' Davydd said quietly; they both grasped me by the hand fervently and left.

I was as usual embarrassed by the emotion displayed as they went. These things always seemed to come so naturally to me, yet the reaction, so kindly meant, was to place me on an unwanted pedestal; a thing so foreign to my nature that this acute embarrassment would always result.

Davydd did come back and see me as I had asked. Although the problem never completely cleared up, as I had first thought, at least his discomfort was kept to a minimum.

Word of this soon got around. At first, one or two of what to me were standard 'headache' cases arrived on my doorstep; then a steady trickle of sufferers began. A radio announcer, who lived locally, became interested in tales that were reaching him through various sources. He came to see me for a chat, interviewed several people who had visited me regarding different ailments, and put his findings out over the air. Soon I was kept busy to the point where I had to consider setting up some form of clinic to deal with the increasing flow of patients. It was becoming more and more difficult to carry on with the rebuilding of our house because of the interruptions, which Peter and I were only too glad to deal with where we could.

I think probably the most dramatic of all my 'cures' – I put this word in quotes, not because the results were in question, but because of the unfortunate 'miraculous' connotation – was the gentleman who was brought to us in a wheelchair, paralysed from the waist down and unable to speak. Now obviously paralysis has many causes, a great number of which are totally outside my abilities, such as viral infections, muscular dystrophy etc. However, in this case it was simply a trapped nerve in the spine, which a few moments of manipulation were able to release. This brief process not only enabled him to get up from his wheelchair and take a few steps, but he was able to speak – slowly and falteringly – with the by now predictable gratitude and emotion. Shortly after this I was interviewed on Welsh television along with several of my patients, who staunchly attested to their relief from headaches and pain.

It was at this point, that metaphorically speaking, little black clouds began to gather on the horizon. An element, ranging from quasi-religious groups to one or two doctors in nearby coastal townships, began to question whether or not I could really do what was taking place. This was soon followed by, comments such as, 'What is an unqualified person doing, working medically with people?'

Now it should be made clear that the areas in which I work are basically in manipulation. However, my psychic senses would often tell me that that the person's complaint or illness was outside my own capacity to help; but at the same time I would instinctively know what was wrong and would often send a person to their doctor saying, 'You have a liver complaint and you need...' or, 'You will benefit considerably from taking a course of such and such...' And, as happened later, I could 'see' such things as a large ovarian cyst which needed urgent removal by surgery to save that person's life. (In this case the person herself was a doctor.)

These recommendations of mine were often getting me into trouble, as they sometimes conflicted with the diagnosis of the individual's doctor. This of course is not intended in any way to decry the excellent work that most doctors and members of the medical profession in this country carry out, and without whom many of us (certainly myself and my husband) would quite literally be lost. Nevertheless, errors can occur in the best regulated of circles, and I found that when this happened, understandably perhaps wounding professional pride, emotional reaction and hostility could be generated. However, I can only tell people what I 'see'; I always emphasise that what I say to them is a result of just that, and that they must make their own decisions in these matters.

While all this was going on an event took place, which was to sadden me considerably. As the steady flow of patients increased, word reached us of a clinic in London that dealt specifically with migraine cases. Having found over an extended period that most cases of migraine fell into basic categories, the majority from displaced neck and spinal vertebrae (either due to falls, or perhaps strain during childbirth), or sometimes from a liver condition necessitating dietary changes, I naively thought that a working arrangement with this clinic could be made. Quite a few of my patients by now were travelling long distances to see me, and some of them told me that this clinic was looking for a solution to the migraine problem. All they were able to do currently was to offer drugs as a means of easing the pain, often with unpleasant side effects.

I wrote to them offering my services, with testimonials from patients and confirmation of radio/television publicity. I received a letter politely declining my services. Being naturally puzzled by this, I asked a solicitor to investigate the clinic's background. It transpired that this clinic was merely the arm of a well-known drug company, its managing and assistant directors receiving salaries of £20,000 and £15,000 per annum (these were very high salaries at this time in 1974–75), and it became quite obvious to me that the last thing these people would want was anyone cured of migraine!

This then was my first experience of the Establishment. My second followed closely when I discovered that no newspaper would accept any advertisement containing the word 'migraine' – the public at large is well protected from any assistance in this direction.

However, my efforts and frustrations had a very amusing sequel. A little later, the managing director of this particular clinic appeared on our local Welsh television, apparently touring the country appealing for funds. Unbeknown to him, the interviewer had not long previously interviewed me, and during the discussion of the appeal suddenly said, 'Why don't you contact Anne Owen? We have recently interviewed her and we have her many letters of commendation for her treatment of migraine.'

The stuttered and inconsequential reply, I'm afraid, did not do a great deal to further his cause!

Although I continued to see quite a few people, I felt progress in this direction was becoming effectively blocked. However, my 'X-ray Vision', as one paper put it, was and had been extending into other areas. My abilities were showing me that we, all of us, have led many lives before our present one. I was finding in many cases that certain illnesses, a person's outlook, conditioning, and even relationships towards people in their present lives, would often have their roots in earlier lifetimes.

In a later chapter I will tell you how my awareness developed into these areas. However, many people have asked whether I was psychic as a child, and how these abilities first manifested. Here then is the story of my childhood.

Chapter 2
The Wheel that Almost Came Off

I was a bonny baby. I weighed over twelve pounds, although my mother was small in height and slightly built. An only child, possibly because my mother couldn't cope with the thought of another like me, I was born with a naevus, a skin pigmentation disorder, which totally covered my head. Mother had to take me to hospital regularly for the first two years of my life to get this burnt off, so I had no hair at all during this time, and everyone thought I was a boy. Fortunately, being then so young, I have no recollections whatsoever of what otherwise might have been a traumatic experience.

My earliest recollection of a psychic nature that I remember was when I experienced what a surprising number of children have – a fairy! These tiny winged elementals or nature spirits are part of our folklore; however, ask around, as I have and it seems that many young people around the age of four or five, as I then was, have had this experience and recall it clearly.

It happened this way. One of my milk teeth had become loose; I would have been about five at this time. It was the custom in those days for parents to hide a silver sixpence either under a pillow or carpet for the child to seek out, if she or he had lost a tooth, which the 'fairies' would have put there. My loose tooth, then, had begun to assume a role of great importance in my life. If I could free it, I could claim the right to seek out my sixpence, which in those far-off days represented a goodly sum, capable of buying sweets or perhaps a small toy.

On this particular day, we were due to visit an aunt of mine not far away. It was during the early part of the war, and the previous night a bomb had exploded in the field opposite where we lived. This field contained potatoes that were just due to be lifted, and the explosion had blown them everywhere. Food of course in war time was in very short supply; a number of local people and my mother had managed to gather a few potatoes that had been blown into the road. Today, she and I were taking some of these to auntie, which my mother knew would be well appreciated.

It was a long bus ride and an even longer walk for my short legs to my aunt's house. However, wiggling my tooth around served to take my mind off this for the most part, and in the fullness of time we arrived. Mother and Auntie had plenty to talk about, and settled in the front room. I was left to my own devices in the back, feeling decidedly bored, when presto! Out came the tooth between my finger and thumb. My excitement was intense; I ran into the front room holding out the tooth. 'Will the fairies bring my sixpence?' I said in my childish treble, hardly able to contain myself.

My mother or her sister – I don't know which, across this gap in time – must have distracted me and slipped a sixpence under the carpet.

'See if you can find it under the carpet then,' Mother said, smilingly, and I stepped forward, eyes sparkling with excitement. As I did this, and before I could stoop down to start the search, I really saw a fairy fly in the air in front of me. She had beautiful blue and turquoise wings and a tiny green filmy petalled dress – just like my picture books! I was overawed by what I saw, so much so that I had completely forgotten about the sixpence. I was shouting, 'Look! There she goes – isn't she pretty?' And as she flew around the room, suddenly she disappeared up the chimney. The tears came to my eyes, and I cried, calling out, 'She's gone, she's gone!'

My mother and aunt were getting cross. 'Stop playing the fool, Anne, and find the sixpence,' said Mother sternly. I looked at my mother and from my mother to my aunt. I couldn't believe it; they hadn't seen my fairy! By now they were getting quite angry, and telling me to get on with looking for the sixpence; but this no longer meant much to me. I was told off for being stupid, and reminded not to tell lies… The hurt went deep, and I learned a hard lesson then; for many years I never told anyone about what I saw, either there or elsewhere. I just couldn't understand why I should be told off for seeing something as real to me as my mother and aunt; however thereafter I kept my own counsel.

Childhood was for me a very lonely period. Born in 1936, I must have been about four or five when London began to fall victim to Hitler's bombs. By this time father was away in the RAF, while my mother worked in a munitions factory; in those days the country's resources and people were stretched to the limit. I was, by force of circumstances, left to my own devices all day in the house in the school holidays. I found being alone like this frightening at times; it made me unable to sleep at night and my parents often found me sleep walking round the house, even on occasion walking down the road. Sometimes I would change into my day clothes from my nightdress and only be aware of it after I had woken up on one of my walks. Knowing how sensitive I must have been in those days, and in the light of my present knowledge, I think a lot of the problems I had were due to the disturbing influence of the house itself. Although in the summer I could play outside, on wet or winter nights I of course had to stay in until my mother came home at 6.30 p.m.

I would often get quite scared on my own, and one night I had particular reason to be. I came into the sitting room – it was just getting dark one late afternoon in winter – and sat down on a chair, having closed the door behind me. Suddenly I was aware of somebody sitting in the chair on the opposite side of the fire. I was instantly petrified. The figure of the person sat there, with a vague, fuzzy outline; the rest of the form seemed to be a smoky grey, rather like fog; but I clearly remember being able to see the back of the chair through this form. I know now that this would simply have been the manifestation of some poor earthbound soul, unable to move on to happier surroundings.

For those unaware of why some people, after they have passed over, remain earthbound or unable to leave the location where they have passed away, the reasons can be many. This could for instance be caused by a person who has never been able to accept the concept of an afterlife, thinking no existence after death is possible; or the condition may be due to the individual being the victim of some deep emotion relating to where they passed away. Persons having committed some grave crime often find themselves trapped in this condition, unable to leave their surroundings where they have lived or where some traumatic event occurred. This is one of the reasons why hauntings take place. Fortunately, there are those on the other side who are eventually able to rescue these unhappy individuals from the situation in which they find themselves trapped, by helping the person concerned to become aware of what has taken place.

However, at that tender age on my own, with no one to explain these things to me, I was of course terrified. In my fright, I wet the chair. I could not move for some time, although probably only a few minutes elapsed. Suddenly the figure was gone; in one fraction of time it was there, and in the next it had ceased to exist. I ran for the door and rushed upstairs to my bedroom. Oddly enough, what was now worrying me more was that my mother was due home shortly, and she would discover that I had wet the chair! With this new fear overriding everything, I rushed back downstairs and turned the seat cushion over. Fortunately it was one that could be turned either way, and my involuntary indiscretion remained undiscovered.

From the viewpoint of later knowledge, I find it quite easy to piece the events together from this early period in my life. About this time, I began to have strange nightmares. They had this constantly recurring theme of a baby dying, being wrapped in cloth, and a long time later buried in the middle of a garden. Many years later I learned by chance about the previous tenant of the house. She was an unmarried Irishwoman who had eight different children by different lovers. It seemed she also had aborted many babies and disposed of them; in the light of my later knowledge it would seem to me I had tuned in to the house's history. Although I could make out no features of the form in the fireside chair, I am sure that the poor soul who had all these problems was this same Irishwoman.

Being forced to play alone a lot as I was, I was left to my own devices. When the weather was fine, I would go out into the woods and pick various plants and herbs. These I would often crush and prepare in the form of medicine for my dolls. I can't remember whether the health of my dolls improved, but I do know how well this fits in with my present-day absorption with Alternative Medicine. Often tendencies such as these are the bringing-through of knowledge from previous lives at this stage of childhood; later on, when I began to recall earlier lifetimes, I found quite a few of them had been spent in Ancient Egypt, where in the priesthood I had tended the sick with many preparations gathered from the fields.

As many of you will know, the early Egyptians were very advanced in the field of what we know as Alternative Medicine today; for instance, they grew cultures containing penicillin for the healing of wounds and abrasions. Healing in Ancient Egypt also extended far beyond the physical, and the subject was regarded by them as holistic in nature, i.e. the whole person was treated on the basis that many illnesses have their origins in the mind of the sufferer.

Many people today ask me about my unusual abilities. 'How do you do it?' is a question frequently asked. Mostly the questions relate to my clairvoyant abilities involving prediction, but included are my abilities to diagnose illness at sight and manipulate displaced vertebrae, limbs and ligaments. As I manipulate a person I can see with my Inner Eye, as I mentioned in the last chapter, how and where a displacement can be. These abilities were learned in very hard schools over many lifetimes; many skills will often show up in different forms early on in most children's lives, as they did with me. This of course is the reason why certain people have a natural 'bent' for doing things, and again in the more extreme cases one finds children of four or five years of age playing piano concertos, solving complex mathematical problems and playing chess brilliantly. The Egyptians knew of these things and would select their priests and priestesses for training from a very early age by a selective process so that souls could carry on from where they had left off in previous lives.

So here were my abilities being rediscovered and brought through, often painfully, as there was no one in my environment who could help me and explain what was taking place. The result was, unfortunately, a lonely and introverted child who was only able to come to terms with these unusual talents much later in life.

However, lest you should imagine that I am feeling sorry for myself, and to show you that my childhood was not one of angelic suffering, no story of early days would be complete without telling you of some of the pranks I frequently indulged in. I had a friend, Patience, with whom I was able to play occasionally. One of our favourite pastimes was to play hide-and-seek among the tombstones in our local churchyard at St Mary Cray in Kent. When this began to pall, we would seek out the graves that had no flowers (I suppose we weren't to know they hadn't been visited for a century or more) and remove the fresh flowers from the new graves to make up the deficiency. I have often thought about the poor people who would have imagined that their graves were being desecrated; perhaps they will read this and realise no harm was intended! Something else we liked to do was to pick bunches of wild flowers and lay them on the altar. The church was a very old one. Built by the Normans, it had a leper window at the back so that lepers of those times could watch the service. In the church, I found a peace within myself that did much to compensate for the bad atmosphere at home; I went there whenever I could to get away.

One day, Patience and I went wading down a local stream that ran into a large lake. On the bank of this lake, leading to the water, was a freshly dug hole with a large pipe sticking out of it. Being inquisitive little girls, we felt that this pipe looked very inviting, so much that we decided to clamber up and investigate. It was but a short step to climb inside; and then of course it had to lead somewhere after all. We squeezed in on all fours, one behind the other. As we progressed of course, it became darker and darker to the point where we wanted to go back; but just then we rounded a slight curve to see a tiny circle of light in the distance. Onwards we pressed, until the angle became quite steep. Suddenly our heads were clear of the pipe – to be confronted by an enormous lorry roaring straight towards us! Terrified, we shot back into the pipe and crawled back as fast as we could. I remember, looking back in my mind's eye at the scene, that there were some wooden trestles close by, and we must have emerged from a freshly-cut culvert; but at that age we were sure we were going to be flattened by that lorry. Dishevelled, with torn and muddy clothing, we really got into hot water that night – in all senses!

Around this time I clearly recall dreaming vividly one night of a large aeroplane crashing. The following morning, exactly as I had seen in my dream, reports of a similar-looking aircraft having crashed were on the front pages of the newspapers. I remember being old enough to find this unnerving, but strangely I didn't question the fact that I'd 'seen' it in advance; and never mentioned the fact to anyone.

Other naughtinesses followed. Today I think I would have been put into care; in those days it was wartime, and a lot of children in my situation were left to their own devices. One Christmas I borrowed my father's saw, and with my friend Patience again we stole out one evening and cut six small fir trees down, which were growing along the driveway of a large house. We then took them away and left them on the steps of poor homes; a misplaced spirit of Robin Hood perhaps, but I hesitate to think of the repercussions that must have ensued.

A favourite trick of ours – nothing novel, but usually attributable to boys – was to fasten a cotton thread to door knockers in a street and operate them by remote control, from behind a hedge. I think if some of those tenants had caught us, we wouldn't be alive today, judging by their reactions at the end of an evening!

Another jolly little game we would indulge in was seeing how late we could leave crossing in front of trains. Blithely uncaring, we would hop across with little to spare; at least the lines weren't electrified in those days, but I can well imagine the train drivers were!

I think the saving grace of my childhood days was when my mother bought me a set of children's encyclopaedias by Arthur Mee. Looking back, they were a turning point in my life; my constant companions, I felt loneliness lifting as I entered many new and interesting worlds. I read about the stars, the universe, and its suns and planets; and in particular the history of Ancient Egypt and Greece.

The many pictures and illustrations seemed to stir long distant memories; it was almost as if I could enter and walk about in them. As I turned the leaves, I could practically feel myself living in certain eras. However, it was the Egyptian pyramids and the Greek temples that fascinated me and held me spellbound above all else in a way I couldn't define; it was only many years later that I was able to understand the reasons for this. I definitely feel these books helped enormously to unlock my memories of previous lives, and enabled me to 'tap in' to psychic abilities developed over many centuries in those times. As I will discuss later more fully, we are all the products of our previous existences, and because of the difficult and arduous lives I have led in the past in the pursuit of psychic knowledge, I am able in this life to use this knowledge to the full.

Towards the end of my somewhat difficult childhood, my father bought a little Austin car. I would have been about eleven at the time, and excited about the prospect of a trip to the seaside. We set off one sunny morning, the old Austin bumping and swaying on its way, springs protesting at the undulations of the winding road. The front seat was rather low for me (mother always liked to ride in the back; she said she preferred the comfort) but I remember how I enjoyed looking out at the green trees and hedges that lined the road, with fields of daisies where sheep and cows grazed contentedly.

Father sat close up to the steering wheel, as he always liked to do, peering through the flat, upright windscreen typical of cars of that period. We had just pulled out to overtake a slower stream of traffic, when suddenly I felt a terrible sickness in the region of the solar plexus, while a brilliant picture formed in my mind of one of the car's wheels suddenly parting company with the car. I shouted, 'Daddy! Daddy! Please stop, the wheel's coming off!'

Father looked across and down at me, irritation spreading across his features. 'Don't be stupid; be quiet!' he said.

I screamed, then grabbed at the steering wheel, and the old Austin lurched alarmingly in the middle of the weekend holiday traffic.

Father, really angry by now, somehow managed to bring the car to the side of the road. Then he got out of the driver's side and started to come round to where I was sitting. As he reached the front of the car, looking extremely irate, I saw his expression change. Following his gaze, I leaned out of the open window and saw the front nearside wheel leaning at a strange angle.

'How on earth did you know that?' he said, baffled.

I couldn't answer; if I had wanted to describe what I had experienced, I would have been prevented by the flood of relief that was engulfing me. The wheel was held on by only one nut; father said very little after that, and although he was able to fix it by using the nuts from the spare wheel, he never referred to the matter again, but looked askance at me from time to time.

I always look back at this incident as being the first time when I was able to use my psychic abilities in a practical, demonstrable manner in the way I do today. I certainly had no inkling of what was to follow later in life; the path, which I was to tread, would lead me through some very strange countryside.

Chapter 3
Everyone in their True Colours

The ward seemed alive with glowing figures, all of them sitting or moving around. They were wreathed in a curious dark smoke-like effect, shot through with angry reds and pale vivid greens shrouded in different shades of grey fog or smoke. I was a temporary night nurse or carer at this time, in a local mental hospital for the elderly. Money was becoming increasingly short in the domestic situation in which I found myself, as a result of my meeting a commercial artist seventeen years my senior during my first job at the photographer's studio.

He was a fine man and I was only sixteen when we met; we married three years later. Shortly after our marriage, we decided to adopt two lovely children, as it was discovered that it would not be possible for me to conceive naturally. During the early years of their adoption, I became a housewife, immersing myself in my children with little time to spare. When my children started school, some spare time became available. I returned to my earlier interest, becoming a part-time fashion photographer. As time went by, I became entranced by many of the beautiful dresses and clothes I was photographing, and a desire began to grow within me to create some original designer clothes myself. Around this time, I became friendly with a woman who introduced me to a source of 'cabbage' – a term used in the dress trade for remnants of dress material that could be obtained very cheaply. I would purchase this and design and make my own designer clothing, selling these by means of private house parties. Unfortunately this relatively lucrative period of my life came to an end when my source of material dried up. For a while we managed, but the bills soon started to mount and it became imperative for me to find some part-time work to help make ends meet. I had found an advertisement asking for carers to work nights at the local mental hospital. I had applied and been accepted, and now I had just come on night duty for the first time.

To me the scene was like a nightmare; I had to pinch myself as a form of reassurance that I was really awake. Mechanically, I started to help the ward sister, turning the patients in their beds; washing bodies, wiping saliva from their lips; changing sheets and attending to bedpans. As I carried out my duties, so real were the auras surrounding these unfortunates that I had to force myself to plunge my hands through this smoke-like effect, wondering if it would do me any harm.

What I was witnessing was the fruit of the preceding weeks, although the dramatic effects were far exceeding any of my previous expectations. Commencing with mild curiosity based on a chance circumstance, I had been led by fate again into a further stage of psychic development to the point that I was unsure of contact with reality.

It is many years now since I experienced what seemed at first to be a trivial incident. The scene was one typical of a Kentish village on a warm Saturday afternoon: the green, with children laughing and playing; an old lady walking her dog and stopping to talk to a neighbour; colourful cottage gardens; and on the far side, a jumble sale in progress.

I have always found jumble sales irresistible, particularly the ones of those times in the early 1970s. Nowadays, of course, the chances of finding that attic treasure are very slim, but in those days granny's silver spoons, a beautiful antique ring, or a dingy but potentially exciting-looking old oil painting would often appear at a cost of only a few pence to help some local worthy cause. On this occasion, however, I was to find a treasure of a different kind. Moving among the little stalls, each with their bric-a-brac, I noticed a small pile of books nestling against a Victorian steam iron. On top of this pile, a dog-eared book with a faded green cover caught my attention. A mysterious-looking single eye peered at me from the top of the cover, with lines issuing forth from it, faintly reminiscent of the type of old religious texts threatening purgatory and various other unpleasantness if you were 'Not Very Good Indeed' during your stay on this planet.

However, its title belied the anticipated threats. Embossed in faded gilt was the legend 'Aura Reading'. Idly I picked it up, and riffled through a few pages. A sentence caught my attention. Written in a slightly dated style, it read something to this effect:

> Once the initiate is able to perceive the swirling mists of the aura, it will not be possible to be deceived as to a person's motives and intentions. The aura reflects the soul; not only the soul's personality and feelings at the time, but also the health and attitudes of the individual will be revealed.

I was intrigued. For tuppence, for that is all that it cost me, I was to be launched on a career that would lead me to meet famous people and travel far; yet the path was to be strewn with thorns and boulders.

After making one or two other insignificant purchases I left, having to become involved in such mundane affairs as family shopping, and the needs of children. A while was to elapse before I could find some time to myself to read the little book, and to start to absorb its contents. Its chapters put forward a system of meditation, in conjunction with certain breathing exercises. As it was one of the requirements, I set aside a little time each day to follow its teachings.

For two to three weeks, very little happened. I then gradually noticed a change taking place within me; more, perhaps, with my whole way of thinking. Something within me was awakening and developing; a heightened awareness at first; then something of a sensation of beginning to unlock a door and see into a room beyond which I knew existed, but had formerly avoided. After each study period, continuing with the meditation and breathing exercises, I felt myself coming much more alive. I could feel, see, and sense more, becoming gradually much more aware of life and beauty around me. The grass was greener, the perfume of flowers more intense, the sky bluer, and life around me had a far more vital quality.

The world looked more beautiful than I had ever seen it. I realised that the world had not changed, but my inner self was developing in such a way that my perception of it was altering. Imperceptibly, I noticed I was becoming much more aware of people and their thoughts and feelings. As my sensitivity increased, I noticed – did I imagine it? – a very faint halo around some trees and flowers. As this started to happen, I would blink and not be sure; however, yes, there was a faint white aura around some trees and flowers. The awareness would come and go, until I arrived at a point where, by allowing my eyes to go out of focus in a certain way, I could discern that the white halo would contain very delicate rainbow-hued pastel shades within it.

This process of discovery continued. Although it was always necessary at this point to become relaxed and in a contemplative mood to achieve these results, progress became steady. Not long after these things started to take place, I began to become aware of the same white glow in certain lights and circumstances around people.

One day I took my children swimming, something my family and I were particularly fond of. In my state of gradually heightening awareness, I noticed that whereas I would see this whitish glow around people swimming and playing in the pool, now I noticed different colours forming within the glow. In fascination, I would watch these colours forming and changing; some had very beautiful colours forming around them like a rainbow in larger or smaller degree; some were so large that the rainbow seemed to stand out around the form for three or four feet; others would have a minimal glow appearing only to radiate inches from the body. Not all had such harmonious colours; some had somewhat muddy or insipid hues surrounding them. A small number would have angry or clashing colours around them – discordant reds tinged with black, violent mauves and nauseating greens.

The weeks that followed, while I continued to practice these teachings, were an ongoing voyage of discovery. I was still, as well as looking after my family, nursing part-time in the mental home for the elderly, as mentioned earlier. It was around this time, during my period of night duty, that I began to see these very discordant colours, in violent contrast to each other, around the patients during the course of my duties. At times, the clashing colours were enhanced by this smoke-like effect, with flickering discordant lights within – dreadful reds shot through with harsh ugly greens, blacks and greys. The smoking effect became so real at times that I felt I was actually putting my hands through it in the course of working with some of my patients.

As time went by, I learned to live in this different world. I became comfortable with these experiences, and found that in addition to sensing the moods and feelings of those around me, their aural colour changes would confirm and enhance my understanding of their innermost thoughts. Someone's depression, for instance, although their outward mood was perhaps happy and relaxed, would manifest in their aura to me as dark-tinged colours; dull reds, dark greys, sometimes smoky blacks. Changes of mood, often due to a person's inner problems, frequently took me by surprise. Greed, envy, malice were all there to see. Greed would show as a similar colour to envy, and envy, well, we've all heard of being green with it! The shades of green, however, were always discordant; never those pleasant greens we like to associate with Nature.

Another well-worn cliché, 'red with anger', can be amply confirmed by any reader of the aura. Strange how these phrases, so commonplace in everyday speech, can be revealed as truth in this light. Their origins, extending back into the mists of time, clearly show that our ancestors were in possession of knowledge that we have for the most part sadly lost. Since becoming aware of these things, I have always viewed the aura as an electromagnetic field surrounding not only the human body, but all forms of life, including many substances we consider to be without life, such as rocks and minerals.

This field has been detected by scientists on sensitive apparatus, which was developed some years ago. As no two people are exactly the same – nor indeed are any living organisms – it follows that everyone will have an aura unique to their own personality. The shifting coloured patterns, each constituent a result of an individual emotion or experience, communicate to the reader of the aura a person's feelings and attitudes and their state of health, including illnesses in such an early stage that they would not be detectable by physical means. Also detectable to the trained eye, as one develops, are a person's former lives, and their futures! Regarding these, which I will deal with later in this book, it is fascinating to see, unknown to the person concerned, how their former lives influence and guide (and sometimes misguide!) their present one; and how, with unfolding knowledge and effort, the apparent future may be changed within certain guidelines.

These things were well known in earlier civilisations in the mystery schools and priesthoods, where knowledge of this nature had to be concealed on pain, in many cases, of some very unpleasant deaths. Rulers in those times were well aware, as are certain power groups today, of what was achievable in these fields.

Although it is not directly related in terms of aura reading, I am going to touch on Distance Seeing – a means of being able to form images in the mind of places and people far away; because once the consciousness has been raised, the individual will frequently expand psychically in other directions. As in the course of everyday life, people will find they are better in certain psychic areas than others. In the same way, study in the psychic fields will produce markedly differing abilities in different areas. Distance Seeing has been commonplace in many civilisations. In ancient times, rulers would employ seers to determine the movements of hostile troops. Our governments use seers today, now known as Remote Viewers, not so much for troop deployment, but to gain military information.

Some while ago, Peter and I were at a party in London. A woman I had never seen before came up to me and introduced herself, saying that she had heard of me, and while not being particularly interested in clairvoyance herself, mentioned that she worked for the British Government in a classified information section. She then went on to say that her department had been using a team of American clairvoyants or Remote Viewers to obtain military information; but of course refused to say in what connection. A picture immediately sprang up in Peter's mind, and he said, 'You work in an office where you have very large maps on inclined boards. On these maps, you have various pink-coloured pins dotted about with unusual shaped heads on them like upturned buckets. These pins denote shipping movements, some of them submarines.'

The lady then went extremely pale, and made as if to leave the party straight away. As she left, Peter couldn't resist adding, 'I can't understand why you need to go to America for the type of information you need – here's my card.'

Needless to say, we didn't hear anything further!

Although we now live in far more liberal times, any form of seeing, or that term with unfortunate connotations of the fairground, clairvoyance, is to a large extent officially firmly sat upon by the Establishment and certain religious groups. In the former case, it is far easier to ridicule any means of uncovering what some of these people get up to, than to be seen to be totally repressive and thus give credence to the whole subject; a considerable improvement on burning various gifted unfortunates at the stake! In the case of certain religious groups, always a touchy subject, the heads of these maintain power and wealth by the simple expedient of maintaining it to be 'evil', and then manipulate ancient texts to substantiate their cover story; whereas in point of fact in many religions the original texts amply substantiate the subject. On the other hand, Buddhism, one of the most ancient religions, practises in many forms the abilities discussed in this chapter. I have to add here that I am not aware of any Buddhist wars undertaken in the name of religion!

It isn't difficult to appreciate that if everyone could recover even some of our lost knowledge of the past, our planet and environment would be vastly different today. Let's look at just some of the basic areas of extrasensory knowledge available to us today:

- Aura Reading
- Our Former Lives
- Our Futures
- Distance Seeing
- Healing
- Communication with those who have passed on to the next stage of Existence

Imagine a civilisation where children are not only educated in these areas, but are able to apply these skills in everyday life. Illness would be anticipated, and therefore treated in good time by means of the aura; former lives acknowledged, and the skills and knowledge from them brought forward into the present life and used in a positive way.

Have you ever wondered how it is that a so-called child prodigy can sit down and perform at the piano in a manner far beyond his or her years? You are hearing the accumulated skills of many lifetimes! There would be far fewer square pegs in round holes in our employment markets if children were thus educated.

Our futures, although planned to a degree before entering this life, are largely governed by free will. Imagine a broad pathway extending before you, along which you are advancing. There are certain obstacles placed before you along this pathway. The pathway is the Pathway of Life, and the obstacles placed therein are for you to handle in the best way possible; the experience gained by so doing, if correctly handled, will lead to a much smoother road and enrichment of the soul. If not, the lesson will have to be relearned at a later time, either in this life or the next.

My husband Peter, who knows many of my clients well, always maintains that they fall into one of two categories: those who have followed my advice for the future, and those who wish they had!

Distance seeing, which I will now return to, can be used in a variety of ways. This is an extremely useful mental facility; Peter and I have used it many times to locate missing persons and objects for the solving of crimes; and sometimes just to find out where each other or a friend has got to! This is achieved by relaxing; focussing your attention on the problem; and allowing an image to form in the mind. Sometimes it is just a very faint impression – did you imagine it? – and often it will be completely different from what you expected. A good way to practise this is to find someone who has a problem that requires solving in this way. If you have arrived at the point where your psychic faculties are working, when the person you are working with (who should have a genuine problem) asks you a question, a picture should come to your mind. You should then describe to the person what you see. As you complete the description, another picture should form and so on until all aspects of that particular subject have been exhausted. Constant practice at this should be exercised until an increasing degree of accuracy is achieved.

However, different people will have differing psychic abilities. Some will find that they are extremely telepathic, and quite unable to do anything else without long periods of psychic development. Others will be excellent at healing, and prefer to work only in those areas. There is a lot to be said for staying with what you find comes easily to you; your awareness will often develop of its own accord in other areas.

In my own case, psychic abilities within me manifested themselves at a very early age in many areas, thus giving me a head start. Intensive study in the priesthoods and temples of former lives, where these abilities were accepted as a matter of course, made my present-life abilities possible. However, intensive and rigorous as these studies were in those past lives, certain areas, such as the reawakening of my ability to read the aura, were required to be brought through again by study and meditation. Other extrasensory faculties, such as my ability to see and be aware of discarnate entities were available to me almost before I was able to read and write.

Returning to aura reading, curiously enough after long practice at it along with all the other psychic study areas, there comes a point in time where instead of requiring to read the aura in detail the required information can arrive, as it were, in a flash from apparently nowhere. Experiencing the intuitive process to those unaware of it is difficult to describe. The only way I can put it is that the thought appears to arrive before you have had time to think it! One of the best illustrations of the intuitive process is telepathy. You are perhaps sitting at home, drinking a cup of tea thinking of nothing in particular, when suddenly you may find yourself thinking about a friend you haven't seen or heard of for some time. A few minutes later, the phone rings. 'How extraordinary!' you exclaim. 'I was only thinking about you a few moments ago.' And you discover that the very friend you were thinking of phoned you out of the blue.

This may be caused in two ways. Either your friend had suddenly thought it was about time he or she contacted you, or they had received the thought you had inadvertently transmitted. In either case, from the originator of the two of you, a carrier wave is transmitted, but at a far higher frequency than is detectable on our present-day equipment. This in turn is received in an area of the mind that is not consciously used by the majority of people, but the signal will often filter through from that area to our consciousness, resulting in our responding to our friend's generated thought.

This area of the mind I always view as being for the majority of people in the form of a rusty filter. Many simply dismiss thoughts received in this way as imagination, but with practice the 'rust' will disappear from the filter, and a remarkable degree of proficiency can develop in many of the areas of the mind I have referred to earlier. All we are doing, of course, is using the areas of the mind, which our ancestors employed as a matter of course.

A good way to embark on the road to aura seeing is to have available a room which you can easily darken and which is quite free from any form of disturbance. You will need a large mirror, one like those used with dressing tables – these are ideal – and a candle. If this is not convenient, simply arrange a table next to the wall and prop a large mirror on it positioned as nearly upright as possible without risk of it falling forwards. Arrange to be seated at the dresser or table, and then place the candle on the surface in front of you so that when it has been lit, your reflection can be seen clearly. Make sure of course that the candle is in a proper holder, in case you happen to doze off!

Concentrate at first on the candle. In the darkened room with all other lights extinguished, look at the flame and allow your gaze to go slightly out of focus. Make sure that you are relaxed; and after a while the candle flame should appear to grow larger, and around it a much larger halo should form. Within this halo should appear very delicate colours after a time, delicate pinks, blues, greens and yellows. Patience and continued practice are the keynotes; and above all, avoid taking alcohol or medication before any of these exercises.

When you feel you have completely mastered this to your satisfaction, now is the time to move on to aura reading proper. After having set up the candle in the usual way in front of the mirror, gaze at your reflection in the soft light. Allowing your gaze to become slightly out of focus as before, and making sure that you are completely relaxed, focus your attention on the outline around your head's reflection. For some people, results may take longer than for others. However sooner or later, in a similar way to the candle, a soft, expanding flame effect should start to show around your reflected outline. In general the first colours one sees are a bluish-white or pale blue.

Do not be disappointed if you do not get results at first; it may take many sessions before any success is achieved. However, I have known a few individuals who have seen a variety of brilliant colours almost immediately; it all depends on your spiritual awareness and development; not only in your present life, but also in your previous ones.

However, I am going to assume that you have either been very lucky, or have lasted out until success has crowned your efforts. Once you have started to awaken your perceptions and begun to see the first subtle colours of the aura, continue on a regular basis, and you should start to see further colours forming within the delicately-coloured halo of light. As I said earlier, the ancients were very familiar with these concepts, which is why saints were always depicted with halos – or auras – around their heads. Yellows, oranges, deeper blues – all will have their meaning.

When you have reached this degree of proficiency, it would be a good idea to ask someone who is sympathetic to the subject, and with whom you have a good rapport, to take the place of the mirror for the next stage in your development. Instead of the mirror, arrange for your friend to sit across the table from you under the same conditions in a darkened room with the candle placed between you. This will be very good experience in the form of a next step; the different aural colours your friend is bound to have will place another perspective in your development.

About this time, you should be becoming far more aware of people and life around you. Although you normally will not get the same results you are getting under the controlled conditions you are used to working with, you will become aware of mental flashes and impressions from those around you. Occurrences of this nature will often come into your awareness, particularly if for instance you are enjoying a relaxing evening with friends, especially under soft yellow lighting – this colour frequency seems to amplify psychic awareness.

Again, as mentioned earlier, a word of warning; as with driving, alcohol, drug-related substances and these fields do not mix! Working with anything in the nature of this subject can cause you untold harm; whatever you choose to do, I would advise you very seriously to leave one or the other well alone, and never indulge in both!

Having delivered this brief homily and you have decided to continue along the road of self-development, here are some of the basic aural colours and their meanings:

POSITIVE AURAL COLOURS

> Warm and Positive Red: a sign of energy and a bright outlook
>
> Bright Warm Green: warmth/friendliness
>
> Cerise Pink: warmth/happiness/caring
>
> Fine Navy Blue: persons in position of authority

Bright Yellow through to Orange: knowledge/learning/wisdom

Soft Warm Blues through to Mauve: the sign of spiritually caring people

Purple: the colour of the healer

Rainbow effect: a spiritually balanced person

Shining White, Gold and Silver These are the colours of highly evolved souls and are rarely seen

NEGATIVE AURAL COLOURS

Muddy Green: envy

Darker Green: jealousy

Muddy Navy Blue: persons of negative outlook

Mustardy Yellow: a sign of sickness and ill health

Smoky Effects: a disturbed personality

Harsh Red, often mixed with a Black and Smoky Effect: a sign of a violent personality

Dark Brown: an earthy person with little knowledge of spiritual matters

Black/Violet Mauve: evil influences/mental disturbance.

Naturally, with all the different emotions people undergo, many of the colours you will be observing will be mixed, and only time and experience, as with all things, will enable you to establish what the dominant colours in the aura are.

This simple breathing exercise will help to enhance your development. Before commencing your aura work each time, inhale and exhale to your fullest extent, then breathe in as much as you comfortably can. Hold your breath for as long as is comfortable, then exhale to your greatest extent. Do this seven times; at no time should you involve yourself in any strain.

As I have said, some of you will find your perceptions awakened quite quickly, due to former lives being brought through to the surface, while others who do not have this background may have to persevere for a long time. Whatever time it takes, your heightened awareness of life and people will give you a completely different viewpoint in relation to those around you.

From fairly early on in this life, I have learned to apply a golden rule. When I first meet people, I ask myself, 'Am I comfortable in this person's presence?' As you have no doubt heard many times before, first impressions are very often correct. Of course, if you have already developed the technique of aura reading, you will not need to absorb what I am saying here; but if you are only a short way along the path, these impressions are the ones that are going to matter. How many times have you got the message correctly when you were first introduced to someone, then said to yourself, 'I must have misjudged this person' – only to find out later how right you were in the first place? Remember; relax and 'feel' those impressions, and believe me, you can save yourself a great deal of grief.

Former lives again. How important are they to our present and our future? Did you misuse the time allotted to you in some of them? Or do you have, concealed within you, talents that could be brought through to the present, that can often bring a sense of great fulfilment?

In a later chapter, Peter and I will discuss with you some of our own and other people's former life experiences. We shall consider how they have affected our present lifetimes and later, using your own time machine, show how you can travel safely backwards and forwards in time in the safety of your own home.

Chapter 4
Of Little Green Men, UFOs and Strange Lights at Night

This chapter would never have been included had it been written at the time of these incidents occurring. The understandably sceptical public of years ago would have heaped derision and scorn on the experiences I underwent. However, in these more enlightened times, where so much evidence on these subjects is now available in bookshops, libraries and on the Internet, these experiences, although frightening and incomprehensible to me at the time, parallel those of many others in today's landscape, as more and more people are coming forward relating similar stories. As with many adventures in life, the route by which I unknowingly approached these events was quite mundane – a simple camping holiday!

I had always been interested in ley lines and the Glastonbury area in general, so, feeling this to be an opportunity to combine a visit with my first husband and my two children with a camping holiday, I put the idea to my family and it was received enthusiastically. Money was still short but the problem of buying a tent was overcome with the loan of one from our very good friend – our next-door neighbour. For our first camping expedition ever, we purchased a small Primus stove, some plastic cutlery and mugs, packed the necessary blankets and food and made ready for the off.

The children were naturally very excited, never having done this before, scampering everywhere with great delight before we set off. This, of course, stood us in good stead, as they soon settled down pleasantly tired once we were en route.

Living in Kent, as we did in those pre-motorway days, the roads west were slow and congested. Slowly, we wound our way across the counties, the narrower country roads giving way from time to time to picturesque little villages interspersed with the occasional large town. The day passed slowly by, progressing to darker skies and a rising wind as the afternoon wore on.

Eventually we arrived at Glastonbury, having picnicked in the car earlier. Now it was evening; the wind was beginning to blow strongly in the gathering dark and it had started to rain. At this point in time the idea of a nice warm hotel began to have considerable appeal; but unfortunately we lacked the wherewithal, and the need to find a campsite became more and more urgent as darkness approached.

As we drove around the narrow lanes we suddenly turned a corner and there it was – a sign on a farm gate saying 'CAMPING'. My husband immediately got out of the car and walked along a muddy path to the farmhouse. A homely-looking woman came to the door, and answered my husband's question by saying, 'You're welcome to use the site, but as it's late in the year, there's no one else there. Let me show you where it is.' My husband disappeared with the farmer's wife, to reappear a few minutes later with noticeably muddier shoes than he had departed with. The farmer's wife disappeared inside the house with a final injunction to, 'Watch out for the cowpats!' I just had time to notice, with deep longing, the briefly opened door with its cosy-looking interior.

My husband drove us to the campsite as instructed – along a muddy track leading from the road, through a dark wood, which led us to a small field. It looked bare and desolate. A single water tap dominated a very muddy area generously interspersed with ominous-looking darker areas. We parked and started to unload our tent. Inexperienced as we were, we struggled first with the tent itself, which was flapping violently in the wind and the driving rain, aided by a discordant symphony from the children, who were by now very tired and very hungry!

A job, which should have taken a little over twenty minutes, managed to keep us occupied for over an hour and a half. Due to the strength of the wind and the softness of the muddy ground, we had great difficulty in securing the tent pegs. As fast as we thought we had secured one, others thought to be well hammered down started to loosen under the onslaught of what was fast becoming a gale. The tent was large and in three sections, and the rising wind would playfully snatch the section of canvas we were working on from our tired and muddy fingers, leaving us to chase the flapping ends through the ooze.

It was now pitch dark, as there was no moon; we were using a torch and the car's headlights. However, the groundsheet finally splashed into place; we fired up the Primus and dined on baked beans and bread and butter, before tumbling into blankets, which caused the ground sheet to squelch under our every movement. Too tired to care, we fell, more or less as one, into a deep sleep.

I awoke with a start as if electrified, becoming instantly awake; one of those times where there seems to be no transitional state between sleep and normal consciousness. Simultaneously, my eyes focussed on an extraordinary figure – apparently male – standing just inside the entrance to the tent. Initially my senses were totally unable to absorb what I was seeing. It was a small, glowing figure, some 3½ to 4 feet high, standing immobile, looking at me. Stockily built, with broad shoulders, this strange being appeared to be dressed in some type of green uniform with military insignia at the shoulders. The uniform was belted with a semi-armoured appearance – almost a cartoon replica of a spaceman, with exaggerated flared shoulders and epaulettes.

Round this person there seemed also to be a greenish glow, in one sense rather like a hologram, but in another appearing to possess a very solid and real quality that totally convinced me of its reality. The figure appeared different from our race, with a form of subtle ridging to the features, which were widened with the eyes, elongated but narrow, a flattish nose and a small slit-like mouth. The head was topped off with a flattish helmet-type device, and there seemed to be no ears. The whole effect of the entity appeared as a greenish-glowing hologram.

My immediate reaction was to throw myself under the blanket in fear. Staying there for what seemed like minutes, I re-emerged to see the figure still standing there. Unable to believe what I was seeing, yet transfixed by fear for a few seconds, I desperately clutched at my husband and shook him violently. To no avail; he remained unconscious, as though poleaxed. I commenced to pinch myself hard in an effort to 'wake up'. Unfortunately, this achieved nothing at all, since I was already only too wide awake! In a final act of despair, I shrieked at the top of my voice; not one member of my family so much as stirred.

However, I noticed a subtle change start to take place in the hologram image; the figure commenced to shimmer, while at the same time gradually losing its appearance of solidity, until it was finally overtaken by complete disappearance. Later, I was able to read of similar accounts by other people where I learned that their being totally unable to awaken others in the same room or dwelling was a normal occurrence with this type of experience.

Amazingly, shortly afterwards, I fell into a deep and refreshing sleep. On waking the following morning, everything seemed so completely normal that I had to ask myself if I had simply dreamed it all – until the stark reality of the experience came home to me again. I was surprised to find myself covered in places by some curious small bruises. Examining them closely with astonishment, I could make out marks clearly made by fingers where I had repeatedly pinched myself in an endeavour to convince myself I wasn't dreaming!

In response to my question asking if anyone had heard or experienced anything unusual during the night, it seemed that no one had been aware of anything at all, as I had expected. I decided, therefore, to keep quiet about the whole affair; reflecting that it would only induce fear in the children, and probably evoke amused disbelief from my husband.

A day or two of struggling around the deserted campsite in the mud, out of season, interspersed with the odd trip to Glastonbury Tor and its environs convinced us that there might be a better way of spending the remainder of our holiday. We therefore decided to drive over to the New Forest in

Hampshire to spend some time with my parents. So we thankfully dismantled the tent and its accessories, extricating the groundsheet and tent pegs from the cowpat-infested swamp as we went. Finally, everything was stowed away, and we set out for what was fortunately a relatively uneventful journey to my parents' house.

It was a wonderful feeling to turn into their driveway, although I couldn't seem to shake off a strange feeling of presentiment that persisted in my awareness. However, it was good to see them and be back in familiar surroundings, and although summer had passed, their extensive gardens were very beautiful. The house was very large, early Georgian and set in some forty acres, and featured large rolling lawns and a walled vegetable garden. It belonged at that time to a well-known actress who had let the old servants' quarters to my parents. An interesting part of its history was that the building of it was financed by the prize money from a Spanish galleon.

It felt good to be with my parents again, and to wander the gardens of my childhood once more. After my recent experience, about which I had told no one, coupled with camping under the conditions we had suffered, the relative tranquillity and home atmosphere did much to dispel the sensation of still not being quite 'centred'.

The remainder of the day was spent catching up with my parents (it was some time since I had seen them) and keeping the children amused. We had arrived unannounced due to our change of plan, and it was an unexpected pleasure to find that my grandfather had already arrived for a brief stay. A fascinating and eccentric personality, he had led an extremely varied life, starting as an assistant coffin maker at the age of ten, and then running away to join a circus! Later, he became a very successful inventor; he developed a nut-cracking machine for Cadbury's chocolate; a revolutionary type of camera, and a quick-loading breech mechanism for artillery guns that was used in World War I. At the time during which these events occurred, he was in his late eighties and still extremely sprightly. I can remember when I was a child, when he was in his seventies, he would unexpectedly start to juggle with six dinner plates at once, or surprise us with cartwheels on the lawn – a carry-over from his circus days!

Thankfully, after the long drive the weather had changed and some late afternoon games in the autumn sunshine helped to see the children off to bed at a reasonably early hour. A little later, everyone else followed suit, and by eleven o'clock, the house was in darkness. Feeling completely relaxed and tired, I fell into a deep and dreamless sleep.

I noticed the time as I came instantly wide awake. It was 3 a.m. and I was able to see the non-luminous face of our alarm clock clearly without any need to switch on the light. Outside, and all around, the sky was bright with the intensity of daylight, but of a slightly different quality that I couldn't quite define. Rising from my bed, I was amazed at the clarity with which I could see at a distance; details of the borders of the extensive gardens, a distant gardener's cottage, outside which stood a wheelbarrow. Although quite a way away, I could clearly see the spokes in the wheel outlined against a fence. All this was at a time of the month when there was hardly any moon; there did not appear to be any source to the light, but the intensity was such that beams were formed in the way that bright sunbeams can be seen to stream into a room in strong sunlight.

I tried to wake my husband; again, as before this was to no avail; nothing I could do would arouse him to consciousness. Just then my little son, Paul, who was about four, came into our room saying, 'Mummy, mummy!' He took me by the hand and led me out of our bedroom into the corridor. Here strode my grandfather up and down, exclaiming repeatedly, 'In all my years, I've never seen anything like this!'

We all stood for some time, marvelling at the sight; there seemed no explanation for the phenomenon. Forty years on, my son Paul remembers getting up in the middle of the night and gazing at the day-like scene outside, standing between my grandfather and myself. After a time, tiredness overtook us all; no logical explanation came to mind, so we had little alternative other than to retire to bed again, falling into a deep and dreamless sleep.

The next morning we slept late, descending in our dressing gowns for breakfast. The three of us – myself, my son Paul, with all the seriousness of a four year old, and my grandfather – chatted away in animated conversation, unable to arrive at any form of conclusion relating to what had occurred during the night. The others, my husband, my small daughter and my mother and father, having slept through it all, couldn't seem to take it on board, murmuring such things as, 'Was it a full moon?' (Actually, it wasn't, the moon was completely on the wane.) 'Were there any army exercises going on?' (There weren't, we checked.) It was all finally shrugged off as fanciful imaginings. Lacking the ability to conjecture further, the conversation moved on to speculation regarding what we should do with the day as it seemed set fair, if a little cool.

All the time that this discussion was taking place, I could not shake off this feeling of not quite being 'centred', but together with this came the beginnings of a sense of heightened awareness that I couldn't really define, tinged with an element of excitement. Pushing this aside as best I could while chatting away with the rest of the family, we all finally decided on a run in the car through the New Forest, stopping en route for a picnic. Accordingly, after some due preparation, we set out in the autumn sunshine, the browns and russets of the forest contrasting in picturesque fashion with the seasonably pale blue skies.

There is something that has always appealed to me about the New Forest; its history of supplying the early naval yards with timber; the ancient oaks that date back for generations; the wild ponies grazing on tracts of open moorland; the scented pines that bend and sway in the breeze. Immersed in my reverie, we continued on our way. Half my mind was engaged in chatter with the children, the other half continuing to dwell on my bizarre recent experiences.

After a time, we swung off the main road onto one of the many delightful narrow lanes that abound in the New Forest, until we came to a suitable clearing for our picnic. We descended from the car and started to set out a little folding table and chairs; packets of sandwiches started to appear and were seized upon by the two children, who at the same time noticed a couple of wild ponies entering the clearing from the far side. Great animal lovers, our two children couldn't wait to wander over and share their sandwiches with the two beautiful creatures, who were only too glad to help themselves!

We didn't realise at this time that we shouldn't have fed them in this way, as food of the type we were offering might well have been harmful to them; in later years, notices started appearing in the Forest asking that ponies should not be offered food in this way. However, my father, who was a great photographic enthusiast, took some charming pictures of the scene. He then asked me to pose on my own for a shot before continuing with the others to complete the reel of film. A quick smile into the camera, and it was over.

We passed a pleasant time, as many families do, for the remainder of the afternoon until it was time to go home. Father, enthusiast as he was, had his own darkroom upstairs and would often, during the evening of the same day, retire there and develop pictures that he had filmed that day. This day, the day of our picnic, was no different, and after our evening meal, he disappeared as usual in such a quiet manner that his departure went unnoticed. Some time later we heard him descending the stairs at some speed. The door of our living room suddenly burst open, and he rushed in brandishing a roll of film still dripping from the developer. 'Look at this, look at this!' he cried. 'A flying saucer!'

At first we could make nothing out; then, as his shaking hand slowly steadied, we were amazed to see, poised above my head, exactly that. Outlined clearly above my head was a large ovoid disc, its topside raised at the centre and beams of light apparently streaming as if from portholes around its rim.

Father, apparently on first developing the film, only saw a tiny dot above my head where there should not have been one. Curiosity getting the better of him, he enlarged it many times to the size shown in the picture, the high magnification leading to the blurred outline. We were all greatly excited; this occurred many years ago when there was little in the way of discussion in the press or in the media on these matters. I became aware much later of the extent of government cover-ups on anything relating to UFOs or extraterrestrial concepts; having been involved directly in a sighting, as I was, I could afford to be amused at the frequent condemning by the so-called official bodies who would invariably rationalise sightings such as these, often by large groups of responsible people, as 'weather balloons', 'the planet Venus' and other fatuous and equally ridiculous pronouncements by persons who were never present.

I carefully kept the developed film and the all-important negative for some years. Unfortunately, I was foolish enough to mention this to a journalist who had links with officialdom; he persuaded me to lend the negative to him on the pretext that he would be able to develop pictures in greater detail. A week or two later he produced a picture of the saucer which was of far worse quality that the one I already had; he, of course, had somehow mysteriously lost my precious negative, which I now suppose is carefully hidden away in some government archive.

However, my encounters with UFOs were not by any means over. One of the most frightening nights I have ever experienced was to take place much later when Peter and I were living in the Welsh mountains, one summer's night in 1974.

Chapter 5
Former Lives – A Deeper Perception

With my awareness growing almost daily, I was developing a thirst for knowledge that was becoming insatiable. I began to want to know why I was different in the way that I seemed to be; other people, somewhere or at some time, must surely have had similar abilities to the ones I was now developing. My desire to know and understand more in terms of esoteric matters was considerably frustrated by the fact that I could find no one among my circle of friends and acquaintances who could identify with my fast expanding abilities.

Further questions began to form in my mind; somewhere, some time previously, I had read in a magazine article the story of a woman who claimed to have had former lives, some of them in Ancient Egypt. At the time the article had meant little to me, but for some reason an inner prompting caused me to recall this article, and that the woman who had been featured had been extremely clairvoyant. Suddenly I remembered her name: Joan Grant.

As soon as I was able, I visited an extensive library in a large market town near where I lived. I discovered that the authoress had written a number of books, among which were many experiences written of her former lives. I was fortunate in being able to order the books quite quickly, and I could hardly wait to be able to get home and start reading about her fascinating experiences. The experiences that I was immediately drawn to were the ones which took place in Ancient Egypt, and I read avidly about her vivid recollections of the rigorous training she underwent as a priestess in the temples to develop her psychic faculties. I found her descriptions totally absorbing, and within me, at a level as yet beyond my comprehension, a stirring was taking place, which I was unable to define. I, like my husband Peter (who at this point in time I had yet to meet), began to develop a compulsive yearning to discover previous life experiences. I had no idea at all how to proceed further along my line of enquiry, so I simply prayed every night to be shown the way to find the evidence of lives I had lived before.

Not many nights passed before I started to have a series of waking dreams, quite different from the muddled and seemingly meaningless ones, which formed the majority of my nightly adventures. I had had, it is true, experienced some vivid waking dreams from time to time, and they were usually predictive and quite accurate, concerning such things as air accidents and national disasters, quite different from what I was trying to achieve at this time – but more of this anon.

In one of the waking dreams I was experiencing now, I found myself dressed in a feathered coat, being pursued and captured by men in steel helmets. Once captured, along with others, we were all chained by the neck and marched off to some sort of underground chamber with a grating high above us. I can recall being tortured to death – something I do not care to dwell on, as the scene was horrendously vivid. I seemed I was an Incan priest, and I was suffering at the hands of the Spanish Catholic invaders under Cortez.

Mercifully, there came a time when the physical body could take no more, and I slipped from my broken and shattered remains as one would discard an old suit. I can clearly remember floating upwards in my disembodied form, looking down with an overpowering feeling of relief at the battered wreck from which I had escaped. I seemed to float through some narrow streets; my next memory of this episode sometime later was that of being an observer at a distance away from my body, watching it being flung from a height into the sea. At the end of this sequence of events, which gave me the impression of being spread over something like three days, I just seemed to rise above it all, and I had no further recollections whatsoever.

These waking dreams persisted over a period, with an impact on my thinking that is difficult to describe. There was a reality about them that personally convinced me I had really lived through these experiences in those earlier times. I did not, as Peter describes in Chapter 7, 'A Tale of Self-discovery', which relates the story of his research into former lives, seek to prove by any form of historical reference the validity of my experiences, being content to just accept the experience for what it was.

During this time, I was bringing up an adopted son and daughter. My psychic development was expanding at a great rate, but it seemed I had acquired an insatiable hunger continually to acquire more. I seized on any books containing esoteric matter, and one day I chanced upon one on how to hypnotise people. It had a particular interest for me at this time because my daughter was suffering from a bad toothache, and an appointment had been made at the dentist the following day, to have the tooth extracted using gas as an anaesthetic. In these enlightened times, of course, this doesn't happen, but at the time of these events this was the current procedure. I was naturally very worried for her, as I had read of various incidents during which gas was used, where things had gone badly wrong – even resulting in death to the patient in extreme cases.

In the daily press, I had heard of hypnosis being used with success on dental patients, and had acquired this book with the idea at the back of my mind of using this to advantage to help my daughter. The practicalities of acquiring the necessary skills and convincing the dentist that this was the way to go in the time available just never occurred to me; how I expected to achieve anything in this way totally escapes me today. Let us just say that this was not one of my brighter ideas, and the problem of my daughter's dental treatment resolved itself in the traditional way with every success.

However, I continued to read the book and study up on the techniques of hypnotism. Remembering that only a short time previously I had experienced my waking dreams relating to previous lives, I began to wonder if recovery of knowledge of previous lives would be possible under hypnosis.

I then commenced to do something I should never ever have done, without realising the implications involved. Using my son Paul as a guinea pig, I used a combination of hypnosis techniques gleaned from the book and my own intuitive psychic abilities to see if I could regress him to a former lifetime. This resulted in instant success in terms of results obtained. Very quickly, in response to my guided questioning, Paul saw himself as a young man in his twenties – my son was aged about eleven at this time – working in a tavern in London by the River Thames. He described the filth and squalor of what seemed to be the London of the late eighteenth/early nineteenth century; the dirt and rubbish littering the streets, and how a lot of this was often just thrown down from the upper floors of buildings with no regard for anyone passing below. My son described his early demise in that life, brought about by a brawl, which ended in a knife fight.

Realising on the one hand that I should not be involving my son in this form of investigation, another side of me was fascinated by these revelations. I continued, against my better judgement, and asked him if he had known me personally in any other lives. He replied easily and quickly in the affirmative, telling me of a former life in Ancient Greece in which he recalled being a young man at the time when the Temple of Apollo was being constructed. He described the partly-built temple in the background, with craftsmen carving some of the blocks. Paul saw himself as part of a group of younger people being instructed by myself as an older man with long grey hair and flowing beard, dressed in a white robe and open sandals, drawing patterns in the sand with a long stick.

Unable to help myself observing this mental form of time travel, and always having had a great interest in Ancient Egypt, I asked Paul if he was able to recall any lives from those times. Once again, he responded immediately, remembering a lifetime as a woman servant. Fear manifested itself in his voice as he recalled working for a woman who seemed to be involved with some sort of occult rites involving mummified cats. At this point I realised that enough was enough, and gently brought him back to the present time, deeply concerned as the realisation hit me about what I had been involving my son with. Belatedly, I asked myself, would any emotional aftermath have been incurred as a result of his relived experiences? I looked at him closely; he seemed a little tired, but otherwise his normal self. 'Did anything of what we've been talking about worry you, dear?' I asked.

'What's that, Mummy?' he said. 'What have we been talking about?'

I gave him a hug and said nothing. Inwardly I was incredulous that such a young child could relive experiences in former lives at ages in those lives far beyond his present age, and also that now I had returned him to present time, it appeared that he did not recall anything we had discussed. I was also greatly relieved to see that, apart from appearing to be a little sleepy, apparently no change had taken place within him that I could detect.

With a vast sense of relief, I resolved never to experiment again in this way with a person so young. However, this experience did give a different and new perspective to the way that I viewed people from that day forward. I realised that we, all of us, are *living summaries of existences going back into the mists of time*, with experiences in former lives showing through in our current lifetimes in the form of acquired skills, tendencies, habits and many other influences. When I encountered people now, I noticed that I would, from time to time, gather impressions from them of their former lifetimes, and began to view people's characters rather as a summary of their previous incarnations rather than just as an individual from the viewpoint of their current lifespan.

It was as if an entirely fresh perception of people had entered my awareness. It seemed that my mind, at times, on meeting individuals had become a scanner in a way that is not easy to communicate. The best way that I can describe it is that often when I met people for the first time, I would mentally step back as it were, and, working at an almost subconscious level, it seemed in certain cases that their features would subtly change before me. Over a period, I began to realise what was taking place. What was occurring was that if, for instance, someone perhaps leading a menial and colourless existence in this present lifetime had had a former life in a much more prominent role, this would show through, and I would perceive this subtle change in the form of an 'overlay' in, for want of a better term, their aural envelope.

The first time that I became aware of this occurring came about in a rather unusual way. My children were at school, and I was out shopping on my own. Having made all my purchases, I decided to go to the café adjoining the store and enjoy a coffee before returning home. I had just sat down, my coffee before me, when I noticed a coloured lady sitting at an adjoining table. She had just given me a charming smile, which I returned, when I suddenly saw a handsome Afro-Caribbean man enter the café and make his way to the lady at the adjoining table. What struck me immediately about him was his immaculate attire; he was wearing a gorgeous navy blue blazer with brass buttons, with an immaculate tie and light-coloured trousers, together with dark tan, expensive looking leather shoes. Nothing unusual, of course, to see smartly dressed people out and about, but as I was taking him in, it idly occurred to me that, apart from his colour, he could almost be taken for an immaculately dressed plantation owner from perhaps the West Indies in the late eighteenth century.

I remember thinking that, of course, such a person from that period would never have worn modern clothes like this, and then it was as if a series of flashbacks superimposed themselves on my consciousness. In my mind's eye I saw his attire change into that of a slave owner of that period, who was something of a dandy. The handsome, smiling dark features of the man before me changed into those of a cruel-looking European decked out in eighteenth-century finery. The superimposed character that I was now seeing was someone with little regard for those slaves in his charge who had been brutally torn from their peaceful ways in their country of origin, shipped in chains under appalling conditions and sold off to be treated worse than animals by their purchasers on the plantations. What I was now witnessing before me, it came to me, was the reincarnation of that plantation owner as a coloured person, so that the soul could experience the other side of the coin, so to speak. I could see the man had experienced a great deal of suffering in his youth, probably having been bullied by young whites, but was now a well-adjusted individual who had overcome the traumas and had integrated well into society. An interesting illustration of the Law of Karma, the word given by many Eastern peoples to the principle we know as, 'As ye sow, so shall ye reap'.

However, in our Western culture this, of course, is viewed as the Biblical principle of the good that we do others being returned to us in life, and the harm we do will be returned in like manner. The difference is, of course, that Karma is the sum total of the good and bad during each successive lifetime. In fact, in the original Biblical teachings, reincarnation was taught, but at a meeting of religious heads at Constantinople in 410 AD, these beliefs were removed, as it was thought that sinners would adopt the view that any bad actions on their part could be atoned for in future lives. So, the message is, whether in this life or future lives, do your best to collect Brownie points!

One day when I was driving through London, I saw a gang of youths aged about seventeen to twenty marching through the streets waving flags with swastikas on and wearing German World War II helmets, and shouting and swearing at passers-by. One of these, the leader, seemed to have particularly cruel features, and I became concerned that he would start to incite his gang to attack some of the shoppers and bystanders, just for kicks. Unfortunately, these days street gangs are becoming more and more prevalent in certain areas, but in this case the mystery was – why the swastika flag and German soldiers' helmets? World War II had ended some forty years previously, and these youths would have been born at least twenty years later.

In a flash it hit me. Young German soldiers killed in the heat of the battle, their minds warped by the frenzied propaganda of Hitler and his entourage, were reincarnated in the land of their enemies! Of course, not all youths in these groups would necessarily have had the same reincarnational background; some of them would have just joined in because it was an outlet for their disturbed upbringing, but there it was – the root cause behind it all displayed before me! This showed me the responsibility that we all have towards ourselves and others; the paths we select through life and our actions towards those around us all contribute to building our futures, not only in this life, but in our next life on this earth.

In later years, I remember reading in the press about a sixteen-year-old boy who had, at intervals, from the age of eleven, been poisoning members of his family and those around him, making them extremely ill. In this article, it stated that the youngster had been obsessed by the life of a nineteenth-century doctor who became an expert on poisons, and who had murdered many victims by skilled use of these, and who remained undetected for years. The inevitable occurred; the man was caught, tried and hanged for his crimes. However, this youngster would constantly visit his local library and take out books on the life of this man, and developed an amazing knowledge of poisons.

I remember the boy was eventually tried and locked away for a long time; I never heard of him again. At the time that I read of these events, it came to me straightaway, leaving no doubt in my mind that the lad had returned from the gallows after a suitable time interval to carry on where he had left off!

These, of course, are very negative examples of how former lives can overshadow and direct some people's lifetimes. The vast majority of my readers will be positive, thinking and caring people, otherwise they would probably not be reading this book! Some of you will have already discovered your natural talents, which often have their roots in former lifetimes, and can put these to good use; but it is unfortunate that many people find themselves square pegs in round holes, having an inner feeling that they should be working in quite another field.

I will always remember one particular client who came to me who had had a rather disturbed background and came from a poor home. Through mixing in bad company during his early development, he became involved in petty crime in his teenage years, such as shoplifting and stealing cars. Inevitably, he was caught and sentenced to serve eighteen months in a youth retraining centre. Fortunately, in this particular centre, the authorities were enlightened people who, although strict with miscreants, encouraged those boys who showed any desire for self-improvement.

Although my client had had a rough education, he was allocated to work in the institution's library and became exposed to books in a way that had previously not been possible for him. Potentially, he had a very keen mind, and he told me that when he first entered the institution, he had a burning sense of injustice against life. Fortunately, much to his surprise, he found that he had an instant rapport with one of the members of staff, who gave him a great deal of encouragement with his reading. Initially attracted to the legal section of the library (apparently there were some four or five books available on this subject), for the purpose of learning how to manipulate the law in his favour if called to account for any future crimes he might commit after serving out his sentence, he found himself fascinated by the subject. This combined with a firm but fair treatment during his stay, caused him to avidly read whatever legal matter was available for him to study. Amazingly, he found it remarkably easy to absorb, to the point where, astonishingly, he started to develop what seemed an impossible burning ambition to become a lawyer. From entering the institution as a difficult, rebellious youth, he became extremely well behaved and cooperative, creating and running a newsletter, with the approval of the authorities.

The institution had a certain number of visitors who formed part of the association, which had been created to help and encourage, where possible, the reintegration into society of miscreants. Again, my client was lucky in having a woman visitor, the wife of a local MP, who encouraged him in everything he did and took a keen interest in his ambition. Through his excellent behaviour, the lad gained maximum remission. Not long before he was released, a member of the visitors' association who had been extremely impressed by accounts of the lad's progress and abilities related to him by the MP's wife, arranged a job for him to train as a solicitor's clerk.

A year or so later, the solicitor who employed him was so delighted with his abilities that he took him under his wing and made a working arrangement with him so that he could qualify as a solicitor in the family practice, it being understood that he would remain within it. The lad worked extremely hard and, after qualifying, became a tremendous asset to the practice.

The first time he came to me – it was for advice on a criminal case he was dealing with – I would never have guessed the story of his youthful lawless escapades. This extremely well dressed and well presented young man, who would have been about thirty-five when I met him, confided his story to me one day when I had imparted to him some particularly useful information, from a psychic aspect, on one of his cases. Towards the end of his account, I began to get the impression that I was talking to a much older man, wearing a wig and the fine apparel of an earlier century, tremendously learned and capable in legal matters. I suddenly saw where his earlier rapid grasp and amazing progress had come from. My client had essentially picked up from where he had left off in a former life – his knowledge from that period being suitably tailored to modern requirements.

Meeting this man brought home to me the importance of the influence our former lives can exert on our present one. Later, I am going to describe how, after Peter and I met, we use this important knowledge to great benefit.

Chapter 6
I Meet Peter

A strange awareness entered my mind as I scanned the room and started to mingle with the crowd. Laughing and chatting between introductions, I merged with the others who met here once a month in the hall to discuss philosophy and promote spiritual awareness, thereby hopefully to grow and learn. At the previous meeting, which had been my first, I had been moved to come by curiosity rather than by any spiritual or philosophical motivation. An association which discussed and promoted these subjects, I felt sure, must surely be composed of a number of people like myself, capable of telepathy, Distance Seeing, Aura Viewing and the like.

The first time that I had come here, I did not get this impression at all. Sincerity in seeking knowledge, yes, but I could sense a form of – how could I put it – *mental coating*, rather like an intangible membrane, that seemed to dim the extrasensory faculties. Everyone, of course, has psychic awareness and abilities to a greater or lesser extent, but unless the veil I have described is parted is some way, no great progress in awareness can be made.

Here I found a hand held out in greeting; there a smile from someone half-remembered from the previous meeting; I moved through the throng feeling a little lost.

Suddenly I caught sight of a man engaged in conversation on the far side of the room – a man remembered from last month's meeting – someone I had felt was very aware, and adept at concealing that knowledge. We had exchanged only a few words in greeting after introductions had been made, and I remembered feeling a strong flash of attraction; something that I had never experienced before in this way.

At the time I had been married for some years to a good and kindly man, very much older than myself. I had met Eddie when I was sixteen, Eddie being thirty-three. Three years later we were married. Eddie was a commercial artist, an extremely good one with a wide circle of artistic and musical friends. Being much older than I was, his friends tended to be in the same age group, and while they were extremely intelligent and articulate and I very much enjoyed their company, I tended to feel a little out of things due to the age gap.

Some eighteen years had passed since my marriage to Eddie. During this time I had become a housewife, adopted and reared two children, and had done my best to fit in with the dormitory community in a developing town in Kent.

However, during the latter part of this period, my psychic faculties, having laid dormant for some time, had begun to awaken. I began to see auras and was becoming extremely telepathic, as well as frequently being aware of events that were taking place elsewhere. Eddie seemed to have a fear of these subjects – something at the time I found very difficult to understand; but with the passage of time and greater insight than I had then, I now realise that lack of knowledge often breeds fear.

This realisation came to me in a very simple manner. One day I was driving quietly along on my own down a country lane. It was a sunny summer's day; to my left there was a large cornfield, with an occasional cluster of wild poppies, their scarlet heads nodding in the breeze. To my right, a narrow verge filled with wild flowers provided a backdrop for butterflies dancing in the sunlight. On the other side of this verge lay a dense row of trees, behind which little could be seen. All at once there was a deafening explosive roar, which shattered my reverie and terrified me to the depths of my being. A brief second or so later, the loud intermittent clatter of a high-speed train brought an overwhelming flood of relief as I caught its reflection through the trees. I pulled to the side of the road to collect myself, and the thought came to me: *when the unknown becomes known, fear will vanish.*

From this point on, I found this simple lesson to be of immense value. Whenever I was confronted by a situation that would produce a sensation of fear in me, I would ask myself, Is there something unknown to me that is causing this fear? In many cases, an examination of the problem would reveal hidden factors which when brought to light would cause fear to evaporate. Simple and obvious examples are fear of water and fear of heights. It would be normal, of course, for a non-swimmer to fear water, but a gradual introduction to the element and some swimming lessons taken to gain knowledge and become familiar with the environment will not only of course often remove the fear, but add a new dimension to living.

I once knew someone who had a great fear of flying. If he wanted to go on holiday with his wife and an airline flight was involved, he would feel sick with apprehension for some days previously; and the actual flight of course was a nightmare. However, so determined was he to overcome this problem that he went to his local airfield and took flying lessons! The first few flights were made with his eyes closed a lot of the time, but determination won through, and very gradually over a long period he became accustomed to the sensation of flight. From this point, he slowly progressed over a year to take his flying licence; and today he is a skilled pilot, flying long distances abroad in his own aircraft.

These fears and phobias are often rooted in former lifetimes, and regression to the incidents causing problems in those lives will often quickly remove them, as one removes weeds from an orderly garden. However, I am going to deal with this subject fully in a later chapter in order to return to my theme.

One day I sat down to talk over with Eddie my gradually increasing paranormal perceptions. I tried to explain how sensitive I was becoming to people's thoughts around me; however it seemed impossible for him to reach an understanding of the concepts. I wanted to explain that I was developing a strange sort of throbbing sensation in the centre of my forehead. It was very strong at times; it almost seemed to be projecting a beam from this point. Bizarre as it may seem, I had the sensation that if I passed my finger or the palm of my hand through the extended beam from my forehead, it would produce a tingling sensation in them. It puzzled and bewildered me, but I had no alternative but to accept this.

Naturally I had a burning desire to talk over these and other aspects of my growing awareness, but to communicate what I was experiencing was something else. I wanted to share my experiences with Eddie; explain to him what was happening to me. This proved no easy task; how can one explain to a blind man differences in colour, or the difference between two objects, without him being able to see them? Yet I knew I had to attempt the impossible; to persuade him that I was not insane.

Eddie's first reaction was that perhaps it would be better for me to leave my job, and that it was obviously becoming too much for me. I told him I was perfectly sane, and that my experiences had started before I had taken up nursing. I said I knew my experiences and new-found abilities were highly unusual, and that I seemed to be able to see and do things that others could not.

However, the more I went on talking, the more he stared at me in disbelief. Irritation and concern showed in his eyes, to the extent that I felt I had to prove that what I was talking about was fact and not nonsense. Asking Eddie to sit down across the table from me, I took a pack of playing cards from a drawer and handed them to him. I asked him to hold the pack in his hands, and look at them one by one making sure I couldn't see the faces of the cards. I told him that I would describe each card in turn and tell him whether it was a diamond, heart, club or spade. Eddie shrugged his shoulders, took hold of the pack, and held the first card in the way I had asked.

'Spade,' I called, as I saw the colour and the suit in my mind's eye.

Eddie raised an eyebrow, nodded briefly and moved on to the next card. We continued together, Eddie and I, as we moved through the pack. I found no problem 'seeing' each one and calling it out (in answer to your unspoken question, I cannot 'read' their numerical values!) as a diamond, heart, club or spade; I read each out in turn.

At first Eddie was amused; this was simply a party game with a difference.

Bewilderment followed as I continued with unerring accuracy; then finally, fear. As we reached the last few cards, he suddenly stood up and flung them to the floor, shouting, 'I don't want to know, Anne! Why can't you be the same as you used to be? It's evil! I don't want to know!'

Eddie was obviously very upset and very frightened. He could not and would not attempt to understand. His reaction convinced me that I had to choose between one of two courses: either I would have to hide the psychic side of my life, or go it alone. To try to turn the clock back was impossible; I had shown Eddie what I was capable of when challenged, and this had altered the entire perspective of our relationship.

From this point forward I learned to keep my own counsel. It was a lonely path to tread; however, as my inner abilities grew and new experiences came into my life, I knew I had made the right decision. Unfortunately, as time went on, the gulf between us widened as I continued to develop; and Eddie, who was a good man but remained in fear of anything to do with extra-sensory perception, found he was more and more unable to relate to me.

It was at this point in time that I noticed an advertisement in the local paper announcing monthly meetings for people interested in the same subjects as I was. This intrigued me. Would I at last be among my own kind? Would they be telepathic, able to read auras and even read the future? What a wonderful thought – to be able to relax, to discuss concepts I would normally have to keep quiet about, and to find common ground with those around me.

This was the background leading up to my seeking out and joining this local branch of a philosophical association. As I mentioned earlier, I was met with a kindness and sincerity that was way above average, but I could sense that the kinship, the mental warmth that I have subsequently learned to experience – which to me identifies the psychically aware – was not there. Earnest discussion with different people, although philosophically fascinating, left me with a feeling, if you like, almost of extrasensory emptiness, a void that needed company – psychically-aware company.

However there was this man – this person – to whom I felt instantly attracted in a way that appeared almost frightening and yet who intrigued me so much and constantly held my attention, in spite of myself. There he was, on the far side of the room, chatting away and seemingly at ease with the world about him. A man of about forty, looking very fit with extraordinarily penetrating blue eyes that were at the same time inscrutable. As I looked across the room at him, he seemed instantly aware of my glance and our eyes met briefly across the crowd, which distanced us. I hurriedly averted my gaze, moving in such a way that my back was turned. I continued a conversation with two women, who were discussing arrangements for the association's annual outing. While I was talking, I remember thinking how very aware this man seemed; almost as if he could read my innermost thoughts. I must be careful what I think because he can probably read my mind, I thought as I chattered gaily on to the others. A moment later I felt a light touch on my shoulder. Turning, I found myself looking straight up into those selfsame penetrating blue eyes!

'You must indeed be careful what you think because I can read your mind,' said the man I came to know as Peter. He had an amused grin on his face, and just as if I was in a romantic novel, my heart seemed to give a great thump; I couldn't think of anything at all to say. Peter put me at my ease quite quickly, however, and I very soon found out that I had met my match in terms of psychic ability. Not only this, but I had the odd sensation of having known him for a very long time within half an hour of meeting him.

Once I had recovered from my initial shyness I found so much common ground with Peter that we continued talking throughout that assembly until the building was closed, even chatting away on the steps outside. The lateness of the hour and the knowledge that our families would be concerned eventually persuaded us to go our separate ways, but as I drove home that night I had the feeling that my life had altered in a way I was having difficulty in coming to terms with.

We telephoned of course, often sharing our respective views on the different areas of psychic perception. It turned out that Peter had been fascinated by the subject since the age of fifteen. Over the years he had amassed quite a library embracing aspects of the paranormal I hadn't even previously considered; and I found it highly interesting comparing notes on our different approaches to the subject.

Over a period of time Peter related his background and experiences to me; like me, he was an only child and had suffered great loneliness during his childhood. Both his parents were serving officers in the Royal Air Force during the War; and Peter, as were so many other boys, was packed off to boarding schools for the duration. After having left school and subsequently taking up an apprenticeship with a view to becoming a design engineer, Peter became interested in philosophy and the concept of life after death during the time he had free from studying.

A year later, he underwent a compelling experience when his father passed away at the comparatively young age of forty-eight. Shortly after this sad loss, Peter had a waking dream, the reality of this remaining with him throughout his entire life. Having gone to sleep in the normal way in his bedroom upstairs, he suddenly found himself downstairs in the living room of the house. Everything in the room seemed much clearer and brighter than normal, with brilliant prismatic colours manifesting in the form of light reflections from certain objects. While he was seated, surprised and amazed at the abnormal beauty of his surroundings, his father appeared through the closed door, greeting him and engaging him in conversation.

After many years, Peter can clearly remember the discussion, which related to financial matters; all through this time he was thinking, This is a completely real and normal situation; here we are chatting away, yet I know my father is dead. How can this be? But wait, he said to himself. If this is a real situation, when my father leaves at the end of this conversation we will shake hands. When I take hold of his hand, I will be able to feel if it is solid; in this way I will know that I'm not dreaming.

During the final part of the conversation, Peter was asked by his father if there was any way in which he could help his son, and Peter replied, 'I would be very grateful if you could help me with my engineering exams; I am having a great deal of difficulty with the study matter.' Peter's father told him that he would do everything in his power to help him, and they got up to say goodbye. (He did pass, by the way.) Peter told me, 'As I took hold of his hand, we both squeezed. The hand of my father was both completely real and solid, yet there was a difference in feel and texture to the hand from a normal hand that I am still unable to define even today. My father left in the same manner that he had entered – through the closed door. The next moment I found myself wide awake in bed with a tingling sensation throughout my body; to me, the feeling was of re-entering my body, almost as if it were a glove I was used to putting on and taking off.'

The reality of this experience convinced Peter totally that life continues after death. However, he realised that a personal subjective experience of this nature, while being a personal proof to him, could never become accepted in a general sense by others, with good reason.

After this occurrence, over a long period Peter experienced a growing conviction that there must be some means of demonstrating a continuing life process. However, some years were to pass before he managed to achieve a breakthrough; and the first links were forged, he told me, in an entirely unexpected manner. How this came about and the story of his unfolding development, leading to recorded proof of one of his former lives, is related in the next chapter.

These things and many others were the subject of much discussion between Peter and myself. We were both learning a great deal, each from the other; and within a short time of knowing him I realised I had met my match. From this time on we both felt we had been engulfed by a mutual emotional storm. Helpless in its all-consuming path, we felt powerless to do anything other than to plan our future lives around each other. The feeling we had known each other for a very long time soon after our first meeting proved later to be true; we discovered that many of our former lives had been spent together.

Chapter 7
A Tale of Self-discovery

Many people have asked us over the years how we both became interested in regression, former lives and their influences on our present lives. Peter and I have often discussed how we developed our interests along these common lines, and because Peter has always had a logical approach to any subject, physical or metaphysical, we thought it would be of interest to follow his early development.

Peter was educated at a private boarding school and later at a certain public school near Haywards Heath in Sussex, undergoing the usual bullying and harsh discipline associated with these places at the time. This caused Peter to withdraw a lot into himself, and he tended to live an interior life, particularly as he suffered severely from asthma and was therefore unable to participate in games. However, unfortunately for Peter, worship in the school chapel was enforced twice a day, and three times on Sundays.

Peter continues: Although Anne has touched on some of these events, which follow, I feel it necessary for the sake of continuity to include and expand on the following significant incidents, which occurred during the development of my understanding. Because of my background, which Anne has mentioned, I developed a deep dislike of all things religious, and, at that young age, neither the hymns, phrased in the archaic language of an earlier century, nor the sonorous and sleep-inducing sermons did anything to arouse any interest in things spiritual.

Fortunately, this most miserable period of my entire life was brought to a close by a sad event in which another boy, older than myself, was accidentally seriously injured by me. This came about in the following way. At different times, classes of boys were singled out to work on neighbouring farms in the Sussex countryside. On this particular afternoon, our class was detailed off to weed a large field by hand. These weeds stood some three to four feet high, and we all became extremely fed up with this boring chore. The master, who should have remained there to supervise, obviously became as bored as we were, and disappeared without notice for a while. This became the cue for the alleviation of our boredom, and some genius among us decided to set up a competition to see who could fling a stone the furthest. All of us set to with enthusiasm; myself as enthusiastically as the rest.

I had just selected a suitable jagged piece of Sussex flint, drawn my arm back as far as possible and launched my missile with all my strength, when to my horror about ten yards away an older boy, whom I did not realise was anywhere near, stood up from his position of concealment among the weeds, where he had been stooping to select his own missile. My stone caught the poor youngster on the temple and severely injured him, causing him to be hospitalised.

The supervising master reappeared a few moments later from wherever he had disappeared to, realised straightaway that he should never have left the scene and managed to successfully direct all the blame onto me, by saying that I had flung the stone at the boy's head on purpose, while his back was turned. To avert the justified wrath of the boy's parents, and to avoid the question of the obvious negligence of the school, the then headmaster backed the story of the supervising master, and I was 'asked to leave' (a term employed for a low-profile expulsion), after enduring a mandatory flogging.

If that lad, whose name I remember as Parkinson, is still around, I would like to assure him that it was nothing other than a terrible accident, which has haunted me for many years.

Under the circumstances, I was vastly relieved when my school days were over, and I remember thinking at that age that if God and the universe consisted of being involved with anything like the religious studies I had endured at school, I would vastly prefer atheism. However, from that point on my life began to change for the better. My health improved; I commenced an engineering apprenticeship and my father bought me a large motorcycle – a 1932 550cc New Hudson GY4505. In short, my life became transformed as I started to make friends and meet new people.

Over the next two or three years, it gradually came to me that we all inhabit a beautiful planet, with its seas, vast forests and mountains, and various races inhabiting it; and all of it, I realised as my awareness grew, was a mere speck in the universe.

As Anne has mentioned, one day an odd thing came to my mind at that age when my father asked me to plant some flower seeds in our garden. Each tiny seed was the same, and when planted they grew into beautiful flowers; each one the same if they grew from the same seed. I realised that here lay something beyond all our comprehension. Something, or someone, had designed and created these seeds and had arranged that they should grow into spectacular beauty. At this young age I had to acknowledge that some Creator far beyond our mortal understanding had somehow brought into being all of these things – and I felt that I had to accept the existence of this Creator.

At around the age of seventeen, someone lent me a book by Joan Grant (something else that Anne and I had in common), which I found fascinating. This author regressed people to former lives, and could remember some of her own former lives, which made me desperate to discover where and when I had lived before. However, the environment in which I found myself at the time did not lend itself to discussion on this subject; undergoing an engineering apprenticeship as I was, most of my acquaintances were of a pragmatic and down-to-earth nature. Also at this time, my father, who was very interested in these subjects, had sadly passed away and I felt that no one around me could throw any light on these subjects, which were really beginning to arouse my interest.

It was not until I reached the age of nineteen or twenty that I was able to obtain my first personal glimmerings on the subject of former lives. At this stage of my apprenticeship, I had left the engineering workshops and commenced work in the design office. Spending my days learning how to do engineering drawings, working as we had to with pen and ink, I was approached by the chief engineer with an unusual challenge. When anyone left the office or got married, it was the custom for the department to present the individual concerned with a gift and a presentation card to mark the occasion.

The presentation card usually took the form of a cartoon relating to the character of the individual and the event. The cartoon was usually fairly basic and not difficult to do, but when I started to work on the illuminated text which was always included with the presentation, I found this incredibly easy, and was able to achieve a higher standard than anyone else had done in the office, including highly intricate flourishes and innovative styles of ancient texts which caused interested comment among the staff. Gradually, while working away on this, an image started to form in my mind of myself dressed in the brown habit and sandals of a monk, sitting on a stool, working at an inclined table for hour after hour writing ancient calligraphic decorative texts. The building seemed to have a high, vaulted roof and the walls had a white-wash effect. High above me there was an open window through which, if I glanced up, I could see the sky. The climate seemed to be warmer than the English climate I was used to, and I had the feeling of being in a Mediterranean country, possibly Italy.

It took me some time, while I was working away with the elaborate archaic script forming under my pen in red, gold and black, to gradually become aware, as the mental pictures grew stronger, that these were my first real experiences from a former life. Nothing else fitted; there was an emotional quality about what had been taking place that was quite different from normal imaginings.

I felt quite comfortable with this, and naturally had a desire to take it further. If I had experienced this life, as I knew I had, I must have experienced others... but how to access them? Also, I realised that if I had had any former life, I must have gone somewhere into another form of existence after leaving the current life, before taking on another lifetime on this earth. All these concepts chased themselves around in my young mind; while other youngsters were taking part in growing up, joining clubs and making their first dates, I tended to remain apart, probably indulging in too much reading and introspection.

However, several years were to pass before an interesting breakthrough came about quite unexpectedly one evening when I was with some friends. This particular couple, a man and his wife in their thirties, were confirmed atheists, not believing in any god or form of afterlife. Somehow, the course of the evening's conversation became orientated towards these subjects, and the man's wife, whom I will call Janet, became almost vehement in her denial of any form of the life beyond our normal physical existence. At this point in the conversation, and to this day I cannot explain how I came to say the words that burst forth from me unexpectedly, I suddenly leant forward and said, 'You committed suicide in a previous life!'

At this point, Janet's voice altered, her expression changed and she said, 'I like to feel the sun on my face, and the wind in my hair.' Immediately I had a picture of a young girl of about eighteen years, with long beribboned hair trailing in the breeze dressed in a crinoline, throwing herself off a cliff and falling to her death.

Janet's husband's features were transformed into amazement. 'I've never heard Janet speak in a voice like that before, or use that way of expressing herself,' he said.

'What's the matter, did I say something?' asked Janet, who, it transpired, had no memory at all of what she had just said.

Neither of them could understand what had just taken place. However, the event for me was highly significant. Somehow, in a way that at this point in time I couldn't analyse, Janet had slipped momentarily into the final moments of a former life, which had sadly ended tragically, although she had no conscious knowledge of the event in her current lifetime.

A year or so later, someone lent me a booklet in the form of a self-questionnaire from which, by asking yourself certain questions, certain words and images would spring to mind in the form of clues to former lives which could be followed up and investigated. Unfortunately, I was only able to borrow this booklet for a relatively short time, as the lender was shortly returning to Australia. I feel now that I should have made more notes then, as the booklet was particularly interesting. Also, I never made a note of its source or title, so I could not subsequently do an in-depth investigation, as I would have liked.

However, during the brief time it was in my possession, I followed the procedures and came up with a former-life name, which I, surprisingly, had difficulty in spelling and writing down. The reason this was so was not the obvious one, the name being French, as I had sufficient knowledge left over from school days to be able to spell and write down a name in that language. Try as I might, I couldn't picture it at all, and even now, with French being a second language (of this, more later), I'm not sure how it should have been spelt. The name was *Jules de Mon Eau* – meaning 'Jules of my Water', which would have meant a water drawer or provider of water for an ancient noble family – or, perhaps, it was Demoneau. I still can't picture the spelling – and the reason for this came to me long afterwards.

In that life, I was illiterate! I lived that life as a blacksmith in the 1700s, living in a squalid building with narrow stairs and working at a large open brazier to beat horseshoes into shape. As it had said in the booklet, scenes would gradually appear in my mind over a period of time. At some point in that life, I left France for the United States on a three-masted sailing ship, enduring a life of sickness and misery aboard. Out there, I became a gunsmith, becoming involved with womanising, gambling and drink, eventually ending up by being shot and killed in a bar-room brawl. These pictures built up over quite a long period, coming at irregular intervals in a series of intuitive flashes in the form of a mental jigsaw puzzle, with various scenes slowly fitting into place to provide an overall picture.

Two points of interest arose from this experience. Firstly, when at school, I had at the age of twelve, made two pistols (which would have been heavily frowned upon had the masters known!), which worked using proper cartridges, and found later that I had an unusual aptitude for speaking French, although I had great difficulty in writing it and mastering the grammar.

While working in the design office where I underwent the former-life experience of living as a monk working on illuminated texts, the departmental manager came in one day and called out, 'Anyone here speak French?' We were all on very good terms in this working environment, and as no one else present said anything, by way of a joke I put my hand up and said, 'I do!'

This was, of course, entirely fictitious, and was intended as nothing more than an interesting diversion from the daily round. In fact, all I had to back up this statement was the diluted residue of some schoolboy French lessons, which, because of the totally unimaginative manner of the approach, had never appealed to me.

'Right!' said our worthy chief. 'For the next six weeks, you will be the company's translator, and will conduct yourself around our engineering works with a team of engineers from the Paris division. They are over here to analyse our production line techniques and to make a comparative study of the two approaches to the problems involved. Any questions they require answers for, you will be on hand to assist!'

With that he was gone, to the accompanying merriment of the rest of the office, who were as aware as I of the extent of my lack of knowledge of the French language!

Realising that my joke had backfired on me, I could do little other than await the outcome. Later that day my boss reappeared with three charming French engineers, made some brief and unintelligible introductions and disappeared without further ado, giving me a fleeting grin as if to say, 'Now sort this one out!'

Much waving of hands and gesticulation ensued, accompanied by Gallic charm. To my amazement, by the end of the afternoon I was finding that a crude basis for communication was forming. I had never previously been exposed to a French-speaking environment, and, as we all wandered up and down the factory assembly lines, exchanging sketches and writing words down in each other's language, I was surprised to find myself beginning to feel at home in this new ambience. One of the team lent me his dictionary, and at the end of the first week, working in French eight hours a day as I was, communication ceased to be a problem.

By the end of this six-week period, when to my sadness it was time for the French team to return to Paris, I had been offered a job in the Paris office, with the French chief engineer saying that after three months with them I should be completely fluent and would have no problems at all with the language! The odd thing was that I had developed a sense of belonging in that language (and still have) in a way that I found very difficult to express.

Regrettably, I was unable to take advantage of their kind offer, due to family commitments; my father had not long previously passed away and my mother had great need of me then. Looking back, this earlier experience, however, strongly reinforced the former life in France, which I was now currently investigating.

Nevertheless, I did not feel that my quest was over. What I wanted was to be able to identify a former life that was traceable in some way, so that I could say to myself, 'That's me, that's where and how I lived,' and locate it recorded and written down in some way in the annals of history. Quite a challenge, and one I wasn't sure was even achievable. For a period of some years I spent many a long hour deliberating and meditating over this problem on and off – interspersed, of course, with the daily round of problems and different projects.

One day, for no reason whatsoever that I could name, I woke from a deep sleep with a great desire to paint – paint, that is, is an artistic sense; and straightaway, with this totally out of character decision, I knew what I wanted to paint, and that I wanted to paint in watercolours. From about the age of seven, I had always had a strong interest in butterflies and insects in general, and these were what I wanted to portray. The desire to do this was quite strong, to the extent that by the end of the same day I had awoken with this unusual inner prompting, I had acquired a box of watercolour paints and brushes and a pad of art paper. Once home with my acquisitions, I chose as a subject a butterfly, basing it on a tiny illustration from an old cigarette card, enlarging it and adding my own background.

I found the work extraordinarily easy, considering that I had never had any training, and at my public school I was ordered out of the art class during the first lesson with the injunction not to return, as I had no ability whatsoever! I had, however, a slight difficulty with a blending of green to yellow on a blade of grass, which formed part of the background. It happened that I had as a neighbour and friend, a highly competent commercial artist and it was to him I turned to ask his advice, regarding the mixing of the colour to achieve the desired effect as a finishing touch to my painting. To this end, I took my effort round to show him, explaining what I wanted to achieve.

He took one look at what I had done, and handed it back to me. 'Another of your practical jokes, Peter?' he asked.

I was genuinely puzzled. 'What do you mean?' I asked.

'It's obvious to me that you've had years of painting experience, and you've certainly no need of advice from me!'

Nothing would convince him that I had had absolutely no previous experience in painting. I had found working with brush and colour so easy that I imagined anyone could do what I could; and some time would pass before I came to realise it was a skill that normally required tuition and practice. By playing around with different colours, I discovered what was needed to complete my picture, and a few days later I attempted another painting, which produced in me a great satisfaction. However, stepping back from it as I was about to finish it, I had a strong desire to paint Chinese characters upon it in the top right-hand corner, to give a sense of balance to the composition. I, of course, dismissed this as fantasy, and thought no more of it, putting the painting to one side preparatory to completing it the following day.

The next morning I put the painting up to give it some final touches. Again, to my amazement, I had a strong instinct to paint Chinese characters in the top right-hand corner. Taken by surprise, and knowing nothing whatsoever about the Chinese language, I asked myself why this had suddenly become important to me, and how on earth could I put Chinese calligraphy on my painting, knowing nothing about the subject? Oh well, I thought; I'll take myself along to a bookshop and see if I can find a book along the lines of 'Teach Yourself Chinese', and perhaps copy a piece of text from that onto my painting. At the time, a thought struck me. If I am receiving such a strong impression to paint Chinese characters on this picture, could I, building on my earlier research, have lived as a Chinese artist in a former life? If so, using the technique I had learned from the booklet on reincarnation, what would have been my name in that life?

To my great surprise, not one, but two names flashed up strongly in my mind. I immediately wrote them both down in my notebook:

TAO CHI

SHI TAO

Immediately after having done this, I remember thinking that the odds of finding names like that in Chinese history in a milieu unfamiliar to Western peoples, written in a Western representation of an Oriental script would represent greater odds against success than winning the lottery. Mentally dismissing this route, I set out to visit some bookshops with the idea of purchasing my copy of 'Teach Yourself Chinese' – if indeed it existed!

Initial enquiries met with no joy at all. No one I spoke to at that time even had any idea as to where to obtain such a book. However, one person I was discussing the subject with mentioned that her shop had a small book entitled *Far Eastern Art*, which she produced for my inspection. At this time in my life I had scarcely glanced at any Oriental art. However, while riffling through the pages of this book, I was immediately struck by the delicate beauty and harmony of the colours – and suddenly I became aware of the beautiful calligraphic texts in the form of poems that seemed to enhance and complement each painting. Why not simply find an appropriate piece of calligraphy from one of the illustrations, and blend it in with my painting to give it the sense of completeness I sought?

I purchased the book and took it home, made myself a cup of coffee and sat down to read. I found the paintings depicted in it beginning to grip me with a total absorption, their beauty complemented by the exquisite calligraphic texts, which I learned while reading the book, were written on each painting in the form of a poem that related to the painting, both in form and content. I felt transported into another world.

Suddenly, a ridiculous thought occurred to me. Impossible, but what if…? I turned to the index of artists at the back of the book. The unbelievable was there. I gazed at the text, unable to take it in at first:

TAO CHI (SHIH – T'AO)

(c1630–c1707, pp.62–63)

The only things lacking in what I had initially written down were the silent 'h' and a hyphen and apostrophe; otherwise the words were phonetically identical!

I discovered later that the name Shih-T'ao was used by the artist Tao Chi in the same way that an author uses a nom de plume.

I looked at some of the illustrations of paintings by this artist. Towering landscapes, mountain tops with pine forests on the slopes interspersed with clouds and swirling mists, seemed to draw me into their spell. Far below, in some of the paintings, would be depicted a tiny lone fisherman afloat in his small craft. These works resonated within me; I felt transported mentally back into those times. I riffled through the pages. Where were the flower and insect drawings I knew were closest to my heart in that existence?

No trace or reference to these was made in the book I had purchased. Intuitively, I felt this to be extraordinary, so I decided to contact the Oriental department of one of the London museums.

The curator in charge was extremely polite and helpful, but informed me categorically that Tao Chi was known only as a landscape artist, and that to his knowledge, no works of his were known to exist depicting flowers and insects. I thanked him for his help, concealing my disappointment, and indeed beginning to wonder if this aspect of my research was incorrect.

However, during the ensuing two or three weeks, a gradual conviction grew within me that my inner feelings were right after all. I therefore decided to carry out some further research of my own into this artist's work and general history.

Somebody suggested to me that a good place to carry out research on the life of this artist would be in the Library of Oriental and African Antiquities in London. Accordingly I took time off, and spent some time reading up general information on the life of Tao Chi. I found quite a store of copies of his various paintings, many landscapes of course, and a number of sketches of different scenes. One of these, a scene depicting a stone bridge over a stream, produced an astonishing momentary reaction within me of violent nausea and sickness, which quickly passed within seconds. I can only conclude from this experience that I must have been extremely ill at the time when I, in that identity, painted that scene.

I continued with my research, hoping to find some clue that would tally with my great interest in flower and insect painting. Suddenly, my attention was drawn to a sketch by the artist of what seemed to me to be an important-looking official. In the accompanying text the following reference was made, stating that, 'Tao Chi made apologies for his inadequacy at figure drawing [the subject of the sketch], writing that he was a good deal happier painting rocks, flowering plants, insects and fish…'

My emotion could hardly be contained. Weeks of research had eventually paid off, and I was confronted with the corroboration of my feelings in the face of expert opinion. Some time later, I was fortunate enough in being able to acquire a rare catalogue on the life and work of Tao Chi. This catalogue corrected some inaccuracies in the little pocketbook from which I had originally been able to confirm my identity in that life, relating to the year of birth which was 1641. The exact date of death is not officially known, but is listed as 'prior to 1720' – my inner conviction is that I passed away in that life in 1719. This later information was brought to light (subsequent to the book *Far Eastern Art* being published, which I had initially purchased and found to contain the original information relating to the dates of birth and death of Tao Chi, later found to be incorrect) in Chinese records which refer to two colophons by contemporary artists, respectively dated 1720 and 1725.

I continued to paint with redoubled enthusiasm, adding long colophons or calligraphic texts to my paintings. Chinese paintings are, traditionally, usually signed with a red seal or seals, and I longed to have my own to be able to sign my work. At the time my research was taking place, I was also paying visits to various London museums to view original Oriental paintings. Opposite one of the museums was an Oriental art shop; from time to time I would drop in there to buy books and prints, as the whole subject of Eastern art was now becoming totally absorbing for me.

I got to know the Chinese lady owner quite well, and without entering fully into my story, happened to mention to her one day how I enjoyed painting in an Oriental style and would like to purchase, somewhere, some seals with my name on, to be able to sign off my paintings in the way I wanted. The owner of the shop surveyed me silently for a moment through fathomless eyes. I waited, not knowing quite what to expect.

'Wait a moment; I think I have something for you,' she told me. She disappeared through to the back of the shop, and, after a short interval, reappeared carrying a small box. She placed it on the counter and opened the lid to reveal two exquisitely carved jade seals. 'As you can see, they have no name carved upon them. They are very old. If you wish, I will sell them to you very reasonably, and, if you have patience, I can arrange to have your name carved upon them.' I was enthralled and nodded my assent. She continued, 'The only place I know in the world where this can be done is in Peking. I can arrange it for you and it will take about a year.'

At this time, in the 1960s, China was under communist rule, and Europeans were not allowed there in the normal way. The Chinese owner of the shop had relations there, and true to her word, a long time later my two seals duly arrived, beautifully carved in antique Oriental script, together with a small sandalwood box for containing the special red ink necessary to print my signatures. The owner explained to me the purpose of the two seals; one represented my signature in raised form; the other in hollowed form, each a duplicate of the other.

The Chinese artist Tao Chi (also known as Shih T'ao) (1644–circa 1720)

Centuries ago, she told me, the emperors kept prints of known artists' signatures to check that paintings offered to them in those days were not forgeries, and this tradition had carried through, often using two seals, each the duplicate of the other, in the reverse sense. I of course treasured these seals greatly, and on first acquiring them felt an overpowering compulsion to wear them in a small pouch around my neck, under my shirt. I felt I had carried my original seals thus, in that former life.

Some years later, confirmation of this arrived when I came across a self-portrait of myself in that former life. A rare exhibition catalogue came into my hands; I had the eerie experience of gazing into my own eyes of hundreds of years ago! A faint outline around my neck of those times in that portrait shows how I wore my seals then.

An odd experience occurred to me during all my researches, long before I met Anne. At one time, I worked in the City, and travelled every day to my office on the London Underground. In each carriage above the windows ran a series of advertisements. I was curiously drawn to one of them, which consisted of a hypnotically beautiful pair of eyes, which seemed to follow me everywhere. The advertisement was by Optrex, a company that still markets eye drops today, but with different advertising promotion. I began to notice that these eyes were starting to follow me on public hoardings, buses, everywhere. I used to gaze back at them in reverie, dreaming how wonderful it would be to meet the possessor of those eyes in person, to the point that she became the woman of my dreams!

Years later, the seemingly impossible happened – I found they belonged to Anne! Her eyes being so unusual, through a mutual friend of Anne's at the time, the advertising company that worked for Optrex had decided to use them for their client – an astonishing confirmation of how dreams can sometimes come true in a way that we would never think possible!

All this, of course, took place quite a time before we eventually met. When we first encountered each other, we felt like old friends; and of course indeed, we were, as we soon discovered we had known each other in former lifetimes. As can be imagined, after our initial telepathic encounter at the Philosophical Association meeting, Anne and I rapidly began to find ourselves more and more on common ground.

Soon we had moved on from telepathy to sharing experiences about previous lives. Anne showed me that we had shared more than one life in Ancient Egypt together, and that she had known me during my life as an artist in China.

I had intuitively realised when first meeting Anne that we had known each other in Ancient Egypt, but nothing more. Shortly afterwards, Anne was able to tell me that I was picking up on a life then when I was a priest, and she in training as a priestess. We fell deeply in love; any relationship was forbidden in the priesthood in this particular era, and once this was discovered by the elders, we were tortured and put to death. Anne with her deeper powers of perception made me far more aware in detail of what had taken place. For some time afterwards, this had the effect of a deep depression on me, and I would lie awake on certain nights with tears in my eyes, while mentally reliving those times. However fortunately, this sad mental state was soon replaced by the deep joy of rediscovering each other as lovers, rather like a joyous and unexpected many-centuries-old reprieve.

Later, other former life links manifested themselves; working together we have discovered, through regressing some hundreds of people that most of us incarnate in groups, sometimes to renew old associations and work together, sometimes to learn how to resolve problems and injustices that were never resolved at the time in former lives.

In the next chapter, Anne begins with an interview with someone who navigated his way through space in a starship – shades of the *Enterprise*!

The eyes that followed Peter everywhere...

Chapter 8
Past Lives – Our Heritage

I gazed in wonderment at the man before me, his eyes closed, studying his impassive features, which were without movement apart from the slight fluttering of his eyelids.

'I am inside this spacecraft. I am one of a crew, which has volunteered to come to earth on a study mission. I am responsible for the navigation. I navigate through the star system by trilocation; we have panels set into the side of the spacecraft which can be either transparent or rendered opaque to show names and numbers of star systems.'

I asked if he could describe the instrument panel to me, thinking in aircraft terms. The reply came immediately, 'We have no need of one. The star navigation panels are all we require to transit deep space between star systems.' The man – I will call him Paul – continued by telling me how mathematical computations were calculated for navigation, which also involved light beams and gravitational deflection, using words and language, which were beyond my comprehension. He went on to describe how each crew member wore a tight-fitting metallic-looking suit; there was a great deal more detail, including how the crew's mission concerned the dissemination of science and mathematics on earth, although how this was to have been carried out unfortunately I did not have the presence of mind to ask.

Paul continued to explain to me how his spacecraft functioned, using such advanced terms and concepts that I was entirely unable to follow him. After about half an hour of this fascinating intergalactic roller coaster ride, the majority of the information imparted being totally beyond my comprehension, Paul stopped quite naturally of his own accord.

One of my deepest regrets was that I had no tape recorder to record and analyse our interview. Curiously, this experience of my most unusual of all regressions to past lives happened the day before the night of the cosmic crash mentioned in the next chapter. Paul, who was an old friend of Peter's, continued to stay on with us and shared our experiences that night. He had no interest in past lives and did not believe in any form of afterlife. This came out one evening, sitting around as we were under stars that shone brightly in a clear Snowdonian night sky, the amazing views stretching from the magnificent mountains on the one hand to the coast some thirty miles away, where the lights of Llandudno and Colwyn Bay twinkled in the distance. With my experience over the years, I had found that people who held these convictions had, during recent lifetimes on earth, suffered a violent or distressing death, which seems in some way to block the former life memory, normally causing the individual concerned not only to reject these wider concepts but to become almost vehement in their denials of them.

Early on in our discussion, therefore, I realised something of this nature had occurred not too far back to our friend during a recent lifetime, although when I mentioned the extensive work I had carried out in regressional therapy, he expressed an interest in experiencing regression to see what would happen. Accordingly, I agreed to a session the following morning, as by now it was getting late and we were all feeling the effects of our day's trekking in the mountains.

The next day, breakfast over, Paul and I found a quiet corner to ourselves in the cottage that Peter and I were restoring. Making sure that he was comfortable and relaxed, I remember him saying, 'I don't believe in past lives, you know; I think you're going to be disappointed in me…'

I began as I often do, snapping my fingers after allowing him to become completely relaxed and saying, 'Describe to me the first image that you can see in your mind's eye.' Normally it is necessary to have more of a preliminary discussion, during which I would determine certain interest areas of my client to give me direction, but for some reason in this instance I forgot to do so. In any case, it is usual for the person being regressed to take a little time to respond, as if they are assembling the first mental images in their mind and wondering if they are just figments of their imagination (occasionally this is the case to begin with, especially with people, as I have said earlier, who have had a traumatic death in a former life).

It takes a great deal of experience and use of my Inner Eye to determine whether it is a genuine regression or a fantasy brought about by the individual's reluctance to confront a previous bad experience. Usually, the individual will gradually 'move over' into a previous life as the session progresses. However, in this case I was amazed by the rapidity of Paul's response, which came without any form of preamble, and we launched into this extraordinary scenario, which I had never previously experienced during some hundreds of regression sessions.

Paul sat there remaining silent, his eyes closed. The feeling I had was that of a child who had somehow managed to start the family car and had now been left grimly hanging on to the steering wheel. I was now left wondering in which direction I should take Paul and where we were both going to end up. However, to my vast relief he responded to the normal technique I use with all my clients whom I regress. 'I want you to return to present time, and to leave the times we have been discussing completely behind you.'

Paul blinked a few times, rubbed his eyes and looked across at me, obviously returned to his normal self. 'That was absolutely fascinating,' I said. 'I have never listened to such an amazing set of experiences.

'What do you mean?' he asked. 'What experiences?' Paul had absolutely no knowledge of what he had been talking about for the past hour; and, even when I attempted in my limited way to jog his memory, nothing surfaced.

This again was something I had never before experienced. My clients almost always remember the scenes from which they have returned; indeed, often these scenes enlarge and expand themselves in the person's mind, particularly just before dropping off to sleep or lying awake in the morning. It seemed that I had by almost random chance, rather like a pinball dropping in a slot machine, entered this particular access route that led, I feel, to an earlier lifetime of Paul's at the beginning of the colonisation of our planet by beings from another star system.

In his current lifetime, Paul is a highly qualified senior lecturer on mathematics and advanced engineering at an overseas university. Much earlier in life he was a senior design engineer with Hawker Aircraft Ltd and was one of those responsible for the TSR2 project, an extremely advanced vertical take-off jet fighter that was cancelled by the British Government – one of the greatest losses to British aviation in our history. I mention this because, in my view, he had carried through some amazing abilities into his current lifetime; tailored, of course, to the technology available to him in our present day. In his leisure hours he is a skilled private pilot and navigates a 36-foot yacht across the oceans.

During the ensuing years, I was to encounter only two other regressees who came through into former lifetimes off-planet, from the many hundreds I had carried out. These were very interesting in themselves; however, they were quite different in nature to the foregoing.

At the other end of the scale however, as one might expect, at different periods in the Earth's history, many people have led former boring and extremely repetitive lives. Perhaps an entire lifetime might be lived out in a remote forest clearing, living in some primitive hut and merely concentrating on survival by hunting or living on berries or the like. Life observed from this perspective during regression of the subject would often surprise me in the early days by not even knowing the year of their experience, the name of any rulers or even what country he or she was living in during that lifetime.

However, it seems that in the majority of cases, we step off our 'Time Machine' to relive during regression some former life or lives that give meaning or colour to our incarnational background. However, before moving on to some more interesting cases, it seems that the purpose of some of the apparently boring and repetitive lives almost all of us have led during our aeons of existence, is to build fortitude and enhance understanding within our 'oversoul', which is the true summary of all our existences, the overall identity that we all are.

Let me now take, as an example, a typical regression case where someone is suffering from an unaccountable phobia, which is seriously affecting their outlook on everyday life. This person, whom I will call Naomi, had a very strange problem, for which neither she nor anyone else could account. Naomi was engaged to be married to a nice kind lad who did not ask to force any form of religion on her, but who had always had a feeling of wanting a traditional family wedding held in a church, followed by the usual reception. This view was held by both families, not in any forceful way, but simply because it was seen to be a traditional basis for the union with the Church of England blessing.

Naomi herself was not against this at all; in fact, she was greatly in favour of the idea. The problem was that every time she went near a church entrance, she was seized by an unaccountable dread that seemed to grip the very core of her being. On many occasions she had been invited by family and friends to visit various very beautiful churches; from one occasion on a school trip to France to visit Notre Dame cathedral in Paris where she was overcome by hysterical terror as she approached the entrance and had to remain outside accompanied by a none too pleased teacher, to others where she had been invited to friends' weddings, some of them in delightful rustic churches steeped in history – true picture postcard scenes – all of which caused her to be overcome by revulsion and fear.

I was intrigued. How on earth could such an innocent scenario provoke such an extraordinary reaction?

Naomi sought my help with this strange and debilitating phobia. I sat her down in a comfortable chair one evening, turned the lights down low, and after a few words to relax her, asked her to close her eyes. I clicked my fingers as I usually do and said, 'What is the first image of a church that you can see in your mind's eye?'

Naomi replied swiftly and unhesitatingly; 'It's more like an abbey than a church but I can see it very clearly. It's very big and it is standing on a slight rise. I'm feeling very frightened.'

I gently asked her what she was frightened of.

'I've been found out, I've been found out!' she said, and started to twist and turn in her chair.

'In this picture, Naomi, how old are you?' I asked.

'I'm about fifteen,' she replied. She went on to describe, unprompted, how she had been meeting a boy monk and they had fallen in love. One of the seniors had come upon them when they were embracing; they had both fled in different directions, and, at this point in time, when Naomi was reliving this former life episode, other monks had been alerted and were out looking for the couple.

Soon she was seized and dragged into a chapel while a row of monks stood on either side. In front of her was a large wooden box, part-filled with sand. She described someone who appeared to be the head monk; a tall, cowled, menacing figure, whom Naomi described as having penetrating, soulless, cruel eyes. He gave orders to the others to bind her, and place her in the box. At this point, Naomi started to become too distressed to continue, so I gently brought her back to present time taking her hand and saying, 'You have left this experience behind centuries ago in another body. You must distance yourself completely from this time period and return to our present time and location, leaving all this firmly in the past, where it belongs.'

I continued to reassure her gently for a while, and Naomi gradually returned and visibly became more buoyant. 'That was absolutely terrifying,' she said. 'They filled up the box with sand and nailed the lid down and I suffocated to death. The strange thing is that I can now look at the scene objectively, as if it all happened to somebody else.'

'Which it did,' I said. 'You can now understand that this did not happen to you as you are now centuries removed from that dreadful experience, but in a different lifetime altogether.' We chatted on for a while, and it was remarkable to see and observe the new, relaxed Naomi.

Some three months later I was delighted to receive a photograph from Naomi of her wedding taken outside her local church, together with a charming thank you note.

I always find it so rewarding when a positive result of this nature comes about, resulting in the release for the person concerned from spiritual fetters of this nature; where a person can have this present life overshadowed by a nameless dread that can often destroy their ability to enjoy life to the full.

Another experience Peter and I derive great satisfaction from is when someone comes to us with no belief in former lives or any other form of existence, but with a desire to 'see if there really is anything in it'. Judy – not her real name – a girl of about twenty, came to see Peter one sunny morning in our Maidstone clinic, expressing an interest in being regressed to a former life. She arrived being completely honest, telling him that she did not expect any results, but that she was interested in 'giving it a go'.

Peter continues: After she had been sat down and completely relaxed, I asked her to close her eyes in the usual way. We have a number of different techniques for sending people back in time, and because Judy had been quite frank in admitting that she didn't expect any results from the interview, I made a very relaxed and casual approach before suddenly asking her if there was any particular period in history that interested her. 'Oh, yes, the First World War!' she exclaimed excitedly and in a manner that seemed uncharacteristic of her.

At what we call the 'entry snap' – the snap of the fingers that will, in the majority of cases cause the participant to mentally tumble down the time corridor and perceive a significant event in a former life, Judy suddenly said, 'I'm getting married. My husband is beside me; he is in uniform and we are walking between two rows of uniformed men who are holding swords above us to form an arch.' I asked her where this was taking place. 'Oh, it's a very long way from where I live. I come from somewhere near London.' Again, I asked her where this place was so far from her home. 'I don't know,' she said. 'It's just so far away. I've never been away from home before and it's all so strange.'

She thought the name of the place began with something like 'Har…', but was unable to remember the rest of the word, which she said had three syllables. I jotted this down on my notepad, which was always kept at hand.

I said to Anne afterwards, 'I went backwards and forwards over this name with her, but could not elucidate any further details. Suddenly an idea came to me. 'To get to this place, what would be the nearest railway station?' I asked. Straight away the reply came back – it sounded like Colbourne or Coleborne, certainly a place I had never heard of. She thought the village was about two miles from this station. I noted it down, then we discussed other details of this life, including a description of her husband's uniform, which appeared to be a dark colour. She was quite adamant that he was a soldier in the army, which surprised me, as the colour of the uniform she was describing would have led me to suppose that he would have been in the navy.

I had always associated khaki as the colour of a soldier's uniform; history was never my strong point at school, and it was not until much later that I discovered this was general in the Second World War, but that many different uniform colours were used for the army, including dark ones, in the so-called Great War. However, for Anne and myself, regression is a totally fascinating subject and one of its most interesting aspects is research into such things, as, in this instance, the type of uniform worn, insignia etc., and from this one can for example find out the regiment in which the individual served, leading possibly to his army experiences and the various assignments undertaken. I continued with Judy but she appeared not to have much interest in pursuing this line of approach. We did, however, discover her name in that life, which I am unable to recall at this distance in time. We concluded the session by my saying that I would do my best to research the fairly scanty information I had taken down in my notes, promising to get in touch with her if I could turn anything up.

Colbourne, Coleborne… I kept racking my brains and searching maps for a railway station of the name, hoping to find a village beginning with Har… within roughly two miles of it. Nothing. Then, one day I happened to be passing a steam enthusiasts' railway station not far from our home in Kent. It was maintained in the manner of the past, with restored steam engines in working condition and carriages from the same era. The train was standing at the station, belching smoke and steam, loaded with excursionists thoroughly enjoying their day out. I don't know why the thought occurred to me, but I remember thinking idly that the railway society might have for sale reprints of the old timetables for steam enthusiasts of bygone times.

Thinking that this was a long shot, I parked the car and went over to make some enquiries. I was amazed to find that, yes, they did sell reprints of old railway timetables and, in fact, had quite a selection. I worked through a small pile of these, covering different railway companies and areas, and suddenly the word leapt out of the page at me: *Coalburn*!

It had never occurred to me to spell the word in this way, so purchasing the copy of the old timetable and slipping it into my pocket, I headed back to the car. Some twenty minutes later I was home and reaching for the *Road Atlas of Great Britain*. I soon located Coalburn (strange how I had never thought of spelling it that way) and found it to be in Lanarkshire in Scotland. Turning to the appropriate page, I soon found the three-syllable village starting with Har… (actually Ha…). It was Happenden, about two miles from the long-disappeared station of Coalburn. Mission accomplished! Allowing for the Scots manner of pronouncing 'Ha' as 'Har' allowed me to slip the last piece of the jigsaw into position.

Judy's reaction was not what I expected. Instead of being excited at the news, as most people are, I felt that there was almost an atmosphere of fear in her voice when I told her of my findings. I had hoped she might take a trip up there at some time in the future to follow up various clues we had discovered together, but regrettably I never heard anything more.

I am returning the narrative to Anne here. It relates to two young men she regressed and led, unlike the story I have just recounted, to an illuminating conclusion.

Anne continues: This experience involves two men who shared with my husband an interest in classic motorcycles. Having met them by chance, Peter invited them down one evening and the three of them thoroughly enjoyed themselves discussing the merits of the various marques. The two of them, apparently, would often go out on a run together, and on many occasions end up at a particular church in Kent near where they lived at the time. Both of them said that they could not account for the way in which they were constantly attracted to it; I had just brought some coffee in and pricked up my ears at hearing this.

'Perhaps you both have had some connection with it in a previous life,' I said. 'Have you ever considered this?'

They both shook their heads. 'Neither of us is religious,' they asserted.

I explained to them that reincarnation and the living of former lifetimes had nothing whatsoever to do with religion. The idea of a permanent identity taking on different bodies at different time periods was completely novel to both of them.

'Would you like me to take you back in time to another lifetime?' I asked. 'In this way perhaps we could find out why you both have this fascination with this particular church?'

They both looked surprised, looked at each other and nodded. 'Yes, we would like to try it,' said one. 'Another new experience, eh, John?' The other assented, and away we went.

Within a moment or two, the first man suddenly became cold and started to shake. 'I'm over a bombed out church – not the one we are so interested in. I'm floating over my dead body...'

As he then started to become very distressed, I rapidly regressed him to a time period four days previously. He replied to my questions easily and quickly. 'I am in army uniform. I am in charge of a group of men and the British are planning an attack on the enemy lines in the next two days or so. Inside we all feel scared, but we feel we are fighting for a just cause.' He went on to give a description of life in the front line and the hell of trench warfare during the First World War.

I gently started to pull him out and away from the battlefields and asked him what the significance of the church was that he and his friend were so interested in. His reply startled me.

'We were married in it,' he said. 'My name was Robert, and Margaret and I were married there.'

I asked him who Margaret was and he indicated his friend sitting next to him. Being familiar as I am with the fact that we all have inhabited bodies of different sexes according to the roles we have planned to play, prior to our taking up the next lifetime, in the ordinary way this would not surprise me.

However, seeing the extremely masculine young man sitting next to me, the close friend of the person I was regressing, and realising that in his last lifetime he had been his wife, was something I found quite surprising! Sometimes changing sex in this way from one lifetime to another can cause problems of homosexuality with the person's stronger female emotions carried over into the subsequent male body, but there were certainly no tendencies of this sort here. In fact, one side effect of these two regressions was that the two men, I understand, saw a lot less of each other after this experience. I feel it produced an uncertainty in their relationship.

However, to continue. Apparently this marriage took place in the Kentish church they had always had a fascination with, in either 1907 or 1908, and they rode in a tall yellow and black car with a completely circular radiator. The story continued, and Robert and Margaret sailed for India, where Robert took up the post of manager on a tea plantation. Life continued happily there, until the outbreak of the First World War. Robert then decided he would return to England to fight for King and Country, and the rest of his story you know. Margaret, after Robert had sailed for England, decided to return also, but sadly a double tragedy ensued. During Margaret's return voyage she was taken ill at Cape Town and passed away. Both their remains were brought back to England by the respective families and interred at the same picturesque little Kentish church where they had been married.

Whereas Robert – John in this life – felt embarrassed at reliving the life, it seemed that Margaret – now Brian – became intensely interested. He later returned to the church that had so interested them both, and thoroughly researched the church records. He found the marriage duly recorded, the two graves where their remains had been buried, and an inscription on a memorial in the church where Robert's name was engraved, along with others who had fallen in that war to end wars.

I found this a touching story; yet another proof that life continues forever across the centuries, and if we really want to see those again we lose, we do of course see them between the lives, although perhaps not always in the same relationship when one is born into the following lifetime.

Fred Williams was a bit of a rogue. My husband met him for the first time at a car auction when they were both examining the same lot. They fell into conversation and it transpired that Fred had several things of interest to Peter, one of which was a mascot for a Hispano-Suiza car, which Peter was restoring. Peter therefore agreed to meet up with Fred later in the week to see if, between them, they would be able to do business. The day came, and between them they came to an agreement over a few items, which Peter duly purchased, being careful to keep receipts as, although Fred seemed very plausible, there was something about him, which made Peter feel ill at ease. A rogue, Peter thought, but a likeable rogue; nevertheless, someone to be wary of.

Some time later Fred telephoned Peter to say that he had an old 1930s-style tourer car in need of restoration for sale, and would Peter be interested? A deal was concluded, and Peter arranged for Fred to deliver the car in a few days' time. After this was effected, Peter asked Fred if he would like a cup of tea, and he came up from the garage to the house to ask me if I would mind making the tea and bringing it out to the garage while they finished unloading. This I did, and met Fred for the first time. He worried me. He had a certain charm, but underneath I felt very mistrustful of him. I could see a side of his nature that was completely unscrupulous, and that even if you befriended him, he would be completely untrustworthy. However, we chatted away over our tea, and it so happened that a neighbour appeared at the garage door, reminding me that she and I had an appointment for a past life regression the next day. Fred had never heard of the concept of past lives, having to ask me, after the neighbour had left, what a 'regression' was.

I explained, leaving Fred somewhat bemused. On impulse, without really considering what I was saying, I asked him if he would like to experience a former life. His comment was that he had nothing against it, if I wanted to 'try it with him'.

Asking myself why I should want to get involved with this man, we – that is Fred and I – repaired to the kitchen in the house and I sat him down. At this point I began to wonder, given his lack of motivation, if I would be able to take him back at all, but to my surprise he slipped easily into a description of being in some very dark woods at night with two other men, all holding old-fashioned pistols.

'What are you doing here?' I asked him.

'We're waiting for a coach to go through,' Fred said. 'Plenty of pickings to be 'ad. We've heard there's gold and jewels being carried, and the gentry always have sovereigns and gold watches with them.'

I was intrigued to think that I was about to hear an account of a centuries-old robbery being carried out.

Fred went on to describe how one of them first heard the rumbling of the coach wheels in the distance, and the sound of the horses' hooves getting nearer, accompanied by snorting, and the mounting excitement of the three men.

'We're waiting at the top of the hill because the horses will be going slower,' Fred said. 'And now we're going to have 'em!' And he went on to describe how they all leapt out, one of them grabbing the horses' heads to bring the coach to a halt. Fred and the remaining man mounted the coach and, apparently, one of the men on the coach tried to put up a struggle.

'I had to shoot him – I didn't want to,' declared Fred. 'But then we went on to get a good haul. I think he was a judge or something – one of the gentry. Gold pocket watch and chain, a purse full of sovereigns, his lady wife's jewels. We did well.' Fred described how they fled through the woods on horseback and recalled how they gloated over their spoils in some hideout.

Some time a few days later he described being in a tavern when some men burst in and arrested him. He was taken and thrown into an evil-smelling jail with some dirty straw on the floor. With the two other men – I think he described this as all taking place at Chichester Assizes in Sussex – he was tried for robbery and murder, and hanged from the gallows.

The curious thing about Fred Williams during this regression was that he seemed to have a strange lack of emotion or even involvement with the scenes he was describing in his life as a highwayman. The other interesting aspect was, although he was obviously reliving former-life experiences, he would not accept that they were what they were, insisting that the experiences were nothing to do with him. In a sense he was right, of course, as these related to another life and another identity; it may have been simply a wish of the oversoul not to accept responsibility.

Sadly, we heard later that Fred had been committed to prison for burglary and theft. I found this to be yet another interesting example of how our former lives shape our present ones, and that we always bring into this world the fruits or otherwise of our previous lifetimes. We have the free will to create either good or bad Karma; so it is always interesting to remember that what we put in is essentially what we get back!

Another interesting regression came my way when Peter brought home someone with whom he had become acquainted again through a common interest in old cars. James Blake (not his real name) was a gifted artist who was generally very bitter with life, as he had been struggling for some years in order to gain recognition for his paintings. One day he brought down some examples of his work in his car, which we persuaded him to show to us. Peter and I were very impressed, and were indeed surprised that he had not been able to gain any recognition.

I was extremely intrigued by James, although he triggered in me some misgivings, which I was unable to analyse. One evening, we invited him down for a meal, and he expressed a great interest in the old Dutch Masters. After we had all enjoyed the meal together, the lights low, his ascetic features illuminated in the glow of table candlelight, I mentioned my interest in past lives and regression. I asked him if I might regress him to find out what connection he had, if any, with art in the past. He agreed; I settled him comfortably and a short while afterwards he was soon tumbling down the corridors of time.

Before long, James found himself walking along the quay of an old Dutch fishing port, describing old sailing ships, fishing boats and various old buildings set in cobbled streets. He expressed surprise as he suddenly found himself wearing wooden clogs, as he had incorrectly assumed that during his regression he would picture himself dressed in his normal present-day attire.

I asked him to return in this former life to where he lived. This turned out to be a very small room at the top of a rickety flight of wooden stairs. It was rather dirty and very sparsely and primitively furnished. In a corner under a window was a board and easel with some sort with a cover over it. It transpired that James in that life was a pupil of Bruegel's, and what was particularly interesting to me in the light of subsequent events was that occasionally he forged the signature of his master on his own paintings, copying closely Bruegel's style and selling them to make ends meet. Interestingly, James did not seem to regard himself as involved with this past life, in much the same way as Fred Williams in my earlier account, dismissing it as fantasy; although some of the emotion he displayed during his experience, particularly when remembering his extreme poverty and hunger, seemed very real.

One day Peter and I were driving in the area where James lived, so we decided to take a chance and call by. James came to the door and, on seeing us, assumed a curious expression, almost of embarrassment. He asked us to wait, and there seemed to be a flurry of activity from within. He returned shortly afterwards and invited us in for a coffee. What immediately struck us was the appearance of utter poverty in the room, with various items covered up on crude benches everywhere with grubby-looking cloths. In stark contrast to this apparent poverty, there stood outside an extremely exotic and expensive sports car, which James had told us with pride that he owned, saying how hard he had struggled to acquire it.

During coffee, we asked if we could admire some of his work again. From behind a curtain, James produced three really beautiful paintings, which we duly admired, expressing amazement that he was not an established artist with well-merited recognition. We asked if we might see some of his other work, which lay around the room covered by these grubby cloths, but James declined, saying that the others were not yet finished and that he would prefer to keep them covered as they were all being worked on. This struck me as a little odd at the time, as surely paint needed to dry, and also if the paint was still wet the cloths would tend to smudge the work. However, we made no comment on this and prepared to leave, as we had an appointment elsewhere.

Some months later we were amazed to read in the press that James had been prosecuted for selling forged paintings by famous artists. His forgeries were only discovered by a bizarre set of circumstances. He had apparently borrowed a particular work after having befriended the owner over a period, made a perfect copy of it and then offered his copy to a London art gallery for sale. Meanwhile, the owner of the original painting had, unbeknown to James, decided to sell his original, and this was on sale at another gallery elsewhere! Consternation ensued when the respective galleries, who had both commenced to market their version of this painting, discovered that there were two identical paintings in existence, when it was of course known that only one could exist!

This led to a full scale investigation by Scotland Yard. James Blake's flat was raided and a large number of fakes 'signed' by the original masters were removed for analysis and investigation. This led to a trial and conviction at the

Old Bailey, where Blake's bitterness at not being recognised as an artist in his own right came out, stating that he saw his forgeries as a revenge on a public who would not accept his work.

The interesting thing to me is that this bitterness due to lack of acceptance seems quite prevalent among certain artists. It seems to me that, spurred on by a subconscious knowledge of former greatness, and an initial arrogance in their lives, followed by bitterness, certain artists have fallen prey to their former greatness, often turning to forging their own works from a previous lifetime.

The man who was acknowledged to be the greatest forger of all time, Hans van Meegeren, appeared to be motivated by the same means. His story is fascinating and has been well documented.

At the end of the Second World War, after the fall of Nazi Germany, an incredible collection of Old Masters was recovered from Berchtesgaden. It had been amassed by Hermann Goering. Many were the result of general looting throughout the war from private collections and art galleries during the German invasion of Europe. A minority had, however, been purchased by Goering himself, and among these was a painting by Vermeer, the seventeenth-century Dutch Master, and entitled 'Woman Taken in Adultery'.

Immediately after the end of the war, there was a witch hunt for persons who had collaborated with the Germans during the conflict. Enquiries uncovered the fact that Goering had paid the English equivalent of £160,000 for this painting from an Amsterdam dealer. Dutch police continued with their investigations and came up with van Meegeren as the man responsible for the sale. Van Meegeren was, at the time, a rich nightclub owner who had made a great deal of money by acquiring previously undiscovered Old Masters and selling them on to a number of major art galleries. In addition to 'Woman Taken in Adultery', which was sold to Goering, he had sold six other paintings signed by Vermeer to various galleries. Van Meegeren was charged with being a collaborator, with the possibility of the death sentence to follow.

He was imprisoned to await trial, during which time he was interrogated for some weeks. The story he gave his interrogators did not vary during this time – he had never collaborated with the Germans, but had swindled them. Goering's painting was nothing other than a fake that he had painted himself, along with many others he had sold worldwide.

When the court heard this story from van Meegeren, which he had steadfastly maintained during his incarceration, they did not believe him, but the judge ordered that he be given a chance to vindicate himself. He was placed under guard in his Amsterdam studio, and given the chance to produce a further 'Vermeer' that would pass muster before experts. When van Meegeren duly produced another masterpiece and called it 'Jesus among the Doctors', the experts, who of course had not been informed of these goings-on, hailed the work as another important discovery in the history of art, resulting in the painter being released unconditionally from prison.

Van Meegeren's victory was short-lived. More and more of his paintings came to light; then he was prosecuted once again, with a charge this time of fraudulently obtaining moneys by deception. He started a twelve-year jail sentence, but, after serving only a few weeks, died at the age of fifty-seven from a heart attack.

Interestingly, before the war van Meegeren held exhibitions as an artist in his own right, but bitterness consumed him as he felt he did not get the recognition he deserved.

Having come across this interesting piece of art history some time ago, using my Inner Eye I 'saw' the unfortunate artist consumed by his lack of general acceptance in this life, much as James Blake had been. I strongly feel that van Meegeren had formerly lived as Vermeer himself. In this way it will be seen that it is small wonder that he found it so easy to recreate his own former life skills, while being understandably bitter at his lack of recognition, regrettably leading him in this instance to a sad end.

Past lives are, undoubtedly, our heritage, and it is really up to all of us to profit from our previous experiences, whether it be to fall back and build on old skills, come to terms with phobias, or simply to avoid previous mistakes – the choice is ours!

The day following my extraordinary exposure to starship technology described at the beginning of this chapter, Peter and I were to undergo the most terrifying experience of our lives. Here is how it happened...

Chapter 9
A Cosmic Crash and the Man in Black

The deafening roar of a mighty explosion, so literally earth-shaking that everyone in the caravan woke up simultaneously crying out in fear, continued to reverberate in a series of dying echoes across the surrounding mountains. Its source seemed in such close proximity to our caravan that we marvelled that the results of any blast hadn't shattered our windows or damaged the structure. The caravan rocked, and from the sensation we experienced, it seemed that the earth itself was moving for a few seconds, as if under seismic shock.

As the reverberations died away, the sound of rain of the intensity of a tropical storm battered like hail on the roof and sides of the caravan, which by now was beginning to rock and sway, this time in response to the buffetings of the rising wind. We peered out through the windows, lashed by the torrential rain, which poured down in rivulets, partially obscuring our vision of the surrounding mountainside. An eerie glow hung over the tops, illuminating the crags in sharp relief through the driving rain.

We feared for our friend who had recently come to visit us from Canada. He was staying in a small building we had recently restored as a studio some yards away, but peer as we might, we could not make out the outline of the stone structure, hidden as it was under the lee of an ancient tall stone retaining wall. No one felt inclined to venture out into that torrential driving rain, which seemed in some way to be strangely intimidating.

Suddenly an electric blue sphere appeared in the sky, described an arc, then hovered motionless before our astonished gaze. After remaining in the same spot for a minute or so, it suddenly accelerated, then shot away from our view out of sight. Only later during the following day did we discuss this extraordinary sight, shocked as we were in the wake of the explosion. What normally would have been the subject of animated discussion seemed, oddly enough at the time, to be of relatively minor importance in the context of what we had just experienced. Looking back, it was extremely difficult to estimate the size of the sphere; it could have been either relatively small in diameter and close at hand, or of much larger proportions at a greater distance. No one present was able to throw any further light on the matter.

A short while later, the rain ceased. All at once, starting to be overcome by drowsiness (the explosion had taken place around 4 a.m.), no doubt brought on by our natural reaction to the deep shock to our systems, we fell back onto our beds and drifted off to sleep.

We woke up, the sun streaming in through the caravan windows. Our immediate thought was, how had our friend survived the night in the little studio?

We slipped on shoes and coats, mastered our respective trepidations and walked the few yards to the studio door, marvelling at the bright sunshine around us, which showed little trace of the horrendous conditions of the night before, apart from the dampness underfoot. With great relief we noted that the structure of the building was untouched, as seemed to be the case with the main house and the rest of the property. We knocked; a dishevelled figure appeared at the door, rubbing sleep-laden eyes. 'What on earth happened last night?' he exclaimed. 'I thought the planet was about to blow apart!'

We compared notes. We all agreed it was one of the most terrifying experiences of our lives. Conjectures were put forward and many common points confirmed; the strange eerie glow, the incredible deluge accompanied by winds, the fury of which seemed capable of much more destruction than had actually taken place.

About us, tranquillity reigned. The sun shone; a light breeze blew against which, under an azure sky, skylarks rose around us with an alternating flurry of wings. Their hauntingly beautiful song went drifting on the wind until, exhausted apparently by their efforts, they would suddenly cease, silently volplaning down to be lost among the coarse tussocky grass of the Welsh uplands.

Suddenly my attention was drawn to a stone wall which bordered our property about fifty yards away. There seemed to be some damage to it; some stones appeared to have been dislodged, and a gap had appeared at the top. A tree that grew at this spot seemed to have acquired a different outline from that which I remembered. Drawing attention to this to the others in the group, we decided to wander over and take a look. We were very surprised at what we found. As we approached the gap in the wall, we could see that some stones had indeed been dislodged. On the other side from where the tree stood was a torn and splintered stump projecting some three feet or so out from the main trunk.

A large branch lay some distance away on the ground, with the severed portion nearest to us. The startling features about the condition and position of the branch were firstly, that it lay some thirty feet away from the main tree (the winds of the night, although strong, were nowhere near enough to bring this about); and there were no burn marks or charring of any description on either end of the severed sections. No other damage was evident in other surrounding trees or structures. What then had happened to bring about this extraordinary event?

Aftermath: the foreground on the left of the Picture shows the broken branches of the tree lying on the ground; the dip in the outline of the wall behind the trees shows where the rocks were displaced and scattered.

The following day Peter and I called into a garage some miles away to refuel our Land Rover. We discussed what had taken place the previous night with the owner, whose house was some distance away from where we lived, and told him of our intense fear when we experienced the enormous explosion. He was able to tell us that at 4 a.m. he had needed to go to the bathroom. In his living room, through which he had to pass, there was an aquarium. As he passed this, he heard the same devastating explosion; even at this distance (some twelve miles away) a tremor shook his house, to the extent that he noticed ripples on the surface of his aquarium!

When we discussed the matter with our neighbour, Mrs Griffiths, who of course had also heard the tremendous explosion, she maintained that she saw some men dressed in black suits, about 3 to 3½ feet tall, walking around the surrounding fields very early in the morning about an hour or so after the event. She told us that military exercises were often carried out in the area and assumed that this was what was taking place. She admitted to being very puzzled as to how the army had assembled a group of men of this stature together, and why they were in black – 'always in camouflage, you know'.

Later she denied this story, telling us the other villagers 'further down' didn't believe her and thought she 'was cracked'.

At the time of which she spoke, we were asleep again; and we could obtain no corroboration from anyone else after having made exhaustive enquiries. Many years later, however, my attention was drawn to a chain of events that had taken place around this time not far away, involving UFOs and the military. A fascinating book entitled *Cosmic Crashes – The Incredible Story of the UFO's that Fell to Earth* by Nicholas Redfern, published in 1999 by Simon & Schuster (UK) Ltd, throws an interesting light on the subject. It seems that around this time (1974), according to this book a series of UFO-related crashes occurred in Wales and surrounding areas. One of these happened more to the south of where we were living (in the mountains of Snowdonia) a little earlier than the time of our experience. Ours occurred a few months later in the same overall time frame.

The earlier crash referred to in this book, like many other reports therein, makes fascinating reading. For instance, this earlier crash, which took place apparently in the Berwyn Mountains, was described by witnesses in the book as involving a glowing, egg-shaped object of some size. It seems that the military appeared almost immediately and the affair was completely hushed up. Were we involved peripherally with an event of this type?

'The whole house shook violently and suddenly. It began quite suddenly, lasted for a few seconds, then stopped quite as suddenly' – testimony from the owner of the village post office, near the Berwyn Mountains incident. A local police constable in the same area testified, 'There was a great roar and a bang… the sky lit up over the mountains. The colour was yellowish, but other people in the village described seeing blue lights.'

There seem to be many common denominators between our experience and that of other UFO-related events. Later, we found out from some more people we knew who lived some five miles away that at the time of the explosion that it had been so violent that three electric light bulbs had shattered, together with several glass window panes. It is very difficult to convey the enormity of the explosion to those who have never experienced anything of this kind and the effect it has on the system. We have been lucky enough to escape the horror and tragedy of war; perhaps there are those among you who will have had the misfortune to experience an extremely great explosion of this nature?

A curious incident occurred prior to all this happening. Our lovely old horse, Fiesta, on the evening before all this took place started to behave very strangely. A big, powerful animal that was as gentle as a lamb, she stood about eighteen hands, and although we were never riders in any accepted sense, we had some wonderful leisurely rides through the Snowdonian uplands on many occasions. On this particular evening, which was fine and sunny before the events of the night, instead of peacefully grazing as was her wont, she came up to our caravan and started leaning on it firmly, rocking it on its suspension from side to side, to the extent that cups and plates started sliding about on the table which was laid for our evening meal. We went outside to try to calm her, giving her a lump of sugar to coax her away, but to no avail. In the end, mystified, we had to lead her away to the paddock, where she remained, pawing the ground and appearing most uneasy.

As you will see elsewhere in this book, my experience has shown me many times over that our pets and animals generally are quite psychic, and Fiesta was obviously trying to warn us of what lay ahead at the time!

Students of UFO lore may well be intrigued to read about my two encounters with a Man in Black. For those of you who have not come across the Men in Black, I should tell you that there are many accounts of these people visiting those who have been connected with UFO sightings. One very famous case concerned Dr Herbert Hopkins, who in September 1976 was working on a UFO case in America concerning abduction.

When he was on his own one evening, his wife and family having left the house on a visit, someone telephoned him to say that he was connected with a UFO research group and asked if he could call round to discuss the case that Dr Hopkins was working on. The doctor agreed, and went to switch on the front door light to help his visitor find his way in the dark. He was surprised to find this visitor already mounting the front door steps, with no visible sign of any transport that would have enabled him to arrive (this was of course before mobile phones were generally available). The visitor looked to him to be dressed like an undertaker in a black suit, black tie and hat, black shoes and a white shirt.

Dr Hopkins ushered him in and the visitor removed his hat, revealing himself to be completely hairless; and as the doctor focussed his gaze more closely he noticed he was not only bald, but had no eyebrows or eyelashes. His skin was totally a hard white, and his lips bright red. At one point the visitor brushed his lips with a pair of gloves he was carrying, and Dr Hopkins was amazed to see a smear of lipstick appear on the visitor's gloves; however, he continued to give an account to the visitor of the UFO incident he was investigating.

When this was concluded, the visitor said to Dr Hopkins, 'You have two coins in your pocket.' (This was correct.) 'Would you put one of them in the palm of my hand, and watch closely.'

Dr Hopkins did so, and the coin seemed to go out of focus. Then, before the doctor's astonished gaze, it disappeared. 'This coin will never be seen again, either by you or anyone else on this plane,' the visitor said.

The two talked a while longer on UFO-related matters, the visitor attempting to dissuade Dr Hopkins from continuing his UFO investigations. Then the visitor got up to go and his speech began to slow down, saying that his energy was running low. He walked to the door and left, walking with an uncertain gait. Not until after the visitor had left did Dr Hopkins begin to feel afraid, almost as if the visitor had used some paranormal means to prevent him questioning the bizarre situation. His wife and family returned later to find him sitting alone, the house with all lights ablaze, and a gun at the ready in front of him.

This is but one example of the Men in Black that I have cited here. Interested persons may make their own further investigations; the American writer, Brad Steiger, made his own and claimed that there have been hundreds of such incidents.

I have gone into such detail to give you some background to my own experience, on two different occasions, of meeting my Man in Black.

Contrary to the recurring theme of warnings not to repeat any information regarding UFO encounters, and a general overtone of menace, my Man in Black was both charming and courteous on each occasion. Curiously, great fear was inspired in everyone involved but myself during both my encounters. The interesting thing is that there is a common denominator – my encounters with UFOs – but oddly enough no mention of these occurred during our meeting.

Both encounters came about during the course of my normal working day, with roughly a three-year interval between them. The first incident, during the time I had a small office in a private house in West Malling, Kent, took place during my usual working hours and was witnessed by my then secretary.

The day started in a perfectly normal manner. I was greeted by my secretary's white cockatoo, which was allowed the freedom of the house apart from my office. A delightfully friendly little creature, she would put her head to one side, and under the gaze of her black beady eye we would be treated to quite a wide vocabulary. On one occasion one of my clients tripped over in the hall – the resulting expletive being repeated over and over again by Polly, to the great amusement of us all!

On this particular day around eleven in the morning, Madge, my secretary, knocked on the door looking very worried. To my surprise, she was holding a rapier – her son was a fencing expert – and she said, 'Anne, your next client is really frightening me. He's so strange-looking that I'm going to put this behind the door – ' indicating the rapier – 'leave the door ajar, and let's change the chairs around so that you are sitting nearest to the exit. If you have any problems with him, grab this and I'll call the police.'

By this time, I was beginning to feel quite alarmed and had begun to wish that I didn't have this client.

Strangely enough, all of a sudden I didn't feel worried within myself. A moment later, Madge showed the man in. My first impression was sheer amazement rather than fear. I should mention that at this point in time I had never heard of Men in Black, so that I had no preconception to influence my thinking. To me his appearance was certainly bizarre. Dressed in a very funereal, immaculately pressed black suit, together with black shoes and tie, worn with a white shirt, he was impeccably turned out and sported a matching black hat. On entering, this was removed revealing a completely hairless head. However, what was very surprising to me was that his whole head and face were a hard white in colour – together they had almost the appearance of a shiny plastic or porcelain. He had eyebrows that seemed to be painted on, and he appeared to have no lips; but where they should have been it seemed that lipstick had been applied with very sharply defined edges. His overall appearance resembled that of a circus clown.

I could not look into his eyes as he was wearing a pair of dark glasses, but when he started to speak he spoke very naturally and with quite a normal and unaccented English-sounding voice. Suddenly I felt quite relaxed. Rather than wanting a reading, my visitor began to talk about the condition of the planet. He was very concerned about global warming and the pollution brought about by most transport systems, including cars, lorries and trains, but most of all about the great number of commercial jet aircraft and the enormous amount of pollution they generated.

I particularly remembered this aspect of our conversation some years later when Peter and I had our own aircraft, and when we flew below about 1,500 to 2,000 feet on certain days, we often found ourselves flying in a misty haze of pollution, the ceiling of which at this height was often capped by an evil-looking black layer; but if we climbed above this, we would emerge into a beautiful clear blue sky. Fliers will be well acquainted with this experience.

My visitor continued to talk about the devastation of the great rainforests across the world in South America and the Far East, and mentioned how everywhere the destruction of our life-giving trees so necessary to our existence was taking place. The gradual warming up of the whole planet; the shrinking of the ice caps and the rapid extinction of many entire species of animals, birds and insects, concerned him greatly. At this point in time, many years ago, I had not been conscious of the extent of the damage man was doing to his environment; this visitor certainly made me aware of what was happening in terms of our ecology and the planet.

My strange client had a curiously graphic manner of making what he was telling me come alive in my mind in a very real way. While this conversation was taking place, which I found truly fascinating, yet at the same time gave rise to my great concern for our beautiful planet, I suddenly found it curious that this person had paid my normal fee to come and see me, but seemed to require no consultation or advice that my clients invariably come to see me for. Another thing that I found curious was that normally while working with clients I could link in telepathically to analyse them; in this case I simply wasn't able to do so. Instead, images of beautiful flowers, fields and scenery were entering my mind in a way I had never experienced before; try as I might I could not pick up on the frequency of the visitor's mind.

At the time when this meeting was taking place some years ago, people in general, myself included, were not aware of the extent of the systematic destruction going on around us right across the globe on such a large scale, in the way they are today. I have to say my visitor raised my awareness of these problems in a dramatic manner, to the point where conservation of life and respect for nature became far more prominent in my everyday thinking from that day forward.

My visitor discussed many more things. The overall health picture of the human race, with the discovery of many illnesses and diseases new to mankind, also gave him great concern. When our interview came to an end and he got up to go, he shook my hand with warmth; there seemed to be an indefinable difference in the feel of his handshake from that which I was accustomed to, and even today I am still unable to put it into words.

As he started for the still half-open door my secretary, who had been hovering a short distance just out of sight, appeared as if by magic, fear still written across her features. On seeing me to be quite relaxed, a flood of relief made itself manifest; goodbyes were said and our visitor departed, his appearance and apparel in sharp contrast to the warmth of the spring sunshine.

So ended my first encounter with a Man in Black. Of course, at that time I was quite unaware of the existence of Men in Black, and was not familiar with the general subject as I am now.

That evening when I went home to Peter I was full of my encounter with the strange visitor. It so happened that he had recently read an article on the subject, and was able to locate it and show it to me. A sketch in the article, plus the reference to the general hairless appearance, the extraordinary whiteness of his features, the lipstick and the fifties-style black 'undertaker's' suit, all linked up with my experience.

The great fear experienced by my secretary seemed also to be linked with other people's encounters, although in my case I felt perfectly at ease. I read through the article Peter showed me; my experience seemed to definitely identify with a 'Man in Black' experience.

Three years later my visitor reappeared. At this time I had moved from the office where he had previously visited me, and started an alternative medicine clinic in Maidstone, Kent; I had a different secretary and a number of staff engaged in the different therapies. The second of the two visits, strangely enough, was preceded by the same emotion in the second secretary as in the first: fear. When the visitor arrived – I hadn't realised who he was until he was shown in a moment later – the secretary whispered on entering my room, 'I'm very concerned about this client; he frightens me. I've warned one of the other members of staff to be on the alert in case he becomes troublesome, and I have my umbrella by me to defend you with!'

Seconds later my visitor was ushered in, and I sensed a flood of relief as I remembered him from our previous encounter. He was exactly as I recalled him: the same funereal suit, hat, white shirt with black tie and shoes; the deathly white pallor of his head and features; the same apparently pencilled-on eyebrows and the same lipless mouth with lipstick applied; the dark glasses, which completely hid his eyes, and the total lack of hair. I still felt completely comfortable with him. However, why did two different secretaries who had never met each other experience the same fear, think in terms of making available an emergency makeshift weapon, insist on leaving the door half open, suggest changing the position of the chairs so that I could make a rapid exit, and mention that they would call the police in the event of a problem, as they both did?

Again, my visitor did not require a reading from me but began a discussion along much the same lines as our last meeting. Ecology and the damage that the human race was inflicting on our planet seemed, as before, to be to the forefront of his thinking; but I do remember on this occasion that he introduced the subject of the human mind and its development as well. I remember again the unusual images of flowers and trees I seemed to picture all the time we were talking, as I had in our previous encounter.

The interview came to a close and he shook my hand in parting, with the same warm but 'different' feel as before, despite his extremely bizarre appearance. Thus ended my second encounter with my Man in Black. I have never seen him since and would dearly like to see him again to ask him questions about himself that I wanted to ask but somehow seemed prevented from doing during our two meetings. I have to say on reflection that I feel his origins were extraterrestrial; the whole orientation of his concern for ecology and the state of our planet seemed to be rather that of an *observer* of our life here rather than as a *participant*, in a way I cannot define.

My life has always seemed to be inextricably interwoven with UFOs and extraterrestrial matters in general. The following chapter continues to enlarge on my and Peter's involvement with these themes.

Chapter 10
More on UFOs – I Meet an Abductee

I have often come across people who are simply not able to cope with experiences outside what they consider to be their known envelope of life. A very good example of this is a story often related by a friend of mine who owned a light engineering business on an industrial estate in south-east England. One day he left his factory to walk across the estate to make a business call on an electrical components unit. As he was crossing the yard, another friend stopped and greeted him, and shortly afterwards someone else did the same thing. The trio had commenced to pass the time of day, when one of them suddenly looked up and saw a great shining, silvery disc suspended motionless at altitude.

'Look,' he exclaimed excitedly, 'a flying saucer!'

The second member of the group looked up, amazed, and exclaimed, 'You're right. Up until now I've only read about them in books and magazines. I feel very lucky to be experiencing this!'

The third member of the group looked up and said, 'Ah, so it is. But I don't believe in things like that,' and walked off!

This is a true story, which serves to illustrate how some people's minds have an automatic cut-off point at the limit of their belief system, which precludes them from absorbing new information beyond the confines of their mental database.

Peter has discussed at different times with me his interest and involvement with UFOs; I use the term 'unidentified flying object' advisedly because his experiences, directly and indirectly, in the main relate to UFOs of a shape or form other than the 'flying saucer' type of sighting. From about the age of eleven he started to read science fiction stories, which greatly aroused his interest in the possibility of extraterrestrial life. Some years later this became greatly increased by the 1947 incident experienced by the private pilot, Kenneth Arnold, which was widely publicised by the press at the time, during which he sighted from his aircraft a number of shining saucer-shaped craft rising and dipping at an extraordinarily high speed for that period in aviation history. Not long after this incident, George Adamski's book *Inside the Flying Saucers*, was published, which included a number of photographs of flying saucers as well as large 'mother ships', which provoked much controversy, but nevertheless listed a number of impressive testimonials by various witnesses which included statements by local dignitaries.

Peter continues: From this time on I started to develop an almost obsessive interest in the subject. Although at this point in time I had had no personal experiences in the way of sightings or phenomena, an incident in my life occurred which fascinated me. I was working as a design engineer with Frigidaire, a large American company with extensive factory premises in the Edgware Road near the old Hendon aerodrome. The office block in which I worked was separated from the factory itself by a private roadway. During the course of their work, the design engineers had, from time to time, to descend to the factory to liaise with the production lines in order to monitor and constantly update the various refrigeration products under manufacture.

One winter's day in November, the weather was fairly cold with a ground mist, above which a faint watery sun could just be seen peeping through. A senior design engineer by the name of Bob Scott, whom I knew well as a reliable, down-to-earth individual, stopped by me to briefly discuss one or two technical product details, before leaving our block by way of the stairs to ground level on his way to the factory floor. Sometime later he burst through our office door and strode up to my desk looking very excited.

'Peter, you'll never believe this! I've just seen an enormous flying saucer! I was just returning from the factory floor and crossing our roadway, when I saw this huge flying disc. It was so big you could have landed aircraft on it. Because of the ground mist, it was almost invisible, and being greyish in colour it blended in very well with the background. I just happened to look up at the exact time its upper surface was slightly tilted in such a way as to catch the sun's rays for a second or two, and after that I could just see its faint outline. I stood and watched it while it was almost stationary, this giant disc.

I looked frantically around for someone else to witness this amazing sight. Normally there would have been a few people walking from one point to another, or a forklift truck or two transporting pallets of equipment hither and thither; as luck would have it, everywhere was deserted. I stood and watched it, totally fascinated. The disc remained stationary for a minute or so, then flames appeared from points on the underside of the rim; seconds later it started to rise with amazing rapidity; the mist consisting of a relatively thin layer, I was able to continue to watch it due to the brilliance of the flames, which shot downwards with increasing intensity. In an incredibly short time, it had disappeared vertically out of sight. It was an astonishing experience, and one to my very great sorrow I was unable to share, as I would very much have liked to have had some witnesses to this.'

Knowing Bob as I did, I unhesitatingly had to accept his story. It would have been so unlike this sometimes dour and pragmatic individual, senior engineer that he was, to concoct such a story set in workaday surroundings such as these. I took the trouble to contact RAF Hendon, a ministry body and the local police in an attempt to corroborate his story, all unfortunately to no avail; but I feel this to be a story well worth recounting.

A few years later, I was lucky enough to undergo a UFO experience, although not of the flying saucer type. One evening, late at night I went out for a walk before retiring to bed. At that time I was living near Wrotham in Kent, which was then a fairly rural area. It was a cool and very clear night, with a moon that was close to full; the stars were shining down with an exceptional brilliance and clarity that threw the surrounding landscape into bright relief for some distance. At the end of the walk as I started to return home, I noticed what seemed to be an unusually bright star very low on the horizon only just above the line of a hedge on a slight rise. I remember thinking this to be the planet Venus, and I continued walking and enjoying the beautiful radiance of the moon's light illuminating the countryside around me.

After a moment or two when I glanced back in the direction of what I thought to be Venus, I noticed that it had moved position from where I had initially seen it, too far for a star and not far enough for a normal aircraft. I immediately stood still to observe what was going on, and sure enough there was a slow but perceptible movement. As I continued to watch, the rate of movement seemed gradually to increase, until the original bright light the size of a distant star became about the size of a single car headlight. Amazed, I continued to watch; at this point in time in the first half of the sixties, helicopters were relatively infrequent, and none to my knowledge flew at night in this particular area. However, the object continued to approach until I estimated that it was less than a quarter of a mile away from me at a height of around 300 feet; however, two things immediately stood out about this machine. Firstly, no noise emanated from it at all; and secondly, the extraordinarily brilliant light, which appeared to be positioned in the nose of the machine, projected no beam whatsoever or any form of radiance.

By this time the machine was nearly side on to me, and now that the intense light of the beam started to disappear in elevation, I could make out a form of skeletal framework tapering towards the rear of the aircraft, while two similar-looking outriggers, one on each side, appeared to taper upwards at a slight angle. At the end of each outrigger, there was an alternately flashing light, one pulsing blue, the other white. This arrangement of lighting was quite different from the normal lighting carried by aircraft at night. Although many aircraft carry flashing strobes, at night all aircraft carry a red light on the port wing, and green for the starboard wing. There was no light at the very rear of the structure, as is usual for an aircraft flying at night. Having had a fair amount of experience as a private pilot, I was unable to relate this machine to anything I had ever seen or read about.

At a forward speed of no more than 35 to 40 mph, the device continued to fly in total silence towards Wrotham Hill; on the hill itself there was a dense ground mist to a depth of perhaps around fifty feet. The machine flew directly towards the hill and disappeared about halfway up it into this low ground mist, and thus out of my line of sight.

I have had a lifetime's interest in aviation, am the holder of a private pilot's licence, and have accumulated a reasonable amount of flying experience; no machine that I could conceive of would be able to maintain silent flight so slowly at night, let alone display the curious phenomenon of a brilliant light without any form of beam or radiance being projected. I have never been able to satisfactorily resolve this experience, which took place in 1963, and there regrettably the case must rest for me.

Another experience that has always remained a mystery in my mind has been one that befell me one autumn night many years ago. At this period in my life I was a representative for a plastics company, and had driven up to Birmingham for a business meeting. On the return journey, the weather started to deteriorate rapidly, with storm clouds forming overhead, and in the distance I could see flashes of lightning from time to time. Soon, rain started to fall, and the skies started to become heavily overcast and dark. By this time, the line of traffic of which I formed part had started to slow to a crawl, as the rain turned into a sudden torrential downpour. Suddenly my engine started to miss, then cut out completely. At the same time, my car headlights dimmed and went out; but fortunately the car still had sufficient momentum for me to pull over to the side of the road.

Having come to a standstill in the torrential rain, I looked about me to find myself in total darkness; all other traffic having seemingly disappeared in the Stygian gloom. The rain continued to fall relentlessly, and I could see no point in becoming drenched while attempting any form of running repair, so I sat it out in the darkness for some fifteen minutes or so. I then noticed through the driving rain a car parked just in front of me, its lights also out, inside which I could just discern some movement. Putting my coat on, I got out and tapped at the window on the driver's side. On it being lowered, I started to explain to the driver, a man of about fifty, that my car had broken down and had a flat battery, and would he be able to give me a lift to the next town?

'I only wish I could,' he replied. 'Exactly the same thing has happened to me!' He flicked his light switch idly, as if to establish his point. Just then the rain started to ease, and my vision began to become accustomed to the darkness. I gradually became aware of quite a number of cars parked in a long line at the side of the road, all with their lights out. This was a main road in a remote area; it seemed there were no houses to be seen, so why, I asked myself, had all these people parked in the middle of nowhere with their lights out?

The answer was that all the cars had suffered the same problem as I had.

Every battery had failed in every car, with the result that none of us could either use the starter or turn our lights on.

By now the rain had stopped, and one or two of the drivers had got out of their vehicles and started to raise their bonnets, poking around in an abstract way without seeming to achieve anything. Suddenly to my astonishment a pair of lights came on three or four cars away. Shortly afterwards this was followed by another, and then another. The whirr of a starter engaging suddenly sounded, followed by an engine bursting into life. I hurried back to my vehicle and tried my lights. They worked! Turning my key in the ignition, my engine followed suit. One by one our cars moved away, restored in some mysterious manner to life. What could be made of all this? I wondered.

Although I saw nothing that night, did some extraterrestrial craft pass low overhead in the storm unnoticed and de-energise all our cars in some mysterious way? Sometime later I managed to confirm my hypothesis. I have subsequently read of several UFO case histories where exactly the same experience was shared by a number of car drivers; however, in each instance a UFO was seen low overhead. Once again, the reality is so much more apparent after a personal experience.

However, my obsessive interest in the whole subject of UFOs was to have a fascinating sequel. I remember a point in time when I would avidly read any material on the subject, going to great lengths to research obscure publications. (There are quite a few references to them in early literature; for example, did you know a monk sketched a UFO in the twelfth century?) I would also spend long hours scanning the night skies, to no avail.

Finally I seemed to develop a desperate yearning for an encounter of what I suppose these days would be termed the 'Third Kind'. I felt that extraterrestrials should be able to be contacted by thought transmissions, and to this end would concentrate on mental imaging of the classic 'flying saucer' type. I kept this up on a regular basis for some months with no feedback of any kind whatsoever, until one night I seemed to receive a clear mental picture of a Flying Saucer in my mind, hovering above some clouds at high altitude. The image was quite clear and shining brightly; after a time this faded, and I was left with the feeling that in some way I had at last established contact, although in exactly what form I wasn't sure.

However, the sequel was surprising, and produced a result I would never have anticipated. For some days afterwards I became quite depressed for seemingly no reason; then to my surprise in spite of myself I started to become disinterested in the whole subject of UFOs. It was as if my mind had started to operate with a form of double perception; on the one hand, I was keen to follow my lines of inquiry relating to UFOs, and yet every time I started to focus my mind on the subject, an immense lassitude would come over me and

I would begin to drop into a deep sleep. If, however, I avoided all thoughts of UFOs, I would not be affected in any way; it was almost as if my mind had received an implant that switched off my consciousness every time I started to focus on the subject. From that time forwards, whenever I watched a film or read a book relating to UFOs, this intense drowsiness would come over me, and I would simply doze off into a catnap. Even awakening from this, and continuing to watch the same film or read the same book, I would lose consciousness within two to three minutes, for periods ranging from roughly fifteen to thirty minutes each time. This curious state of affairs has persisted even until the present time; if nothing else, I have my own personal cure for insomnia!

Interestingly, from about the same point in time, I discovered that I had acquired an entirely new faculty – telepathy! I mentioned earlier that at one point in my life I had worked for a plastics company as a sales representative and progressed later to sales management. I became aware on more than one occasion that I would know in advance what my potential customer was about to say. For a while I was sure that I was imagining things, and disregarded the impressions I was receiving. Then I came across a book entitled *Psychic* by Peter Hurkos, who discovered that he had become suddenly telepathic subsequent to an accident.

He wrote of his discovery of perceived impressions by thought transference from people that on subsequent analysis proved to be correct. After having read this book, his descriptions of his experiences seemed so startlingly familiar to my own that I began to analyse in a critical way the impressions that I was receiving from people. I noticed for example that if I was putting forward certain advantages of the products that I was selling, I would receive an impression of what the client was thinking about the points I was making. Another time I would experience this, and the client would confirm in subsequent speech exactly what I had sensed. At other times I would sense what he was thinking, and I would receive no spoken confirmation of this thought; and yet I would feel quite positive that he had experienced a particular thought in his mind without expressing it.

After a time I became quite skilled at this, and one day I became particularly perceptive. I had telephoned the chief engineer of a well-known international food chain, with the objective of selling him my company's new insulation product. This product was a board material used for building and lining the floors of cold stores. It was unusually strong and would take heavier floor loads that the competition, and was superior in terms of insulating quality to existing competitors' products. It was odourless when correctly sealed, and cheaper to employ, because far less of it needed to be used in terms of thickness to achieve a given insulation value. I have gone into this detail because these technical facts are relevant to the understanding of what took place during my sales meeting with the chief engineer.

I called at the company's spacious offices, and as I had previously made an appointment, I was quickly shown through to see the chief engineer. He rose to greet me, extending his hand and at the same time ushering me into a chair. A smiling, genuine and likeable personality, he put me at my ease, and we soon settled down after the usual pleasantries. Knowing that he was a busy man, I encouraged him to steer me in the direction of the product, which was of course the purpose of my visit. I started to describe the product, saying what an effective insulant it was in relation to heat transfer. Into my mind came the sentence before he spoke it: *Yes, but it is very expensive per unit.*

Without thinking, I replied to his unspoken thought, 'Yes, on the face of it, it is, but because the material is so efficient, you will need to purchase a lot less of it than the normal type, and for this reason it is cheaper.'

The next unspoken thought came from him: *I know your material has as a constituent sulphuretted hydrogen gas; this has a particularly bad odour and would contaminate food in our stores.*

Without thinking, I again replied to his unspoken thought, 'Although this gas has a terrible odour, it is completely non-toxic and won't taint food in any way. The gas is only given off if the material is damaged in some way, but in any case the material itself will be completely sealed off by the concrete floor of the cold store itself, and it wouldn't be possible for any odour to escape.'

I hadn't realised the extent to which I was mind-reading, carried away as I was by the excitement of possibly achieving a large sales contract. The chief engineer, I noticed, had become extremely pale. He suddenly rose to his feet and threw a pencil he had been absently toying with onto his desk. 'I don't know how you are doing this,' he exclaimed, 'but you are reading my mind in some way. You're really frightening me!'

For a moment I was taken aback; obviously the last thing I wanted to do was to frighten my client away. Hastily I went to reassure him. 'Not at all,' I lied: 'I only wish I could! It's just that I'm so familiar with the standard objections against this material, I'm afraid my answers were just too pat due to experience. Please accept my apologies for presuming to provide your replies in advance for you.'

Slowly the colour returned to his face. 'You really had me worried there!' he told me. 'I was beginning to feel quite spooked, but I suppose as you say if you have as much experience as you have, you must know virtually all the answers and the probability of the order of your client's questions. Perhaps I'm cracking up.'

I laughed and passed the incident off, noting well that in future the new ability I had strangely developed would have to be more effectively concealed;

the interview was successfully brought to a conclusion a little while later. I was fortunate in obtaining some impressive orders from this client, and I made a mental note to be a little more subtle in future.

I became very interested in the fundamental nature of this ability. Having trained as an engineer, I am always interested in what makes things tick. So how did those thoughts arrive? In what manner did I become aware of them? After an in-depth study of the phenomenon, I realised that my telepathic faculty would only become activated *when a person's thoughts were concealed from me*. It seems that the action of concealment appears to stem the free flow of thoughts in some way, much as the effect of a dam in a river, creating a carrier wave that somehow I could directly tap into. The concealed thought borne by this carrier wave itself appears to be generated by the concealment, and it seems to me the carrier wave appears to enter an area of my mind, which then translates it as a thought form in the normal thinking mind.

Once I had been able to rationalise the ability in these terms, it seemed to crystallise and accelerate the process by leaps and bounds. As soon as any type of concealed thought came about during a conversation, I found that I was able to read it and modify my approach to any subject matter to great advantage.

After a time, now that I could consciously use this faculty, I discovered that a certain small percentage of people whom I encountered in daily life also have this ability, to a greater or lesser extent, without necessarily being aware that they are in possession of it. A characteristic they exhibit is that in listening to you, their head is slightly turned away and their eyes often averted and distant; but in nearly all cases they are not consciously aware of what is taking place. With this new-found ability and heightened awareness, I was able to conduct my affairs to much greater advantage, as I am sure many successful businessmen do using the same abilities.

Many more people have this as a latent ability without being aware of its existence. I am now convinced that most of us can develop along these lines; when talking to people, allow yourself to relax and mentally take a step backwards, allowing any impressions emanating from the person with whom you are conversing to rest lightly on your mind. Can you sense worries and concerns around this person for instance that are not necessarily related to you? Try to feel how this person feels towards you. Is there a feeling of warmth, or is there an element almost like a barrier between you? However fleeting the impression, hold it and analyse it, and see how it relates to the general conversation. In this way, by constantly analysing the changing impressions you are receiving and comparing them with the reactions and courses of events that ensue, you can develop these skills to definite advantage.

Anne continues: Telepathy – yet another of the common threads woven into our lives. At different points in our lives, before we had even met, Peter and I had undergone experiences involving an extraterrestrial background. I personally feel this involvement has for both of us considerably heightened our extrasensory abilities at all levels, and interestingly I have read of a number of accounts where other individuals have had similar experiences, leading to the stepping-up or the acquiring of heightened paranormal awareness.

A different aspect of interaction with UFOs is that of abductions. There are countless cases of abduction on record, going right back through history; the most important one of all known to mankind in our recorded civilisation is referred to in the final chapter of this book. However in modern times the world became aware of these happenings during the sixties when Betty and Barney Hill experienced a loss in time during a journey they were making by car. A full account of this incident is written up in the book *The Interrupted Journey* by John Fuller, where the couple, who were returning from a short break in Canada by car to their home in Portsmouth, New Hampshire, in the United States, suddenly noticed a UFO pacing them along US Highway 3. They stopped the car, and viewed the craft through binoculars. It was a very large vessel 'like a big pancake' with a double row of windows. It landed not far from them, and Barney again focussed his binoculars on it. Through these he observed the occupants at the windows; they were dressed in dark military-style uniforms. He was suddenly convinced he was about to be captured, and fled back to the car. The couple then drove off at high speed.

Shortly afterwards, Betty Hill reported the incident to NICAP (National Investigations Committee on Aerial Phenomena). She commenced to have a series of nightmares in which she and her husband were led aboard the spacecraft and medically examined. During one session with NICAP investigators, they realised their journey home had taken two hours longer than it should have.

Under hypnosis, both of the couple told the same story. They had been taken aboard the spacecraft by grey-skinned, black-haired humanoids with small, flattened noses, blue slit-like mouths and large wrap-around eyes, who then gave the couple some medical examinations. During this time, they were able to converse with the occupants of the craft by telepathic means, only realising this later having been under the impression at the time that they were conversing normally in English. After this experience, they were led back to their car and watched the UFO depart 'like a glowing orange ball'.

What is of highly significant interest, and what firmly places the stamp of authenticity on this encounter, is that during one of the hypnotic sessions, Betty related how she was shown by one of the spaceship occupants the star system from where they had originated. She was able to make a sketch of this system, but after exhaustive research by contemporary astronomers, the sketch resembled no star system known at that time. However, six years after these events took place, an expanding space research programme was able to identify this star system, which today is known as Zeta Reticuli in the Reticulum constellation.

A US Air force base not far from where the event took place confirmed that their radar had shown an 'unknown' in the air at the exact time of the incident.

Since this time, many experiences of this type have been undergone by individuals, to the extent that groups have been formed to discuss and share their experiences. It seems there are several different types or races of interplanetary visitors to our planet; some are benevolently inclined to us, others are not. Abductee experiences seem to vary, with some individuals meeting with benevolent beings on board their spacecraft, who acquaint them with the interior of their ships, sometimes taking them for a short voyage. Others undergo quite terrifying experiences, being forced to take part in experiments involving advanced surgical operations, being told that they are necessary for the continuing development of the human race, involving hybridisation with certain space races.

It seems that at least two types of abduction occur. One is the 'missing time' type, where persons who, after having set out on a car journey somewhere unaccountably find themselves driving along a stretch of road they are not familiar with, involving a missing time period of some hours. The events normally remain a complete mystery until the information relating to the event is recovered by hypnosis. The second type appears to be, as mentioned above, contact by benevolent beings who conduct contactees aboard their craft, or express concern for the deteriorating state of our planet, as happened to me.

There are also quite a few cases on record where young women have given birth to a child after an abductee experience, with no possibility of normal intercourse of a human nature having taken place. Children conceived in this way often develop abnormal psychic abilities and capabilities well beyond the norm.

Another type of abduction occurs with the person being taken while they are sleeping by space visitors. The person concerned is levitated from their bed, and beamed through any structure such as a wall or closed window by process of dematerialisation up to the waiting space vessel, where events take place in a similar way to those outlined above. Persons sleeping in the same bed or room are never able to be awakened, as I found out for myself in my experience related earlier, although I have no memory of any abduction.

There are many books obtainable today on this subject, and those of you who are unfamiliar with it will find plenty of material available from which to choose.

Many accounts are available of people who have experienced abduction and recovered the knowledge of this by hypnosis, where the abductee has subsequently acquired a curious triangular mark on the underside of their forearm, bearing a resemblance to a birthmark.

Neither Peter nor I have any conscious knowledge of abduction experiences ourselves, but I became very interested some time ago when a mother came to me for a reading involving problems with her eleven-year-old daughter. She explained that her little girl was having constantly recurring nightmares, where strange-looking spacemen, who looked as if they had emerged straight out of the pages of science fiction, would stand looking at her from the foot of her bed. She then dreamt that she floated through the walls of their house, and continued to float up to a hovering giant spaceship. She could never remember what happened once she was inside the craft, but always felt uneasy. Neither the mother nor the girl, after questioning, had ever had any exposure to any literature concerning abduction, and simply thought that the recurring nightmares were just that, and no more. They were only looking to me for a means of psychological explanation, with the objective of finding a cure.

I heard the story through and asked if the girl had been watching any science fiction or horror films. This was met with an emphatic denial, the girl saying she didn't like them because they reminded her of her dreams, and had indeed never watched them, having no interest whatsoever in the subject. I deliberated on what to say, realising the worry and concern that would ensue if I made them both aware of the true possibility.

A thought suddenly occurred to me. Taking the girl's hands as if to comfort her, I turned them palm upwards. It being a warm summer's day, she was only wearing a T-shirt and her arms were bare, allowing me to observe the underside of her forearm. Under her right forearm was a curious triangular red mark, very like a birthmark! I struggled to maintain my composure. Believe me, it is one thing to read about such happenings, but when confirmation of these events is evident before you, the reality brings about an entirely different perspective.

This was one of those rare situations where I was at a loss what to do. I felt that to make both of them aware of what was taking place would be just too frightening, so that, still holding the little girl's hands, I told her I was going to give her some healing which would cause her mind to forget her nightmares. I treated her as I had many of my other patients, involving prayer and asking that the child could be spared these terrible nightmares. Both the mother and daughter seemed relieved at this, and after a few more comforting words they left feeling reassured. I did not feel entirely happy within myself, but felt that this was the only route to go.

I heard afterwards that the little girl's sufferings were considerably alleviated but not completely eliminated. It seemed that our meeting had allowed her to be much more at peace with herself, and her memories of those experiences became far less frequent, so that I felt the best had been made of an extremely difficult situation.

Interestingly, both the girl and her mother were from South America, world-famous for UFO activity. Oddly enough, it never occurred to me to examine the underside of my own forearm at the time. Some time afterwards, someone asked me if they could look to see if I bore this curious triangular mark myself. I turned my arm, and to my surprise there it was – a curious triangular indentation in the flesh, which I bear to this day!

Not long after this incident, I came home one dark autumn evening on my own and started to cook. As I did so, a strange picture came into my head on my mental screen – something the like of which I had never seen before. The picture was of an extraordinary-looking entity, with a pallid grey skin and fathomless wrap-around black eyes. This image remained in my mind's eye like a strong photo-image that I was completely unable to dispel, for something like two hours.

During this period I carried on doing things around the house. I remember thinking how incredibly bizarre this image was, like nothing I had ever seen. Strangely enough, although I was completely unable to dispel this mental picture during the two hours or so that it remained on my inner screen, I was unafraid, wondering if this was some extraterrestrial image that I was mentally viewing. At the end of this time it disappeared from my mind as suddenly as it had appeared.

At this time, Peter was away on a short business trip. The following day early in the evening, I underwent almost the identical experience, except that this ET – at the time I never realised how apt my use of the word was – had a slightly darker skin, but even larger black wrap-around eyes, who remained in my mental screen in the same ultra-vivid photo-image manner that I had experienced the previous evening. This image remained for a longer period – roughly four hours – to the point that I began to wonder if I was under some form of alien investigation, a thought that was beginning to unnerve me.

I started to experience a feeling of fear. Would this intense image always be with me, in such a way that I would be unable to dispel it?

At this point I began to pray, and continued to do so for some while. Suddenly this extraordinarily strong image disappeared from my mind, leaving me with a vast feeling of relief, while at the same time causing me to wonder at the origin of this baffling experience.

The following day Peter returned from his business trip. I related my experience to him, showing him a clear sketch that I had made of the amazingly strong images I had been experiencing.

ET – *Communion* book cover
Copyright Ted Jacobs

Peter was equally puzzled, saying to me that he had never seen or read about such images as those I had sketched for him. We discussed what I had experienced, but had to leave what had occurred without coming to any conclusion.

Some eighteen months later, Peter and I decided to take a holiday break in Florida. We had been working quite hard, and the idea of relaxing for ten days in the sun appealed to both of us. Disembarking at Orlando Airport, we decided to have a coffee in the airport lounge. I picked up a paper, while Peter got up to go to the bookstall to see if there were any flying magazines on sale. A few minutes later he returned excitedly waving a book at me. 'Look at this, Anne! Look at this!' he exclaimed.

It took me a moment or two to focus my attention on the book cover. There, staring back at me with those fathomless black eyes, was the very photo-image that I had sketched from memory eighteen months previously. The book *Communion* had just hit the stands for the first time in the USA, appearing subsequently the world over amid a storm of controversy.

For those of you who have not read this book, the theme communicates an ongoing interaction between author Whitley Strieber and extraterrestrials of an identical appearance to the ones in my experience. Interestingly, I kept this book on show on my desk at the Maidstone clinic without making any comment to my clients about it. I was fascinated when several of them over a period mentioned to me, 'Do you know, Anne, I thought I was going mad. I've seen images identical to this book cover in my mind's eye several times...' and many interesting discussions would ensue. These conversations with clients began to take place well before the book was on sale in the UK and continued up to the time I had to close the clinic.

Chapter 11
Time, Ladies and Gentlemen

Another fascinating experience I underwent during our time in Wales for which I have no explanation was that of the Whispering Lake. Peter and I would often go for long hikes in the North Welsh mountains, an area known for its remoteness and wild rugged beauty. Up there, far removed from any habitation, lies another world of rugged rocky landscape interspersed with short wild grasses flattened by the winds, while here and there miniature wild flowers bloom in a dazzling array of blues, purples and yellows.

On this particular day, we separated with the idea of meeting up at a certain summit to admire the spectacular vista, which would extend on a clear day for some thirty or forty miles across many peaks and ranges to the horizon lost in a purple haze. In this area there are quite a few mountain lakes; many are fairly deep and of a curiously remote slate-blue-grey fathomless nature. I commenced a steep climb to the right of one of these, admiring the way that the sheer rock face tumbled to meet the seemingly bottomless lake surface, when suddenly I became aware of a curious whispering that reached my ears. Pausing on the slope, I strained to find the source. Turning my head to different positions, I couldn't determine any change in intensity of the sound, or the direction from which it came.

I climbed a few more paces and listened again. The whispering was still there, and I could hear it quite clearly; yet it maintained its lack of apparent source. It seemed to be composed of a single whisper in a language totally unfamiliar to me. It continued without pause during the time I stayed within the vicinity of this lake; it didn't seem to sound like the Welsh language that I was used to hearing, and I have since wondered what the language could be; it certainly sounded like nothing I had ever heard. Perhaps ancient Brythonic or Celtic; I just wasn't able to tell.

I continued my climb to the ridge. At a certain point when I was leaving the lake the whispering just ceased; not wishing to give Peter any concern before I rejoined him, I didn't linger any further. When we met up at the summit we talked the incident over; neither of us could throw any light on it.

However it had an interesting sequel. After we had reached the summit and enjoyed the spectacular views, we descended together by a different route, calling in to the little farmhouse where Kath and Huw welcomed us as ever with one of their delightful teas. We told them of my experience by the remote lake and described where it was. 'That's the Whispering Lake,' they said. 'Many people have heard what you heard; it stems from ancient times; it's well known to the locals here.'

So, at least I hadn't imagined it. Is there some ancient time warp up there from the distant past, where a powerful event took place in those mountains?

Time warps do exist, you know. It seems that under certain conditions that we don't yet understand, a few privileged people have physically entered an entirely different time period in the past and undergone real experiences back in that time. There is the well-documented case of two schoolteachers, one of whom taught at Oxford, who visited Versailles together and found themselves on two separate occasions, one in August 1901 and the second in January 1902, walking through the famous gardens in the time period of 1789!

Not realising at first that this had come about, they assumed the people that they saw were in fancy dress. However, they noticed that the layout of the gardens, which they had previously visited, differed considerably from what they knew. Becoming lost in certain sections of the gardens, they continued to see people dressed in period costumes, and even spoke to some of them, one of the teachers being a fluent French speaker. As they left the gardens later on, they found themselves back in familiar contemporary surroundings. After they returned to England, they made maps of the gardens as they had seen them at that time, and found many of the features they had noted did not correspond with the present-day layout.

Pursuing the matter further, they discovered that no maps existed of the layout of the gardens at that earlier period, so were unable to corroborate these sketches and descriptions. However, in 1903, one year later than their last visit to the famous gardens, by one of those extraordinary coincidences that seem to occur in life from time to time, an old map dating from that period was found stuffed up a chimney in a long-disused building on the outskirts of Paris, showing the layout of the gardens at Versailles dating from that period! Examination of this exactly corroborated the sketches that the two teachers had made earlier, showing a bridge that had long disappeared, the Trianon as it was at that time, and various other features that no longer exist today.

An interesting addendum is that a French family living in proximity to the gardens during the years 1907–1908 moved away from the area because they couldn't cope with the inexplicable time lapses that occurred from time to time when they found themselves suddenly in an earlier century. The whole story is documented in a rare out of print book entitled *An Adventure*, by Miss Moberly and Miss Jourdain, and prior to its publication in 1911 the original notes and sketches relating to the entire experience were deposited at the Bodleian Library in Oxford before the old map was discovered that corroborated the story.

Because the subject of time travel is so little known outside the works of H G Wells and science fiction epics, I am going to relate one more example with which I was personally involved in the sense that Peter and I knew someone extremely well who physically experienced travelling back in time. Some years ago, because Peter was interested at the time in classic motorcycles, he joined a club to gain further information about a particular machine he was rebuilding. He was introduced to a retired company director who was passionately involved with the collection and restoration of these machines, and received a great deal of help from him with his project. One day, after working together on the project, a lunch break was felt to be due; accordingly they repaired to the local café. Later, when they had settled down for a coffee, for some reason the subject of their conversation turned to the paranormal, owing to the fact that the café owner had referred to an alleged haunting in the building next door. Tom – I shall call him that – then started to relate his fascinating story.

'My love for motorcycles started during the war when I was serving with the RAF. I struggled for some time on Air Force pay to save up the funds to acquire one, and having purchased it not long before Christmas decided to travel up to Norfolk for my Christmas leave on it, to visit some relatives who had bought a pub there. Accordingly I set out in good time, and arrived in the general area as dusk was beginning to fall. It being wartime, of course, all road signs had been taken down as a precaution against the possibility of a German invasion. I had only a rough idea of where the village lay that I had to reach when I started out, and to cap it all snow had begun to fall. I continued through the lanes slowly – not a person to be seen anywhere. Suddenly I rounded a bend in the road and saw to my amazement – although it was Christmas Eve – a large manor house, ablaze with lights, and the sounds of a very merry party coming from within. It was the sight of the lights streaming from the windows that completely stunned me. The blackout regulations were stiffly enforced at that time, and this spectacle would have attracted any stray German raider for miles. However, my prime need was to obtain directions for my destination, which I knew was not far away, so I rode my motorcycle up the drive and pulled it up on its stand in the snow outside the front door. I then grasped the knocker to announce my presence, and the door was opened by a sweet young thing of about twenty, dressed in the flapper style of the twenties. Behind her, couples were dancing, it seemed, all dressed in fancy dress of the same period, to the strains of a three-piece jazz band.

' "You look cold," said the girl. "Come in and join us for a Christmas drink."

' "I would really like to," I replied, "but my relatives will be very worried about me. I really must be on my way. Could you please direct me to…" and I named my destination. She gave me detailed directions, wished me a Merry Christmas, and I was on my way, rolling the motorcycle off its stand and kick starting it into action as I went. Following the easy directions, I soon arrived at my relatives' pub – a delightful tavern set in the middle of a rural village. After the initial joy of us all meeting up once more, and some jars of ale distributed all round, I mentioned my stroke of luck in finding the old manor house ablaze with lights and obtaining directions from there.

' "By the way," I said, "don't you bother about blackout regulations around here? That house could have been seen for miles by enemy aircraft." During the previous few minutes, while I was describing the house and its approximate whereabouts, my relatives and the others gathered around had become very quiet, and one or two were quite noticeably pale.

' "There's nowhere around here with a manor house such as you're describing at all," said one of the bystanders. "There *was* one, however, that fits your description, but that was burnt down twenty years ago one Christmas Eve just after the First World War. You must have been having a pre-Christmas drink on the quiet somewhere before you got here!"

' "It would have been very welcome," I retorted, "but let me take you to the house in the morning. I can soon find it again." With that we all retired to bed.

'The next morning we rose early and breakfasted, and set out to view the old manor house that I had visited the previous evening. This was wartime, so traffic was almost non-existent, and with the light fall of about an inch of snow that had fallen the previous day it was easy to follow my tracks; the more so because one of my motorcycle tyres had a large patch on it which made a very distinctive impression in the snow. After retracing my route for some three to four miles, the tracks turned into an ancient gateway leading to an open field. Some hundred yards into the field, we found the marks in the snow where I had pulled the motorcycle up on its stand, where there was now only open grassland. This field, however, proved to be the exact site where the old manor house had burned down.'

Tom, having related his story, went on to reflect, 'I have often wondered what would have happened if I had accepted the invitation and stepped inside for a drink. Would I have been trapped in that period, and lived out my life as a traveller from another time?' He shook his head in bewilderment, adding, 'Incredible as it may seem, this was a real experience that happened to me. I often reflect on it, but can never arrive at an answer.'

Interestingly since then, in recent years, I have heard two or three experiences of a similar nature related on television programmes. One of them concerned two men who were interviewed on television. They had been searching for buried artefacts at night with a metal detector, and related this experience of going back apparently physically in time. They had located something in the soil that they had unearthed, which had proved to be an ancient form of stirrup. At the moment that they had prised it loose from where it had lain embedded for centuries, they heard a rumbling of what seemed to them to be a great number of horses pounding towards them. Becoming worried that they might be caught up in the pitch darkness with them, they turned to run back to the road where they had parked their car... to find a solid wall blocking their path, where nothing had existed on their way to the site! Feeling their way along it in the blackness of the night, they were greatly relieved to find that it ended after a few yards, and they were able to continue on their way back to the road where they had parked their car. However, on reaching it and putting the lights of the car on, no sign of any wall that they had just been feeling their way along was evident! The rumble of the horses' hooves had died gradually away as they had felt their way past the wall.

Enough people have come forward now in situations often where more than one person at the time has shared the common experience of being physically in another time. I have to say that I have always felt time travel to be possible, and I am sure that quite a few people who have never come forward will have experienced incidents of the type mentioned.

All of the above events have involved more than one person experiencing the time shift, with the exception of the Norfolk incident, which had a number of witnesses who observed the tracks of the motorcycle in the snow. However, one unwitnessed incident recounted to me in recent years has always intrigued me, and I feel it is worth relating, if only to alert our minds to previously unconsidered possibilities

It concerns an individual who was alone walking along a beach on the South Coast of England very early one morning; unfortunately no one else was around at the time. Suddenly he noticed out at sea in misty conditions a strange greenish-grey glow, which seemed gradually to approach him, so he stopped to observe whatever this was. As it grew nearer, it appeared to be some sort of futuristic-looking vessel, which seemed to be just above the water rather than in it. It was apparently also unusual in that it had no external hatches or projections showing on its hull.

The vessel came almost to the beach, and at this point a section opened in the top of the hull. A figure appeared, according to the witness, dressed in a form of suit that reminded him of a sci-fi television epic. This person addressed our friend saying, 'What year is this?' Unfortunately the individual concerned was completely overtaken by panic and ran off to inform the police, who were not impressed when nothing was evident to substantiate his story!

What was established however was that this person was not under the influence of any alcohol or drug-related substances; and his terror was very real, from the accounts of people, including the police, who later witnessed his emotional state.

However, using the Inner Eye, it is possible to view mental images of scenes from the past, and to travel through time in this way. In a later chapter I shall describe how this is done, and readers may experience this for themselves if they wish.

Something else has always intrigued me, and that is the disappearance and reappearance of objects such as keys and certain other small items. Peter and I have experienced two such occurrences, where all possibility of a physical explanation has been completely eliminated. In the first instance, we needed to go to the States on business, and for this trip we required a visa at short notice. To obtain this we were required to take our passports to the American Embassy the following day; at this point in time I left the house to do some shopping, leaving Peter to his own devices.

Peter continues: It occurred to me to check that our passports were where they should be, ready for our trip the following day. They were always kept, together with things such as driving licences and medical documents, in a small drawer in the top of our writing desk. I pulled this out, expecting to see the passports in their normal place, and was very surprised to see that they were not there. This drawer being quite small, it did not take long to remove and empty it; I riffled through the remaining papers to see if our passports had in some way been caught up in them – nothing. At this point in time, I began to become quite concerned, as a lot depended on our trip to the States. I began to wonder if by chance our passports had not been returned to the drawer from some previous trip abroad, and then began to search through suit pockets, various wallets and travel bags around the house, again without result.

I returned to the original drawer, emptying it yet again and even searching around the interior top and sides where it entered the desk in case they had become wedged into the interior joints – again no result.

I was still sitting at the desk with mounting concern at a loss what to do next, when Anne returned from the shops.

'My love, we have a problem,' I announced. 'Our passports, which we need for tomorrow, have gone missing. I have searched everywhere throughout the whole house and they're just not around. You and I both know that our passports are always kept in the top left-hand corner of the bureau – here.' I leaned forward to open the drawer to its full extent. Two red passports, the gilded and embossed lettering on the covers glinting dully in the full light of day, rested on the papers beneath and seemed to stare back at me in an attempt to belie my statement

Inexplicable as it may seem, such were the facts. No one else was in the house, as in the case which follows:

Anne continues: My father used to own a mobile home, which he kept in our garden in Kent. He had a beautiful white cat called Snowy, which he doted on. One weekend he decided to go away to visit some friends in the New Forest area, and asked us to feed and look after Snowy during his absence. Before leaving, he came to the house to leave us the keys to his mobile home, where Snowy's cat food was kept. The three of us – that is, Peter, my father and myself – agreed that the keys to the mobile home would be left on top of our kitchen worktop, which was otherwise kept completely clear of any objects. This agreed, we all made sure the bunch of keys was left in this position so that Peter and I would have no difficulty in locating them when feeding time came around. My father said his goodbyes, and we duly busied ourselves with the remainder of the daily round.

Six thirty soon came around (Snowy's next feeding time) and I went to the kitchen to collect the keys to the mobile home, as Snowy was already making known what was required by a series of insistent miaows. To my amazement, the kitchen worktop was completely bare. I peered over the sides to see if the keys had accidentally been knocked down. Nothing to be seen; so, pursuing the obvious course, I found Peter working in the garden to ask if he knew if anything had happened to the keys. Knowing that we had carefully agreed between us exactly where to leave them, I was hardly surprised when he told me he had no knowledge of their having been moved.

We searched everywhere we could think of, knowing that it was impossible for them to have been moved. Completely unable to rationalise what had happened, we decided to assuage poor Snowy's hunger with a tin of sardines from our own cupboard. After an hour or so we were forced to give up the search for the missing keys, simply because as far as we were concerned there was nowhere else to look and no one else had been on the property during this time.

The evening came and went leaving us completely mystified. At eleven o'clock we turned in as usual, and after a deep sleep, I came awake with a need to go to the bathroom. The kitchen door was between our bedroom and the bathroom, and wishing to know the time I flicked the kitchen light on to look at the wall clock positioned over the worktop. Four o'clock – and a bunch of keys placed exactly where they should be!

Because Peter and I are so used to investigations while working on behalf of our clients, every known avenue was explored to find a physical reason for those keys to disappear. No explanation other than a non-physical one was possible in this instance.

So, do these disappearing objects simply dematerialise and go into another time dimension, or were we simply victims of some extraterrestrial prank?

Chapter 12
Between Two Worlds

Could you take a talking parrot seriously? If anyone had asked me this question before a certain evening had taken place involving one of my clients, my immediate response of course would have been not to take the speaker seriously at all and wait for the punch line! However, on this particular evening I had an experience that made me revise my whole concept of what was possible between the next world and this.

It began when a lady client came to see me for a general reading. As I often do, I requested that I be given an object to hold; in this case it was a ring that was handed to me. After I had picked up on a few everyday situations with which my client was involved, I heard a voice in my head asking me to give a message to her. The message concerned a pet parrot, which the family had apparently had for some years. The impression I received was that the person communicating was her father, so that just to check this was so I asked if the lady's father had passed over. She confirmed this was so, and I started to continue only to wonder to myself if my ability to hear communications from the Beyond had somehow begun to become scrambled, as I distinctly heard the words, 'Tell my daughter I gave the parrot a bit of help.' I relayed these words, expecting to meet with ridicule; however the reverse occurred.

My client, after confirming that she knew exactly what her father meant, commenced by saying that one day she had had an extremely lucky win at bingo; a win of £800, which of course delighted the family. On re-entering the house with a friend, the family parrot, an African Grey, which normally had a fairly limited vocabulary consisting of brief phrases such as 'Hello', 'How are you?', 'Goodnight' etc., astonished them both by saying, 'How did you like your surprise?' Not only was it so apt, but the parrot had never been heard either to repeat this particular question previously, or even to repeat a series of words of this length before.

A few days later, my client's daughter, aged about eleven, was about to attend secondary school for the first time. The great day dawned, and the girl busied herself in preparation for this new adventure, very much looking forward to going. With everything finally packed into her school satchel she readied herself for the off, when to everyone's astonishment the parrot called out, 'Are you excited?' – another expression, perfectly timed, which no one had ever heard the bird use before.

Confirmed as it was by the father (the grandfather of the child) speaking to me as he did and telling me that he had influenced the parrot to say these things, I had to accept what had taken place, my client saying that she had had the feeling that her father had influenced the bird in some way.

I have never come across anything like this in my life, either before or since. Could this particular African Grey have been the world's first example of a parrot working as a medium?

One day I was asked to see a lady in her late eighties. I had been contacted by a friend of hers who told me that although the person did not believe in any form of afterlife, she wanted to try to contact her deceased daughter Hazel (not her real name), and she had contacted me through this friend to see if this was possible. Accordingly one sunny day I arrived at a picturesque bungalow set in quite a large area of land featuring rolling fields and woodlands. After the introductions had been made, over a cup of tea my client confessed to a lack of belief in anything concerning the afterlife, but had felt compelled to get in touch with me, as someone she knew had passed away in mysterious circumstances, and she felt that possibly through me she could achieve some inner peace if any light could be thrown on the matter.

We continued to chat for a few minutes while I started to mentally scan. In this instance I found it quite difficult to pick up any signal – often the reason for this is that the person with whom you are working does not think communication in this manner is possible, and without realising it puts up a mental barrier that makes communication difficult. However, after a while I heard with my Inner Ear the word 'Mum'. The lady indicated that she knew who I meant when I relayed this, so I asked her how long ago her daughter had passed on. I was told she had passed away two years previously, and that this was the anniversary of her passing. The daughter was able to tell me that there had been several unusual occurrences in the house. On one occasion her husband had felt her presence very strongly in the bathroom, and on quite a few other occasions a number of old clocks, which had been in the family for many years, behaved strangely by stopping and then restarting on their own – something almost impossible for the old type of mechanical clock – and chiming out of sequence and then reverting to normal timekeeping afterwards.

I relayed this information to the mother, who confirmed that these events had actually taken place. The daughter then went on to tell me she had owned three dogs over the ten years preceding her passing; one initially, which died after about five years of being with her, and two others which she had acquired later, both of which had passed away not long after the daughter's death. I again passed this information to her mother, who confirmed all these facts to be correct, expressing some surprise.

Once communication had been properly established, Hazel went on to describe something of her life over there. She talked of the cottage she lived in, in some woods with fields close by. All of her three dogs were apparently with her again, and many birds and owls lived in the woods surrounding her dwelling. She told me she had been a great lover of nature on earth, and had been delighted to find when she had 'settled in' over there how it was very like the life she had enjoyed on earth, but much more enhanced in terms of beauty and quality of living. She continued by saying that she could realise her great love for children and animals by rescuing them. Her work consisted of taking them into her care after passing over from sometimes difficult and tragic deaths, introducing them into a loving and caring environment, and helping them to adapt to their new way of life.

I would have liked to question her more on what life was like over there, but Hazel was more concerned in getting her mother to put behind her not only her death but any thoughts of pursuing the matter further.

I asked her what she meant by this. Hazel went on to explain to me that she had given up her teaching job due to the lack of means of controlling pupils brought about by today's educational system, and taken a job with the cross-Channel ferries. One day, she told me, a staff safety exercise involving over one hundred people was carried out, and a simulated passenger evacuation implemented. The flooding of a compartment was effected, but her planned escape was not possible as one of her feet became trapped in a piece of equipment. Attempts to cut her loose in time were to no avail, and she drowned. Hazel's mother confirmed all this to me, adding that the company should be brought to justice over this, but as Hazel suffered from asthma this illness was falsely blamed for her death. Hazel spoke to me again saying that her mother should on no account attempt any form of legal redress, as she would have no hope of winning, the cover-up having been too clever.

As a matter of interest, because of my involvement with the Zeebrugge ferry incident discussed in a later chapter, I had become very familiar with the dismissive cover-ups carried out in distressing situations of this nature. A book written by a Zeebrugge survivor entitled *Disaster at Zeebrugge – the Crew's Story* by Stuart White throws an interesting light on the attitude of some of the ferry companies to tragedy. The lack of hope of any form of redress in these types of situation is starkly outlined, making interesting reading... but I digress.

On the basis of the evidence I had previously given, the mother decided not to proceed any further with the matter. The conversation then took a change, the daughter telling me she had a collection of objects concerning animals, which were still in the house. The mother confirmed that Hazel had always collected horse brasses from an early age, and that they remained in her room. Hazel rounded off her fascinating series of communications by saying that she was concerned for her mother living in such an isolated situation, that she would like to see her sell the farm and land on which she lived and move to a village where she would be less isolated. However, Hazel's husband preferred to remain on the farm, which created an obstacle to this being achieved. I was unable to mediate on this between-the-worlds discussion, and Hazel suddenly said, 'Goodbye – I must go now.'

There was a brief postscript to this interlude. I received two further communications destined for the mother from people who had known her on earth.

This can often happen when a communication has been established between two people, one on earth and the other discarnate. I have been told that when a link has been established between the worlds, this in some way transmits a signal to others who have passed on who have links with the person I am working with. In this case, following on Hazel's departure, two further communicators came through: the first was a relative who was a sailor in the Second World War, who made himself known by two or three references – all correct – to times when he knew the mother in her younger days; and the second was an older cousin, who showed me mental pictures of growing some particularly fine vegetables. It then transpired that the mother had given over a portion of her land at the time to this cousin for vegetable growing. The cousin then went on to say that everyone normally who had passed over continued to do what they enjoyed best, and he was continuing to do just that – growing vegetables – in the same way that Hazel was continuing to look after children and animals.

When I am working in this manner I am always intrigued by the way, almost at the drop of a hat, I can find myself quickly immersed in yet another interesting and complicated situation. Naturally, a lot of my work consists of fairly mundane matters, perhaps concerning the work or emotional problems of people; but in this chapter I am including some of the quite dramatic situations and challenges with which I have been confronted. One such incident came about one day quite by chance, when a long-standing client suggested to a friend of hers that she might like to contact me regarding her considerable problems. When this person arrived, an American, I certainly never realised that a web of intrigue of massive international proportions was about to unfold before me.

As with many of my new clients, she was very sceptical at first. However quite quickly I picked up that her husband had passed over, and that she had not had any children. She confirmed that this was correct. I moved on to say that I felt he had been involved in construction in quite a big way, and she again confirmed this was so. I then sensed that her husband's death was not a normal one, and it was at this point I received a strong mental image of a man I described to my client. She immediately recognised my description of the man

I was seeing as her husband. He then told me that his death had been planned very carefully to look like suicide. This was certainly not what I was expecting to hear, but I relayed what had been communicated to me, wondering what my client's response would be.

'This is very interesting,' she said. 'I always had a feeling he never committed suicide, but that was the finding at the inquiry.'

Meryl (not her real name) became quite emotional at this point. 'I want to tell you how it all began,' she said, doing her best to withhold her tears. 'We met on an old steam train in America – I have always loved those old trains – and this was a Scottish one brought over from the UK by a wealthy steam enthusiast. We all wore kilts during the ride, and I was thoroughly enjoying myself when this tall, handsome stranger from the storybooks came up and started talking to me. Although I was only seventeen at the time, I felt straight-away he was the person for me, and it seemed he felt the same way. Not long afterwards I introduced him to my parents – it was something of a whirlwind romance – we had a storybook wedding, and he took me back to a beautiful part of England to a lovely old house with low ceilings and oak beams, something I had always wanted.'

David (again, not his real name) apparently worked for a large international construction company, and lived between England and America, working on some quite massive luxury housing projects. His company was building him a fine house to his designs in the States. It was at this point that the fairy-tale existence for the couple took a downturn. On one of his trips to the States while working on a project, he came across some documents hidden at the back of a filing cabinet, which related to an enormous fraud, involving very large sums of money being tracked to subcontractors unrelated to the main company. David immediately raised questions with the management regarding this; he was told that the matter would be looked into, the documents were removed and he was no longer allowed access to them.

David then feigned a complete lack of interest in the matter, and continued with his work in the usual manner without saying a word to anyone. However, he had made careful notes, and at the first opportunity returned to England on leave. He then made a personal appointment to see the titled owner of the multimillion-dollar enterprise – which was a household name – taking his notes with him. He presented the material, explaining the details of the enormous fraud taking place in the States.

After the meeting, the man said, 'Trust me. Don't say anything to anyone; I'll investigate the situation.' The meeting was concluded; the two men shook hands, and David went on his way, feeling that he had done the best he could to resolve this difficult and delicate situation.

David travelled back to the States to his home there, a very desirable rented property where he was staying while his own property was being built for him and his wife to their own exacting requirements. It was at this point that some very strange things began to take place. He found on his return (Meryl had stayed in England) that many items he had specified for the interior of his house, which he had planned together with Meryl, who was a talented interior designer, had been completely changed. Colours they had specified had been altered, and items such as kitchen tiling and certain fittings had been laid in the wrong colours or in the wrong places. The kitchen units arrived in the same manner; the wrong components were supplied to the wrong designs. David began to realise that this was no coincidence. He then attempted to contact the head of the concern with whom he had dealt in England; he was just never available.

At this stage of the affair he was no longer permitted access to any documents or paperwork relating to accounts. The project he was working on involved millions of dollars, and in the normal way his responsibilities would have included careful budgeting to maximise profit. His exclusion from accessing accounts effectively tied his hands in relation to budget control.

He began to feel particularly uneasy with regard to his chief assistant, a man who was always smiling effusively, wore gold rings and a large gold chain on his wrist.

Around this time it was suggested to David that he bring his wife over, so that the company could use her services as an interior designer. David thought this a little strange, as the American company normally employed their own people, but was delighted that Meryl was able to join him at this difficult time.

A lot of company entertaining went on, and David was surprised to notice a particularly charming man often flirting with his wife. As time went on, his attentions became more and more evident, with the man often telephoning their home asking for Meryl. Sadly, Meryl became completely infatuated with this person, and left David to live with him.

Much later, both Meryl and David realised that a very clever plan had been set in motion. The man with the gold chain became very sympathetic and commiserated frequently with him. David, besides being interested in steam engines, had a great love of vintage cars, one of which he had shipped over to the States so that he would not be separated from his hobby. Due to his wife having left him and his work situation becoming worse and worse, David threw himself more and more into working in his spare time on his vintage car.

The man with the gold chain started to come round more and more to David's rented house in the evenings (the house he had attempted to have constructed and completed was developing more and more problems, and remained incomplete). One night a maudlin session of commiseration developed between the two men, the one becoming extremely drunk on bourbon... and the other not so drunk, as we will see.

The following morning David was found asphyxiated in his vintage car, his garage door closed and a suicide note left beside him on the car seat.

Meryl suspected at the time that David had never committed suicide. She knew his character would never have allowed him to take this route, and that he had been extremely skilfully murdered. The scales then began to drop from her eyes. Her 'extremely charming man' ditched her almost immediately after this tragic event, and she began to realise she had been duped. Remorse set in, and she had periods of uncontrollable weeping, as she realised she had indirectly contributed to her husband's death, appreciating what she had thrown away.

David's body was flown back to England, and he was buried at his birthplace. Quite apart from the remorse and emotional stress left in the wake of this tragic series of events, Meryl was subjected to new fears. Her house was broken into on more than one occasion and her husband's office was ransacked; it became very evident that her telephone calls were being tapped, and her rubbish bins were collected before the normal collection days.

The strong mental image of her husband had never left me. I could sense his concern that the matter should be allowed to rest, that no amount of investigation would return him to life and the Earth he had been forced to leave. Any further probing on Meryl's part would only result in her death. He asked me to reassure Meryl that she should not blame herself for becoming a victim of infatuation; that he loved her, and that he was concerned that she must now make a new life for herself.

Meryl's remorse was very sad, but she realised the wisdom of the other-world counsel. Nothing could change the situation, and she thanked me, saying that she felt a great weight had been lifted from her shoulders. By chance, I heard some years later that she had successfully made a new life for herself, had remarried and returned to settle down in the States.

One day someone whom I knew asked me if I would be able to help on a local murder case, handing me a local newspaper report. One evening a man had been killed with a knife not far from the centre of a busy market town. The police were baffled, and had no information to go on, the man having no family. The only link that could be traced to him was that he had been born in the Channel Islands and had lived there for many years, and had spent the 1939–45 War there as a young man. He had left the islands some while after the war, since which time he had settled in England, apparently leading a solitary life without any family.

The person who had drawn this incident to my attention knew someone in the local police who was interested in following the matter up using my abilities. An informal appointment was made at our friend's house, to see if I could help in any way. Peter came with me, as we often work together.

We arrived, and were introduced to the officer, a detective constable, who had expressed an interest in meeting me to see what might transpire. He had a pleasant and relaxed air, and as is the wont of many members of the police force with years of experience, a non-committal manner. After we had exchanged pleasantries, to my surprise he produced an identikit form from his briefcase and asked to interview Peter and myself separately.

Peter undertook the first session, and using the same mental imaging method as I do, over a period of about twenty minutes communicated to the officer his impressions of the features of the murderer.

I of course was not shown the result that Peter had achieved, and I sat down facing the officer and started to mentally 'scan' with my mind's eye to see what I could come up with. To my surprise, a voice in my ear said, '*He deserved it!*' I concealed my astonishment as best I could, realising it would not be appropriate to relate what I had just experienced to a police officer I had just met for the first time. Closing my eyes to better focus my attention on the mental images that might appear in my mind's eye, I mentioned to the detective constable that I would need some time to remain quiet in order to concentrate, to which he nodded assent.

I then heard the voice again in my head, which spoke in an accent that I recognised as Jersey, saying to me, '*During the war he worked for the Germans. I was one of the many people he had killed for helping the Allies.*'

I then began to experience a grisly, sickening sensation of people being beaten up, tortured and shot… I hastily closed down the mental pictures that had started to flood in, and tried to concentrate on what was going on around me. Fortunately nothing more of this nature came to me; my mind became blank. However, I began to feel within me an indignation that without realising, I had started an enquiry within myself to bring to so-called justice the perpetrator of a long-deferred execution that was intended to right the wrongs, which the murdered man had committed. This was a strange experience for me, having suddenly had thrust upon me the responsibilities of judge and jury together! However, so strongly did I feel that justice had been done that I felt I could play no further part in any way tracking down the executioner, for that was the light in which I saw the affair.

At the time this occurred, it was of course many, many years after the War, and I marvelled at how the execution had been carried out after such a long time interval. Was it because the person or persons concerned simply couldn't trace the perpetrator of these war crimes until recent times, or was it because the individual had simply bided his time until this late date, nursing the grave injustices, so that no links with the past could be established? Nothing further came to me, and I just felt that the matter had resolved itself into a closed book.

After all these reflections had taken place, I suddenly realised the detective constable was beginning to become restive, after having waited so patiently while all these events and thoughts of mine had been taking place. I 'came to', as it were, apologising for my long silence and merely saying that the circumstances around the case seemed so complex that I was unable to make any sort of headway. The man smiled politely, slightly raising his eyebrows as he did so, as if to say; 'I should never have wasted my time on this; what could I expect if I start coming to clairvoyants to solve crimes?'

I didn't feel I had done my reputation any good as we said our goodbyes. However he thanked both of us; Peter had evidently not picked up anything relating to the type of information I had been privileged to receive, and by simply using Remote Viewing, had built up an identikit picture with the help of the DC. Later of course Peter and I compared notes; he felt quite mortified when I told him what I had managed to pick up, feeling better when he realised we had been using entirely different approaches, Remote Viewing not of course involving any form of other-world communication.

We never heard anything further relating to this matter, and as far as I know the case has remained unsolved to this day.

One evening I was working with a group of people, when a woman came in and sat down opposite me, looking careworn and sad. We had exchanged a few initial pleasantries so that I could 'tune in' so to speak, when I began to get the feeling that there was a substantial court case in which she could be involved somewhere ahead in time. I asked her if she had any connection with a legal dispute, and her reply was that she had been turning a matter over in her mind for some time, whether to go ahead or not. Suddenly I heard a male voice quite clearly in my Inner Ear, saying, *'Tell her to go ahead with it. There are a lot of us over here because of what happened! We were used like guinea pigs in a form of laboratory experiment after which many of us died a slow, lingering, terrible death.'* The voice paused there a moment, as if to allow me to relay the information, which of course I did.

'That's my husband,' the woman said excitedly, 'He was involved in an atomic bomb experiment at a place called Bikini Atoll in the Pacific Ocean.'

The voice continued, as clear as a bell in my head. *'We were all ordered to turn our backs to the explosion; the flash was of such a searing intensity that we could clearly see the bones through the flesh of our hands, and the detonation which arrived seconds later seemed to reverberate through our bodies in such a way that we thought we were going to vibrate to pieces. It was a terrible experience, which should never have been allowed to take* place. In addition, the inhabitants of the area had been forced to leave their homes that their families had inhabited for generations, for an environment some distance away totally unsuited to their way of life. Many of them suffered and died due to this. As for ourselves, over the next few months and years, we all became extremely ill, dying slow and painful deaths.'

His wife took up the story. 'His illness was shocking. He seemed to take on the appearance of jaundice. Of course, we weren't allowed to know at the time, but it was a form of cancer due to the intense radiation they all underwent. He was admitted to hospital and kept in an isolation ward; the examining staff all wore protective clothing.

'When my husband died, I was not allowed access to his body or to remove it for burial. The whole affair was a crime against humanity and nature itself, and to think we vote people in to power and give them a free hand to commit misery and mass murder on this scale, all in the name of government! You can imagine how I and many other wives and relatives suffered, not just from the loss of our loved ones, but watching them suffer and waste away because of the thoughtless irresponsibility of those who, by virtue of their position and responsibility should have known better.'

I was overwhelmed with sadness by this tragic story, which continued to haunt me for a long time afterwards. I could feel her husband's intensity of purpose that the cudgels should be taken up in the name of justice for those who died in vain, their loved ones left in the wake of misery.

I am happy to say that following this episode, although this took some years, my client arranged to get together all the members of the families affected; a successful action was brought against the British Government and compensation awarded to the bereaved.

About a year after my father had passed away, Peter and I received an intriguing physical communication from him, which, although brief, certainly took us by surprise at the time. During his lifetime, his passion was radio and electrical equipment; this background may have accounted for yet another experience we were fortunate to undergo. Peter is an experienced private pilot, and at the time of which I write, we owned a four-seater aircraft in which my father, who loved flying, would often accompany us. Some time after his passing, we were on our own in the aircraft when we clearly heard his unmistakeable voice in our headsets! We heard only four words: *'Hello, how are you?'*

We were so surprised, Peter and I; we looked across at each other at the same instant. Apart from the fact we knew his voice so well, the aircraft headsets were switched to internal only, i.e. we were not able at that point in time to receive external calls either from other aircraft or ground stations – this was definitely from beyond the grave. There have of course been many other instances of this occurring; but it certainly was fascinating to experience it first-hand.

Chapter 13
I Can See Through You

As soon as my client entered the room, I could sense the scepticism. She had come to me for a reading, as the bulk of my clients do, which normally consists of analysing situations around them concerning relationships, emotional problems, business situations etc., and, strangely enough, a health check!

I took my client's hands and turned them palm upwards, as I often do. Using a basic knowledge of palmistry, I will perhaps start by tracing certain lines on the palm, which indicate trends and tendencies within their lives, and at this point flashes of intuition will rise within my consciousness, revealing to me situations surrounding the client. I mentioned one or two sets of circumstances that were taking place around her and known only to her. I saw her expression change from disbelief to one of surprise and astonishment. For something like fifteen to twenty minutes I continued to unravel her life, which was rather complex at this time, and advised her how to handle various situations which were causing her some difficulty. At the end of the session I was glad to see that I had gained yet another convert as she admitted to being very impressed with what I had told her.

'Your health,' I said, 'Let me just run my eye over you.'

I had told her earlier that I knew she was a doctor, and she immediately said, 'Thank you, but I have regular health checks, and there's nothing wrong with me.' I said nothing, but set my 'scanning system' in motion.

Because so many people have asked me how this happens, I will do my best to describe what takes place. As I turn my mind to mentally checking over a person's health, a mental image forms itself in my mind of their body, rather like a skeletal representation. If an organ is malfunctioning or there is for instance a bone or joint deformation, I get the impression of a small red blob, rather like a laser beam, showing the malfunctioning area. Automatically, my mind will blow this area up, magnifying it; let us say the image is that of the liver or pancreas; then I will know there is a problem with this particular organ. Sometimes when there is difficulty in identifying the problem, a 'silent voice' in my head will say 'blocked artery' or 'inflamed colon', for example.

In the case of this particular client, both processes occurred. From the initial skeletal representation in my mind, I followed the appearance of the familiar red blob in the lower half of her body off to one side; the image rapidly expanded and a silent voice in my head said 'ovarian cyst'. 'You have an ovarian cyst forming,' I said to her. 'You must get it checked immediately.'

Disbelief appeared again on my client's features. 'This can't be so,' she said. 'I've recently, as I said, had a complete check-up, and the hospital would have picked up on that.'

'Please listen to me,' I said. 'Go and have what I have told you checked out.'

Unconvinced, my client settled up with me and left, promising however that she would do as I said. A few days later she telephoned, thanking me effusively. 'It was just as you said; an ovarian cyst had formed, and I was able to be operated on just in time, as it would shortly have burst. I can't thank you enough.'

This process of internal scanning would prove to be available to me in almost any field. At the time that Peter and I first met, as I have mentioned earlier, Peter had a business purchasing and selling antique and classic cars. One day I accompanied Peter on a buying trip to view a sports car in North Wales. We arrived at the owner's home and there the car stood looking resplendent in gleaming paint and polished alloy. The price seemed quite reasonable for such an attractive car, and Peter was very taken with it. He inspected it very carefully, lifting up the bonnet and peering here and there in all the nooks and crannies, and was asking questions about its maintenance history, when for some reason my mind was drawn to the engine, the bonnet being in the open position.

Suddenly something happened that had never previously occurred to me since childhood during the incident of the wheel on my father's car mentioned in an earlier chapter. In my mind's eye, I saw something akin to one of those exploded diagrams shown in car magazines of the car's engine. On one of the cylinders a red blob suddenly showed, and in the same way that images of the human body expand in my mind's eye, this particular cylinder expanded up and I could see a hairline crack running through the cylinder wall. With some alarm, I could see that Peter was about to close the deal. Quickly, I caught Peter's eye and beckoned him over. It wasn't easy at this late stage of the intended purchase of the car to draw Peter to one side, so I could see no alternative other than not to beat about the bush and say to him, in front of the owner, 'Peter, this car has a cracked cylinder!'

Although I had never at that time used my abilities for detection of mechanical faults in cars, Peter immediately accepted what I had said. He turned to the owner, saying that he trusted my judgement, and what did he have to say about it?

Both of us expected him to become angry and say something like, 'What does this woman know about cars?' or 'No one can see inside engines!' To our intense surprise, the colour drained from his face and he said, 'I can't understand how you know that,' thereby admitting that he had known of the serious flaw in the engine all along. Totally bewildered and embarrassed, he watched us drive away after we had politely said our goodbyes.

Since that time, Peter has been often amazed at how my gift can frequently solve engineering and mechanical handling problems, with no training whatsoever. On one occasion, Peter had purchased a large and very heavy V8 car engine for installation in one of his projects. He collected it in our Safari Land Rover, having had it loaded onto the vehicle by means of a crane at the place of collection. This engine had to be delivered to a friend's house, where it was to be stripped and overhauled. We arrived and reversed our vehicle as near as possible to the workshop where this work was to be carried out, and Peter and his friend suddenly realised there was no crane available to offload the engine. They were both standing about scratching their heads over the problem, when suddenly my Inner Eye showed me in a series of quick flashes how to resolve it. Almost out of sight in the distance was a porter's barrow, leaning up against a fence, half concealed by some bushes. When I pointed this out to Peter's friend, who owned the property, he told me that he had forgotten the existence of it! I suggested to them that they should place the handles of the barrow against the rear floor of the Land Rover, and put a blanket over the floor and handles together. I asked them to slide and lever the engine onto the barrow handles over the blanket, and the two of them managed to slide it onto the blanket to the step of the barrow, causing it to become erect. The Land Rover was then moved away, and the two men then manoeuvred the barrow, with its load, into the workshop where it was required to be.

Both of them were amazed that I had suggested this solution. I can't explain how these things occur to me, other than they are a series of sequenced images which just flash into my mind.

Over the years, I have been flattered to have a very great number of magazine articles written about me, involving everything from murder inquiries to robberies, people's health problems and the location of missing persons. To my everlasting regret, it is impossible to cope with the resulting flood of mail, which comes to me from all over the world. Contained in the proportion I was successful in handling at the time was a letter accompanied by a clipping of horse's mane. It was from a lady who wrote to me telling me that her horse had been sporadically ill for some four or five years with a form of intestinal infection, and in spite of numerous visits by a number of veterinary surgeons, no one had been able to arrive at a means to end its suffering.

Immediately I touched the clipping from the horse's mane, I received a vivid mental image of an inflamed intestine. This was followed swiftly by a mental enlargement of the inflamed area, and I could distinctly 'see' a splinter of wood lodged deeply in the centre of the inflammation. I contacted the owner, Penny Goring, and she passed the information on to her vet. She told me that Yogi, a horse well known in international dressage circles at the time as 'Lord of the Dance', had recovered sufficiently well after a few weeks to compete once more in international competitions.

This story and many others have been written up in the national press, having been checked out by various reporters.

Subsequent to this, many horse owners got in touch with me, asking me to identify the mysterious ailments that their animals had been suffering from. This grew at one time to such an extent that I had an arrangement with a local riding stable for owners to bring their suffering charges to me on a day that was set aside once a week for me to view them and diagnose their complaints. This 'horse clinic' was a growing success, but due to pressure of work at my Maidstone clinic, having so many human sufferers, I was forced to reduce this to a working minimum every now and again, owing to lack of available time.

Dogs too featured in my daily round. A patient of mine, who had heard of my success with horses, asked me one day if I would be able to help her Alsatian to recover the use of its back legs. It is of course well known that Alsatians often have a weakness in this area, due to inbreeding, so that I was concerned that I would not be able to do anything to help the suffering animal. The problem had become quite advanced to the extent that my client's husband had made a trolley for it to drag itself around on, which it was managing to do quite successfully. However, I agreed to see the animal to try to help it in some way, so one day shortly afterwards I called at the owner's home.

My heart sank when I saw the poor animal. I offered up a prayer, and passed my hands palms down over its back without touching it. Through my palms, I could sense a slightly greater heat wherein the source of the arthritic condition lay. Asking the owner to hold my patient firmly by the head (at least my human patients don't often bite!) I started to manipulate the spine area with my fingers.

I began to sense that some joints were loosening, and as I continued for about ten minutes, after which time the dog was freed. At least he was wagging his tail and looking happier. I thought some movement seemed to have returned to his back legs, so we took them off the little trolley. There was definitely movement; as I was pressed for time I had to leave, but promised to call back.

I did so twice more, at intervals of roughly a week, continuing the treatment. In the final event the animal was able to walk using his hind legs without the little trolley. His walk was not perfect, but he was able to get about and seemed quite content, licking my hand in gratitude. As with other certain extreme cases, I felt rather that I was the instrument of some infinitely powerful influence, and felt very privileged to be able to contribute in some small way to ease this animal's suffering.

One day I was out shopping, when a neighbour came up to me telling me that she had heard about the good results I had achieved by my work with animals. She was very attached to her little dachshund, who went by the name of Bobby. She told me that her dog had been knocked over by a car some months previously and had to be treated by a number of visits to the vet. There had never been any wounds as such, or bleeding, all the injuries being internal. Bobby had recovered to quite an extent, but had been dragging his back legs a lot. This affliction had remained with him and showed no signs of improving. Would I be able to take a look at him? Without demur, I agreed to see the animal the following day.

When I arrived at my neighbour's cottage, Bobby greeted me effusively, barking enthusiastically and rolling over on his back, tail wagging furiously. When we managed to calm him down, I watched him drag his hind legs, and marvelled at how well he coped with his affliction; certainly a lesson for some of us humans!

Stroking him to calm him down, my Inner Eye scanned his back, entering the area of the spine, running along it and seeing a number of red blobs indicating deformation caused by the accident. My heart sank. I was beginning to feel that this was going to be too much for me to cope with. I asked Bobby's owner to hold him by the head – although he had a very sunny disposition, if I needed to touch an overly sensitive area there would be no telling what might happen – and started to work my fingers firmly into his spine, following the course of the little red blobs. I was very concerned to feel for myself just how severe the deformation was, but gradually, almost socket by socket, bones began to click back in place under firm manipulation. One by one they went in, poor Bobby giving a plaintive yelp from time to time. I felt somehow Bobby knew I was trying to help him; he never growled or showed his teeth.

Finally, I had finished. Giving him a little pat and a caress, I told his owner to let him go. Bobby shook himself – always a good sign in a dog – stretched, and walked absolutely normally over to his bowl and commenced to drink. His owner was in tears, and I felt very embarrassed. I explained that I felt that we very much had luck on our side, because if Bobby's spine had been left for a much longer period, it might not have been possible to re-manipulate his vertebrae into position, which had been so badly displaced by the accident.

Some weeks later I saw Bobby out with his owner, trotting cheerfully at her heels. I was delighted to see that he had no hint of a limp – one lucky dachshund!

At this point I would like to bring about an abrupt shift from the animal kingdom to what many people have found to be some highly interesting encounters with certain illnesses, apparently at or beyond the limit of current medical knowledge.

Some time later and in another country, someone had suggested to a wealthy Dutch industrialist that he bring his wife to me, to see if I could help her in any way with a serious health problem she had. He telephoned me at my house asking if I could call at the guest house where he and his wife were staying on holiday, saying that he would prefer to leave any discussions of her problem until the time of my visit. Most intriguing, I thought, supposing that her problem proved to be completely outside my working areas; perhaps the couple would have been better off seeking help from conventional medical sources.

I drove to where the couple were staying. A form of country club, it sported tennis courts, a swimming pool and riding stables. The Dutchman was a man of about fifty, and his wife, who hailed from Equatorial Africa, was extremely attractive and intelligent, and twenty-five years younger. They conducted me to their room and told me their story. The husband had been on holiday on a guided tour of a safari park, and his wife had been the guide of the party. After a whirlwind romance and an African wedding, she had accompanied him back to Holland, where she had adapted to her new life extremely well, becoming fluent in Dutch and involved herself more and more in helping him to run his business. One thing, however, marred their happiness. She could never wear dresses, only trousers, because both her legs had become dreadfully disfigured with large blistering bubbles under the skin, and the legs had swollen to half again their normal size. In addition to all this, they itched permanently and the poor girl was at her wit's end in endeavouring not to scratch them. She told me that the problem had started roughly three years before she met her husband. During that time she had visited many doctors, and since she had settled down in Europe with her husband, they had together sought out many medical opinions, without achieving any success. The condition had been diagnosed as an extreme form of psoriasis, and was thought to have been contracted by standing in one of the African rivers, which the girl had done quite often, being a lover of water.

They asked me if I thought I would be able to do anything for her. At this stage I had not been able to view her condition, and after what I had heard I was starting to feel a little apprehensive about what I would be able to do. We repaired to a bedroom, and the girl slipped her trousers off. I was appalled at what I saw, and also very surprised that no medical treatment had been found to alleviate this terrible condition, which now that I was viewing it for the first time was far worse than I had imagined possible.

My instinct was to recoil from the situation and make my excuses and depart. Realising what it must be like to be in this poor girl's condition, I steeled myself and tried to get a grip on the situation. I could see what seemed to be large white blistering bubbles everywhere under the skin, with bleeding here and there where my poor patient had yielded to the intense desire to scratch the sores. Never having previously been confronted by such a situation, for a few seconds I was at a complete loss as to how to proceed. Then I felt an inner calmness take place within me, and I offered up a prayer for help. A silent voice, which I had experienced on occasions previously, said, *'Use the magnetic treatment.'* (At this stage I did not know what this meant!) *'Breathe in and imagine your hand as a magnet. Hold your breath and pass your hand about a quarter of an inch above the skin, slowly moving it over the leg you are beginning to work on.'*

My Inner Perception started to perceive what appeared to be small brown shiny balls under the skin. All I could do was to continue under the instruction of this silent inner voice, which while telling me what to do produced within me an inner calm and detachment; this in turn gave me an assurance that although I was the instrument, the responsibility lay with a power beyond my comprehension.

I changed position and continued with the other leg. My patient seemed slightly surprised at what I was doing, no doubt wondering how on earth passing my hand over her without touching her was going to bring about any improvement.

During each pass of the hand, I received the impulse to shake the hand at the end of each pass, as if to free myself of some invisible clinging matter. I continued in this way until I had completed the series of passes over the second leg, and I became aware of the silent voice again. *'It is essential that you wash your hands thoroughly as quickly as possible. After you have done this, go home and shower yourself. Continue in this way for two further days.'* Then silence.

I left as soon as possible, as instructed. The couple was very friendly, but naturally seemed a little incredulous, as was to be expected. 'I have to leave now,' I said briskly. 'I must see you again tomorrow and the following day to complete the treatment. Shall we say ten o'clock?'

The couple assented, and I took myself home for a thorough shower, as I had been told to do.

The following day I returned to where I had left off. As soon as I entered the premises and met the couple again, I received an extremely warm greeting from both of them. Having been very concerned about how I would be received on my return, I felt very much reassured, and was ready to continue the treatment with eager anticipation. The girl told me, 'We are amazed at the improvement in my condition! Come and see.'

The husband ushered us both back to the bedroom, trousers were slipped off, and although I was supposed to be the healer, I was myself taken aback by the improvement. What I can only describe as the angry, frightening appearance of the skin surface of the legs had considerably lessened; the evil-looking white blistering bubbles under the skin were appreciably diminished, and as I started to 'tune in', I could 'see' that whereas the previous day the small shiny brown spheres under the skin had been massed together everywhere, I was getting the impression that in some way they were now coalescing and starting to dissolve.

Greatly encouraged by this, but at the same time attempting to convey the impression that this was to be expected, I continued, 'I am very glad to see that you have made such good progress. If you will just lie down again and relax, close your eyes and we will continue where we left off yesterday.'

I repeated what I had done the previous day, passing my hands slowly over a period over both legs, maintaining a distance of roughly a quarter of an inch from the surface of the flesh. I continued in this way for something like fifteen to twenty minutes and then, remembering the experience of the previous day, I rushed to wash my hands thoroughly.

After exchanging a few pleasantries, I left as soon as possible so that I could shower as I had been instructed, confirming the last and final appointment as I went.

On my arrival for the final episode, the couple were ecstatic in their greeting, the girl having tears in her eyes. 'I've suffered for years with this dreadful problem,' she said. 'I just can't believe what's happening. Come and look!'

We repaired to the bedroom once more: it was true. The flesh was starting to look healthy again – in some areas it was even necessary to peer closely to see that there had ever been a problem. The remaining afflicted areas were greatly improved; the rate of progress along the road to recovery was truly astonishing.

I carried out the third and final treatment. The couple had to return to Holland that afternoon; they telephoned me a couple of weeks later, effusive in their thanks, saying that the affliction had completely cleared. 'You know what,' said the girl over the telephone to me, 'the thing I am enjoying most now is that I can wear skirts again! Thank you so much.'

Thus ended an episode that had initially given me great concern and a feeling of inadequacy, followed by my instinctively placing a trust in some higher entity beyond my knowledge, something that was to happen to me more and more in the future.

Another interesting incident, which had its amusing side, took place a few weeks later. Peter and I were visiting friends in a large general hospital not far from where we were living at the time. As we passed by the reception area, a woman we knew slightly came up to greet us. After exchanging a few pleasantries, we asked her why she was in the hospital. She told us that she had brought her husband in as an emergency with bad head and chest pains, possibly a stroke, and an excessive ECG readout at their local doctor's. It was thought he might have to be admitted as an emergency. Naturally I was immediately concerned, and asked if I might have a word with him while he was waiting to be seen by the hospital doctors. She readily agreed, and we followed her to where her husband was sitting outside the consultant's room. He was obviously in a lot of pain, and was sitting doubled up, clutching his chest. I took one look at him, and said, 'Would you allow me to help you?' and he nodded assent. 'Don't worry about what I am going to do, just follow through with what I say.' He nodded again.

Sometimes I find it difficult to communicate what takes place in my mind; I could perhaps describe it as a shift in levels of consciousness; in this case I received an impression of certain acupressure points on the head, which relate to the heart. I placed my left palm on his forehead, and intuitively felt for these points with my right hand on his head, neck and body. I worked in this way for a few minutes, then the attention of my Inner Eye was drawn to two or three points of dull red in his right shoulder. I then grabbed his right hand, moving his head and arm in a roughly circular motion using both my hands, and distinctly heard a click as a ligament or sinew snapped back into place. The man was astonished to find that full movement had been restored to his right arm and shoulder; his wife then saying, 'I forgot to tell you that my husband had a bad shoulder sprain some three or four months ago, as I was so concerned about his head and chest pains that came on earlier this morning. I haven't seen him move his arm about like that for a long time.'

At this point she looked over my shoulder, saying, 'Quickly, here comes the consultant; we mustn't keep him waiting.'

Fortunately, I had just finished everything that I had to do; so we quickly said our goodbyes and Peter and I wended our way home.

Three days later the husband rang me, thanking me profusely. 'I have never felt such a strange mixture of emotions after you left,' he said. 'Relief at suddenly being free of all pain; disbelief at what had taken place, and acute embarrassment after the consultant had examined me. He could find nothing wrong with me anywhere. My blood pressure had dropped to normal from its previous high level, my ECG rate was normal, and I had no pain whatsoever! I felt something of a fraud; the consultant looked at me curiously after he had finished examining me, and I was left with the impression that he considered me to be nothing other than a hypochondriac.

I walked out of there feeling free as air, and I have never looked back since. Thank you so much, Anne.' And with that he rang off.

I was deeply moved, and yet could not put out of my mind my amusement when he had told me the reaction of the consultant after the examination. I could well imagine my erstwhile patient's embarrassment when he found himself during the examination feeling perfectly fit after having been admitted a short while previously with what appeared to be life-threatening symptoms!

Chapter 14
The Party Circuit

I am often asked: 'Anne, can you predict your own future?' The answer, unfortunately, is no! In this respect, strangely enough, I sometimes quite envy my clients; at least I am able to tell them what lies ahead, and then it becomes their own decision as to how they handle things from then on. Not so in my case, however; if I had known what was in store for Peter and myself when we started our market garden in Wales, our bags would have been packed for the return trip with the speed born of fear!

What happened briefly, was this. In the period immediately after the fuel crisis in the early 1970s, there was a great upsurge of interest in growing fresh vegetables, as it was thought that the energy crisis would lead to a general breakdown. Living in North Wales as we were, we noticed there was great interest shown by hotels and restaurants in good quality vegetables. It seemed that supplies of these were delivered daily from the Liverpool markets; the problem being that the people closest to Liverpool always got the best quality produce, while those further away were sold progressively inferior goods.

It seemed a good idea for both of us to set up a market garden in North Wales; enquiries for business among the local outlets were met with enthusiasm. With the remaining money we had, we purchased twenty acres of good land, together with two tractors and other necessary equipment. To cut a long story short, we were beaten by the two successive fierce droughts of '75 and '76. Although Peter was out at five o'clock each morning watering the growing crops, it just wasn't possible with the facilities we had to water them sufficiently. The unforeseeable prolonged heat killed everything; at the end of the second year we reluctantly sold off the land and equipment and returned south to Kent again.

Life wasn't easy at this time. With our little remaining money, we decided to purchase a derelict cottage again and renovate it; we were used to doing this after our adventures in Wales. This one was in the suburbs of a large market town. It had been unoccupied for many years, with holes in the roof, broken windows and a tree growing out of one wall; we still thought it reasonably priced. Shortly after we purchased it, however, we found there was a boundary dispute concerning the property, together with a very aggressive neighbour, who had, we saw from the deeds, been gradually moving his fence across our garden in a move to gain ground. Every time Peter replaced the fence where it belonged, our neighbour would break it down and throw it back. For good measure, he would also 'accidentally' fill the freshly dug foundations of our house with water overnight by jamming his overflow; it eventually became necessary to call the police to restrain him. However, step by step, by careful legal manoeuvring, this situation was resolved and our cottage, after much hard work, started to become quite charming in appearance.

While all this was going on, Peter had attempted to restart his earlier business, but with only partial success. With the cost of rebuilding the cottage, money was running short; I had nowhere to work with clients, and problems were mounting.

Our neighbours, Pat and John, on the other side of our property, however, were kindness itself and sympathetic to our problems. One day I was talking to Pat about our difficulties – in particular how to find somewhere to work, as I had done in Wales, with patients again. A number of them had traced and followed me from there, and were desperate to have treatment. Pat herself had been a migraine sufferer, and I had been able to help her with my special gift in the way I was used to. She had never quite got over the way in which the constant pain had disappeared, and said, 'Look, Anne, why don't you use my house to see your patients in? It's quite big as you know; I can easily let you have a couple of rooms.'

The tears came to my eyes and I said, 'Pat, are you sure?'

'Of course I'm sure, Anne; ever since you took my headaches away my life's begun again. I know what it means to people with a gift like that.'

Pat had solved my problem for me. I gratefully accepted her kind offer, and within a short space of time, as in Wales, I became very busy again. History then repeated itself once more, as the local radio station was contacted by one of my patients who had come down from Wales. She told them of her migraine and the relief I had been able to give her from the pain. I was then invited by Brian Faulkner of Radio Medway to talk on his weekly show, 'Personally Speaking'. The local papers took the story up, and the 'Larkfield Clinic' was launched. Once again I was inundated. Pat put out chairs in the corridor of her house, which was kept fairly bustling with patients; I used her dining room for consultations.

One day, one of my patients was virtually carried in by two helpers. I had no idea of her history or background; to me she had a badly displaced disc with a swelling in the area around the vertebrae, causing a nerve to be trapped. I remember getting this young lady to put on a pair of slacks and asking her to lie on her stomach. I kneaded her spine, stretched and pulled: then told her to stand up, asking if it still hurt. 'Ouch!' she said.

'Never mind,' I assured her, 'let it hurt; keep walking.' I gave her a few very quick lessons in yoga; one exercise lying face downwards, followed by another one after she had rolled onto her back. My parting words to her were to do this five times every morning and again at night and at all costs to keep walking; then the pain would go away.

What I was not told was that she was just out of hospital, after lying on her back for three months. The next step was to have an operation to remove the offending disc; I had known nothing of this. The poor girl had only just that day got out of bed to come and see me after the hospital stay; had I known this I'm sure I would not have taken it upon myself to tell her what I did, or instruct her to keep walking. However, within the next two weeks she visited me again, telling me the true story and praising me, saying she had no pain and was walking. She had now taken up yoga, and because of her 'great triumph', as she put it, had started a class herself twice a week at her home with other people who had back problems in the village.

Shortly after this, a chain of events came about that led to the beginnings of what we came to call the 'Party Circuit'. A patient visited me one day who had a very bad chest problem. The treatment she had received from her local doctor was having no effect; I told her to go away and insist on an X-ray. I was sure she was suffering from pneumonia, and the antibiotics were not working on her. I also told her to try for an examination at a specialist chest hospital. Sure enough, she called later to say she had followed my advice and that I had been correct; it had been a pneumonia 'shadow' that wouldn't clear up. However, the course of action I recommended had proved successful; her health was steadily improving. She then asked me if Peter and myself would visit her home professionally for a party of her friends. We agreed to go, and a date was set.

This party turned out to be quite an evening. There were a number of people with various minor illnesses; a poor battered wife with a black eye; a couple of pregnant mums, and many others asking me what I could do for them and asking for help with their problems.

My first readings were a mixture of medical diagnosis and fortune-telling (a word I have come to detest, due to its unfortunate association; later on, Peter coined the term 'paranormal analyst' which seems to sum up my abilities nicely). I found that I could tell almost involuntarily if they were married or had a boyfriend, how many children they had; in fact almost anything about anyone who had come to see me. The information just seemed to flow from my lips, and astounded even me.

After this, Peter and I placed an advertisement in the local paper advertising a 'Party Plan' for clairvoyant readings in people's homes, much along the line of clothes or Tupperware parties. Quite a few of our friends thought the idea something of a joke; we were told many times that it couldn't work. However, the first advertisement brought quite a few enquiries. I can remember being somewhat nervous when Peter drove me to those first early parties. For some reason, my greatest fear was that my ability to 'see' clairvoyantly might evaporate, leaving me to stutter helplessly.

Fortunately this didn't happen. The first few parties ran surprisingly smoothly; Peter would drive me to the flat or house where the party was held, and we would always be received very well. I found as soon as I held a person's hands, palms upwards, in front of me, a stream of pictures would start to flow which I could easily interpret. These pictures would start by showing me the circumstances or situations surrounding a person.

I would describe what I saw; often the person was quite startled, but, thank goodness, never ever worried by what I told them. After looking at their palms for a time, I found I could continue on better by holding an object such as a watch, ring or item of personal jewellery. The pictures would keep flowing; sometimes faster than I was able to describe. People had difficulty in writing down information at the speed I gave it to them; often, later on during these readings, they would ask me to repeat the same information I had already given. I realised that they hadn't been able to absorb what I told them, but found it very frustrating to have to keep covering the same ground. The reader will ask, 'Why didn't you use a tape recorder?' I do now, but at this time there were problems involving the equipment which I was only able to resolve much later. These problems have their proper place further on in this chapter, at which time I will tell you all about them.

Not long after Peter and I had started out on our Party Circuit, we had one which we later christened the 'Fish and Chip Party'. It was a pleasant autumn evening, with a hint of mist in the country lanes as we drove to the address, which was in the Medway district in Kent near the mouth of the river of the same name. A tree-lined street of suburban terraces greeted us, and we drew up outside the address we had been given. Judging from the noise coming from within, everyone was thoroughly enjoying themselves, and when we had knocked and been shown in we saw there were something like twenty people inside, laughing and joking, with drink flowing freely everywhere. I was a bit concerned, as I find it difficult to work with too much noise around; Peter stayed with the clients while I was shown to an upstairs room, where fortunately the sounds of revelry couldn't penetrate.

As I started to climb the stairs, I noticed a mobile fish and chip van pulling up outside. With exclamations of delight, several members of the party went outside to queue, while I got settled with my first client. Soon I had taken her palms, and was telling her the various circumstances surrounding her job, much to her surprise. I was also able to tell her that her husband was having an affair with a girl, and described this girl in detail. The lady with me became very quiet; I concluded her reading and she left to go downstairs to send the next person up. Much to my amazement, I recognised the girl as the one I had just described to the previous lady! I then started to describe the previous lady's husband to the girl. At the time the implications never struck me. The evening wore on and several people, including a man, came up to see me. I was in the middle of telling a seventeen-year-old about two jobs that were shortly going to be offered to her, when I found it was becoming difficult to concentrate due to the increasing roar downstairs. Just then, Peter knocked at the door and came in. 'I think we have some problems here,' he said with a little smile, inclining his head to the stairs. Taking my hand, he said, 'This could well be a good time to leave!'

Through the now open door, we tiptoed down the stairs. The woman I had seen earlier and the man and girl were hurling pieces of fish and handfuls of chips at each other. The air was quite blue; people were standing around in various attitudes sipping their drinks and shouting encouragement. Luckily, all attention was focused on the contestants; Peter and I slipped out quietly through the kitchen and got away unnoticed.

I learned from that night; and from then on was able to tactfully skirt around such situations involving domestic intrigue. I can only remember one other incident where an upset occurred through a domestic intrigue, and this was many years later. It was brought about largely because two men decided to take a rise out of me.

One winter's night we pulled up outside our venue for the evening as usual. We knocked, and were warmly received by the hostess, who showed me to where I was to work, while Peter remained with the clients in the usual way. The evening started quite normally, with everyone well satisfied with their readings. Towards the end of the party, Peter told me afterwards, two men appeared, one being the hostess's husband. They were both quite merry, having obviously spent a convivial evening at the local.

'What's all this then?' said the friend to the husband.

'Some sort of party my wife's having. Think it's a fortune-teller or summing.'

'I can't believe it; your wife having a fortune-telling party?' said his friend incredulously. 'Surely they don't believe in all that rubbish?' He made a dismissive sweep with his hand, 'Some people have got more money than sense to spend it on having their fortunes told,' he added contemptuously.

Suddenly the husband paused, light dawning through the alcoholic haze. 'Tell you what,' he exclaimed, slapping one hand across the other. 'Why don't we have a laugh? You go in and have your palm read, and I can listen outside – I'll go fifty–fifty with you.'

'I like it,' said the friend, grinning.' You're on!'

They waited, chatting and joking, until the party-goers had all finished having their readings. 'In you go then,' said the husband: 'I'm looking forward to this!' Peter told me afterwards he was feeling apprehensive while all this was going on, but couldn't see how to avoid the situation.

I, of course, was oblivious to all this. I heard a knock at the door, and called out, 'Come in. Do sit down and let's have a look at you.' I saw a man, obviously the worse for tipple, but quite friendly and looking amused. 'Now, let's see your palms.' I reached for them, and the impressions started forming. 'You have a slightly unusual job; you hand out money.' A look of faint surprise crossed his face. 'I see a counter with a wire grille across it. Now I see shelves. On the shelves are food and groceries. I would say you have a post office and general store.'

'Yes,' he said. 'That's absolutely right. You amaze me.' He leaned forward now, his eyes alight with interest.

'I'll tell you something else,' I said, 'you're having an affair with the lady of the house, aren't you?'

'That's right,' he said, his expression conveying rekindled memories. 'She's gorgeous. I come round in the day when the old man's working; she has these lovely frilly nightdresses...' All thoughts of the listener at the door, whose existence I was unaware of, had flown out of the window; he continued on at some length, his tongue well loosened by alcohol. Finally he turned to go, to be confronted by the figure of a man standing in the half-light, his features black with fury.

Not being tuned in to the situation, I smiled sweetly and slipped by the man in the corridor, the reading I had just given being the last. Peter stood there waiting, ready for me to go. Suddenly a loud crashing sound erupted behind me; at that moment we were saying our goodbyes to our hostess. I saw her expression turn to alarm of a type that registered the whole situation instantly to me; I almost pulled Peter out through the door and quickly closed it...

To be fair it is very rarely I embarrass my clients. As my abilities developed hand in hand with experience, I learned to skilfully avoid awkward situations, and became able to handle them with tact and understanding.

Peter, being outside the room where my clients have been waiting, was of course able to gauge people's reactions as they emerged from seeing me. I am glad to say I was almost always told they came out quite pleased and amazed. However, every now and then a little pattern would occur. It would happen like this: two or three people, one after the other, would emerge clutching the sheets of paper containing their notes for the future (this was during my pre-tape-recording period). They would be radiant, and come out with remarks such as, 'Guess what she told me! I'm going to have a wonderful holiday in

Australia,' followed by someone else saying, 'I'm going to marry a rich man and see the world – imagine that!' Then a poor, dejected little lass might emerge, saying disgustedly, 'I didn't think much of her. She hardly told me anything!'

Peter used to get quite worried at times like these, until he analysed these situations and realised that the person who would say this had in fact been told quite a lot of information. Unfortunately, what he or she had been told did not fall in line with what they wanted to hear; the reading could tell of a possible marriage break, a need to cut back financially or some other hardship. Contrasted with the glowing futures predicted by their friends, it produced a bitter disappointment. Peter and I from then on made it clear to clients that *I can only predict, and not provide, the future*; however, I always emphasise that I can only go so far ahead in time. As a guideline I suggest that a person comes back to see me after six months or so, although with certain readings some things I predict come about much later in time.

The timescale of my predictions had always been a problem, and something I won't normally commit myself on. People tell me that things I have told them have happened so much later in time that they had forgotten all about them, and others... Let me tell you about the fastest-happening prediction I can ever remember.

One night we were at a party given at a poor home, where a sincere and hard-pressed mother, whose husband had sadly long deserted her, had two sons to bring up but made an income by fostering children from broken homes. When I had sat her down to sort out her many problems and give her a reading on them, right at the end I had a mental flash and had to tell her that her eldest boy would unfortunately soon be in trouble with the police.

'Now that's nonsense!' exclaimed my hostess. 'He's a good lad, never been in trouble and the last one to run foul of the law.'

She got up to go, opened the door, and the telephone which was close by in the hall started to ring. She pickled it up, and her expression changed to stark dismay. She made no reply and just put the receiver down.

'I'll never disbelieve you again, Anne,' she said. 'That was the police. They want me to go down to the station and collect him; he's being held for vandalising cars.'

Another problem which people of a certain disposition always worry about before they see me is, 'Will she tell me anything bad?' What they mostly mean is, of course, 'Am I going to die?' I have to say that I never ever get an inkling of anything like this. Many years ago I had to tell a young lad of eighteen that I was totally unable to read him. Three weeks later, to my distress, I heard that he had been killed on a motorbike. Why I hadn't been able to foresee this, I am not able to explain. Perhaps some things are not meant to be known. And yet, on a few other occasions over the years I haven't been able to read some people at all, but those same people have come to me on a later occasion and I have been able to give them a perfect reading. Yet again, I gave an extensive reading for a lady a long time ahead, and yet she passed away from a heart attack three months later; was this the future she would have had? As I mentioned earlier, I feel some things are not meant to be known, and are hidden from both myself and my clients; at any rate neither Peter nor myself know of a single case where a client has been sent away with unsolvable nameless worries.

I always enjoy the stark disbelief with which my readings are sometimes met. At another of our parties in May one year, I gave a woman a reading to the effect that her husband would be working abroad successfully with his own business – by the end of August (it isn't often I can be this specific on time!). She came out and vehemently declared, 'She told me a lot of nonsense about my husband working abroad for himself in three months' time. He's worked for the same firm for fifteen years; he intends to stay there until he retires because he's so happy there. What a waste of money!' And she stamped off.

She returned to me a few weeks later. 'Anne, I've come to apologise. I was very cross when you gave me a reading a little while ago; to be honest I thought I had been ripped off, as my husband was so settled.' I couldn't remember her reading at the time at all, but she went on to say, 'I went around telling people what you had told me, right up to the end of July. At this time my husband came home, very sad. "Love, I'm afraid I've been made redundant. I can't believe it after all these years, but the firm has been taken over and I've had to leave tonight."

'Later in the evening, and very despondent, he rang a friend to tell him the bad news. "Have you got a passport?" enquired the friend. "Yes," my husband replied, mystified. "You're a qualified electrician; I need one for my company in the Middle East on a three-year renewable contract basis. Interested?" He then mentioned a figure for my husband's services that he couldn't believe. On the first of August he was on a plane for the Persian Gulf,' she concluded happily. 'And I'm going to join him soon; at the end of three years we'll be rich enough to come home and live in style. Thank you so much; and I'm sorry for what I said and not believing you.'

It was lovely to hear her words; she shook my hand and left almost in tears of happiness.

Peter and I seem to meet with a most interesting variety of people. For instance, I have done a number of casts of West End theatre shows, which of course include many well-known stars. One show, *The Sound of Music*, stands out in my mind. A prominent member of the cast had been very impressed with a reading I had given him, told the others, and I had been asked to give nearly all of them a reading. These readings were arranged in such a way that they were given to each actor and actress at a time when they were, of course, off stage. Now it happened that a senior member of the production team disapproved of my presence; with the amusing result that I was literally smuggled from room to room, and even at one point in time had to hide behind a laundry basket between readings!

Another amusing incident for me was when I came face to face with a number of half-naked nuns, some of them smoking cigarettes, rushing along a corridor; I had to do a double take before remembering they were part of the cast!

A problem I had for a long time while I was giving readings to people was that many of them could not write their notes quickly enough, and some occasionally not at all. I was finding it was a struggle for me to keep stopping while they wrote, as it seemed to break the thread of my concentration. Why not tape it, you ask? Yes, I do now almost exclusively, but when I first tried working this way I encountered all sorts of difficulties. When using a tape recorder, I found that some tapes reproduced perfectly, while others were inexplicably quite blank, although they had been tested and found to be in first-class order. However, what was completely mystifying was that a percentage, when played back, had acquired voices on them which sounded a long way off, half obliterated by rushing sounds. Yet others had faint music in the background, although there was nothing in the environment that could have possibly caused any of these things in the normal way.

At one party, there happened to be a lady who owned a television shop that also sold tape-recording equipment. She was quite an expert in this field, and insisted that her reading be given on a tape recorder which she had brought along, together with of course a new tape. I explained that I didn't give recorded readings (this was before I had learned how to solve the problem), that I usually had trouble with the recording equipment and therefore would prefer it if she took notes instead. However, she was adamant, and set her equipment up, which included a large commercial microphone on a stand. I gave her the reading she asked for in the normal way, and the tape was played back. At first nothing happened.

'Oh, darn,' said the expert, 'we couldn't have had the machine on "record".' Just as she had said this, a male voice spoke slowly and deliberately, saying, 'I – am – Fred!' in an odd sort of falsetto whisper.

I had by now become used to this sort of thing, but the poor woman was understandably flabbergasted. 'I don't understand it – that's totally impossible!' she said. 'I am something of an expert on this type of equipment, and that voice could have been no more than an inch or two away from that microphone!' Lost for further words, and shaking her head in bewilderment, she left.

However, although I was never given cause for concern by their efforts, my other-world visitors unfortunately had to be eliminated somehow from my tapes, otherwise I could never be sure my clients would be able to record their readings. Some time later, Peter and I cracked the problem. We found that if I put the tape recorder on my lap, or personally held the microphone, my visitors and their strange music would disappear, and the tapes then recorded perfectly. The only remaining problem was that for another unexplained reason no microphone that I held would last for more than three days or so. This expensive overhead disappeared when I simply used the built-in microphone on the tape recorder; and this is the way I have worked for some years.

During this latter period, Peter and I have only had one very strange experience with recording equipment. One night, in a party of people whom we had visited several times previously and knew well, two women, a mother and daughter, were present whom we hadn't seen before. They were only known slightly to the group, and had come a long way to see me. About half-way through the evening, the daughter came in for a reading. I asked her what her age and birth sign were.

'You tell me – you're the clairvoyant,' she said, nastily and sarcastically. As I cannot work well with people with whom I am not 'in tune', I politely told her I was sorry but I couldn't read her as a person, and that of course I wouldn't charge her. She got up and stormed out of the room, slamming the door behind her.

Shortly afterwards, her mother came in and sat down, looking very disgruntled, but saying nothing. I took her hands and started to read out what I saw.

'You are thinking of buying a hotel a long way from here, and it's near the sea,' I said.

'It's nowhere near the sea,' said the woman, and leered at me aggressively.

I sighed, and tried again: two people like this in one evening? However, after a few more tries, I gave up. 'I'm sorry,' I said again, 'but you must be one of those people I can't read, like your daughter.'

'I don't think you're much good,' she said, and she too stormed out, in the same way the girl had.

I was very relieved to see that the next lady was one of my old clients.

'Hello, Anne,' she said. 'Don't take any notice of those two you've just seen. Everyone in the room with them out there, including your husband, has had a headache since they arrived.'

This both surprised and relieved me. 'Thank you for telling me that,' I said. 'I was beginning to think I'd lost my psychic abilities.' I picked up her hands and found that once again I could read easily and correctly.

Outside, Peter told me later, he was very relieved to see the two women leave – although, as he hadn't been in to see me, he wasn't aware completely of what was going on. I heard them go, and as they left my headache, which had begun when I first encountered the daughter, and everyone else's in the room outside, including Peter's, lifted!

At the end of the party, something happened that no one has ever been able to account for. While Peter and I sat talking afterwards with the remaining members of the party, quietly sipping a cup of tea, everyone was very sympathetic.

'I don't know what was wrong with those two,' said one, 'but something definitely lifted after they went.' There was a noise of general agreement. 'Don't worry, Anne,' they said. 'We've known you for years and we've always found your readings correct. It'll be a good thing when those two move right away and buy that hotel in Paignton they've been talking about.'

I pricked up my ears; Paignton was a seaside resort, and any hotel they were thinking of buying there had to be near the sea...

Just then someone noticed that a tape was lying on the table. 'Whose is this?' they asked.

'Must belong to that last woman who left,' said someone else. 'Let's play it and see what it says.'

She picked it up and placed it in the machine, switching it on. After a short pause, a raucous rendering of a tune by Chaz and Dave burst forth. Everyone in the room turned to look at each other.

'That woman plays nothing else at her home,' someone said. 'I was over there at her place some weeks ago, and the constant repetition nearly drove me mad.' (I should perhaps mention here that I had recorded this interview with my own brand new blank tapes supplied by my own wholesaler, as I normally do unless otherwise requested.)

In a stunned silence, the tape was removed from the machine and placed back on the edge of the table. 'Look!' said Peter, his finger pointing at the tape. Slowly, the tape ribbon, of its own accord, was uncoiling from the spool. As we watched, it broke up and disintegrated into confetti-like fragments all over the carpet under the table edge.

Looking back now, I am amazed that no one, including myself was frightened or scared. There was just a feeling of incredulous amazement, yet an atmosphere of friendly peace seemed to prevail.

Suddenly someone broke the silence. 'There are more things in heaven and earth,' she murmured; and everyone there felt, myself included, that she had summed it up rather well.

Chapter 15
Death on the Party Circuit

The body lay huddled on the pathway, the violence of the passing evident from its posture. In contrast, the suburban respectability of the house, with its neatly tended lawns and flower beds, contributed to the starkness of the scene.

The familiar sense of déjà vu ran its fingers over my spine. How is it, I mused, that advice and counsel, sought and paid for with such forethought and determination, could be so deliberately ignored?

Just like almost all my other parties, it had started pleasantly enough with a simple phone call. A woman with an agreeable manner and a slightly foreign accent had telephoned and asked if we would be prepared to travel to North London. I agreed, and arrangements were made for the following week.

Peter was intrigued when he noticed the address. Contrary to what I had thought, the venue was to be held in quite a select area. It turned out that Peter had served his apprenticeship in mechanical engineering not far from where we were going, and he knew that the district was a very exclusive one.

A fortnight later we arrived. The house was quite substantial in its proportions, and when we entered, it was evident that this was an environment in which there was no dearth of funds.

The women wore expensive dresses and jewellery, while the subdued glint of gold watches and cufflinks of the men folk reflected the sparkle of the imposing chandeliers.

Peter was left with the assembled gathering, while I was shown into a smaller room. On the polished period table rested an elaborate gold pen, together with a notepad. I noticed as I entered that Peter did not seem to be welcome; this was unusual, as normally people accepted us as a couple; Peter would keep the guests entertained while I gave them their readings. He told me afterwards it had been made clear that it would have been better if he wasn't present. As he joined the waiting group of guests, some of the assembly started to speak French, as if to pointedly exclude him. Unfortunately for them, as he has discussed in another chapter, he speaks this language fluently. However, as the group changed languages, he realised that confidentiality was involved, and murmured a few French pleasantries. Immediately a ripple of tension ran through the group; Peter was then abruptly left on his own with a drink, while the group evaporated into the kitchen, closing the door!

At this stage of the proceedings he hadn't realised what we were becoming involved with. Left to his own resources, he sat down in a corner with a book; something he always carried with him in case of just this sort of eventuality. Meanwhile, I was left to continue to give readings at what was to prove one of the most dramatic parties of my life...

That night there was only a small group of people, about five or six; a lot fewer than a normal party. When the booking had been made, the woman made it clear that she was prepared to pay well; in fact a sum was mentioned that was greatly in excess of a normal party booking.

It seemed that some members of this small group of people had flown in from all over the world. While I was waiting to begin, the door of my small room had been left ajar. A small warning bell began to sound in my head, and I could both sense and see that Peter was not welcome, as he began to be left high and dry in solitude.

Soon, however, my first client came in and sat down. He was small, dark-skinned, and slightly built; almost weedy in appearance. I began to sense violence around as soon as he began to talk. Ostensibly, he was involved with a large 'business deal'. Essentially, he wanted to know if it was going to be successful; however he would discuss almost nothing in connection with it. I found this frustrating, for when I discuss complex business aspects I need to 'bounce off' certain details, as these generate a reaction in some way which helps me to form my pictures. However, there gradually formed in my mind a feeling of violence and bloodshed that was bringing about within me a feeling of sickness and revulsion. At this stage I began to experience the first feelings of fear. I had a strong feeling that if I didn't handle this situation in the right manner, Peter and I might just not be able to get out of the place alive.

I decided to act the unsuspecting innocent. It came to me that the key to the whole situation was 'Mr Big' – the large man with a massive diamond ring. The small, weedy man (he was apparently South African, or had connections there) needed to convince Mr Big of the success of whatever operation everyone had come to consult me about. The group's problem was that they were not familiar with the way I worked. My impression was that I was thought to be a form of yes/no machine which would react accordingly to questions put, without my actually realising what my answers related to. Quite how they arrived at this conclusion was difficult for me to understand; but whenever I am asked questions by clients, my pictures start to form in a way that enables me to study any problems put to me by becoming aware, in the majority of cases, of the complete background to the story lines.

This was again proving to be the case in this instance. Despite the veiled questions of 'Mr Weedy', couched in a reassuringly bland manner ('Do you think the operation will be a success?' Do you see much risk attached to the deal?') I could see that there was not only a very considerable risk to the participants, but to ourselves as well, because we'd been made aware of what was going on. The extensive use of arms, violence, bloodshed – all these things began to manifest themselves in my consciousness.

I was able to confirm that Mr Big – he of the many carats – needed to be convinced to part with a very large amount of money indeed. I continued to act the innocent, pretending not to know what was going on. I can remember telling Mr Weedy that he would be wasting any money that would be invested in the 'deal', that he would have blood on his hands, and blood on the doorstep, and that he should do everything in his power to back down. The significance of my words was to return to me later with a sureness of a boomerang to the hand of the adept.

At this stage the plot began to thicken, as I became aware that the weedy man was the brother of the lady who owned the house. At the same time I realised that the native home of the majority of these people was a certain group of islands in the Indian Ocean. As my pictures continued to form, I saw that Mr Weedy either owned or had owned many houses and hotels in these islands, and he had had to leave in a hurry to go to South Africa. As the 'film' unreeled, it began to show again pictures of bombings, violence and bloodshed. To my horror, it came to me what the 'deal' was about. It was to finance a coup; Mr Big needed to be convinced to part with some of his vast wealth to pay for a small army, weaponry and bombs.

I found out later that there had been an earlier attempted coup which had failed; at this time Mr Weedy had been thrown out and his possessions confiscated.

A little later, the owner of the house also came to visit me. I remembered saying to him, 'Don't get involved; there will be violence and bloodshed, and some of the people in this house will die if you go forward with your plan.' He told me he was a financier and moneylender, but did not have the resources to finance this coup, and had brought all the people concerned together tonight to help his wife's family. I could sense that his heart was not in this matter at all, but that he had been drawn in willy-nilly, in the fashion of a spent match cast into the vortex of a whirlpool.

I felt saddened as I sensed the inevitability of events. Although the matter of choice still lay with the organisers of the coup, my inner knowledge told me that nothing would deter these people from setting out along the path of self-destruction.

Although during that evening I saw only five people or so, it was hard going because they all came and saw me in turn several times. Each time one of them would come in to see me and discuss the 'deal', as they continued to call it, as soon as their reading was concluded they would return to the kitchen for another conference.

I arrived at the point when I was beginning to wonder if I would ever be allowed to escape from the room. Back and forth came the same five or so individuals; as so often happens, all the people present wanted their readings reversed, and to be told that their venture would be crowned with success. Perhaps they hoped that by sheer persistence with me their futures could be altered, and that I could be convinced, as some form of arbitrating deity weighing their destinies in my hands, that this cause was just and I would be able to bestow success on this venture.

At last it seemed they could think of no further questions. The last client left me, and as the door was opened for her to leave I could hear the heated discussion continuing in low voices from the kitchen. A silence fell as I emerged, and Peter was summoned from his lonely vigil in the deserted room at the back.

Our farewells were, as might be imagined, somewhat curtailed. As we got into our car and drove away into a gloomy downpour which reflected the mood of the evening, Peter and I compared notes on the night's events. Peter of course had not been able to be quite so much in the picture, but had naturally picked up that there were some strange undercurrents, coupled with secrecy. I explained what had been going on and mentioned what I had predicted for the assembled group in the house: if they went ahead with their plan, and I again repeated the phrase that I had emphasised to the group – *they would have blood on their doorstep*. From this point on, events would have to take their course.

With the passing of time, the events of that evening faded into obscurity. Quite a while had elapsed until one evening we chanced to switch on our television to catch the evening news. The announcer's voice went unheard by both of us as the camera focussed on the attractive North London house we had got to know so well in the space of a single evening. There, on the paved pathway leading to the front door, was a huddled figure lying assassinated in a pool of blood – one of the group I had advised so strongly against pursuing this 'deal'.

The words I had uttered on that memorable evening came back to me: 'Pursue this course of action, and there will be blood on your doorstep.' Sadly, it was another example, if rather extreme, of advice unheeded. I reflected how these people had gone to the lengths of contacting me for advice; how I had so strongly warned them against going ahead with their plan; and how they had ignored everything I had said, in spite of my dire predictions.

'Death on the Lighter Side' was to be the theme of a reading I gave to two men who came to see me for a consultation. Very unusually, I had agreed to see them both at the same time; normally I can't work this way because I find that with two people at the same sitting, their frequencies tend to mingle and one person's future will sometimes wrongly appear in another's! However, these two had especially requested that they could both see me together, and it proved to be of those rare instances where it was the right thing to do.

One of them started the ball rolling by asking if I could tell him what had happened to his mother-in-law. With startling clarity, a picture of a quarry flashed into my mind. I could see a body, wrapped in something and heavily weighted down, being flung into this quarry and disappearing into the murk below. I described what I saw, trying to break the news as gently as possible. However, to my amazement they both smiled broadly. 'We have to tell you we knew she was dead,' said one of them, 'but we never knew what happened to the body!'

For a brief moment I misinterpreted what he was saying. Had the mother-in-law been brought to an untimely end by these men? However, as soon as the thought occurred to me, it was dismissed; these men were open, honest and kind. As I started to tune in to the events leading up to the quarry, they began to unfold a tale with a curious combination of the macabre and the comic.

Vic (not his real name) started by telling me that he had never got on with his mother-in-law. Apparently she had been against him from the start; prophesying disaster for the marriage, which in fact had worked out very well. However, she had recently passed away due to a short illness in Scotland, and for family reasons the burial needed to take place in the South, near London. Some time previously, Vic and his family had moved down to London, and a problem of economics had confronted him. The expense of transporting the body was considerable using conventional funeral companies, so Vic had obtained permission from the authorities concerned to bring back his mother-in-law's body himself. He had therefore driven up to Scotland in the family estate car with a friend, and found that in addition to bringing the body back, he had to clear his mother-in-law's flat of her possessions.

There were more things than he had allowed for to bring back, and he and his friend had ended up by filling the rear of the estate completely with furniture and effects, leaving quite a few things such as china and bric-a-brac still to be removed. However, a solution presented itself. Mother-in-law, presumably past caring, was consigned to the roof rack, the remaining china and odds and ends were carefully packed around her and the coffin lid replaced. Feeling that the sight of a coffin speeding along the motorway on the roof of a family estate might create undesirable interest and concern, Vic and his friend decided that Mother-in-law's presence might be better concealed from prying eyes. To this end, the coffin and its mixed cargo were wrapped in a carpet and carefully tied down.

It had been decided, again for economic reasons, not to overnight anywhere, but to continue driving down all the way, taking turns at the wheel. Once they had started on their journey, they began to have a problem with the carpet surrounding the coffin. Above a certain speed, it seemed impossible to contain the flapping loose ends; after several attempts to confine these, a compromise speed was attained well below that which had been anticipated. This of course resulted in the journey becoming much slower, so much so that even taking turn and turn about, the two men began to quickly feel very tired.

A decision was taken to pull off at one of the motorway stops south of Birmingham. Owing to the prolonged journey, of course, not only did the men feel extremely tired, but very hungry as well. Throwing caution to the wind (there is of course nothing worse than eating a heavy meal when one is very tired, and a need to continue driving afterwards) they ate very well and inevitably drifted off into a deep sleep…

One of them awoke with a start some hours later, in time to notice the sun settling well down on the horizon through the café window. In a brief motion, he awoke the other and they glanced at their watches. Realising how much time they had lost, they quickly collected their things and made to go. Arriving back in the car park, they had some difficulty in locating the car, a common problem in a large car park where the vehicular landscape changes as cars come and go. After a prolonged search, the thought came to Vic that perhaps, in this tired condition, they had crossed the motorway bridge and they were now searching the wrong car park. Crossing the bridge, they searched for their car with its carpet-wrapped cargo. Belatedly it occurred to them that their car should be extremely easy to spot, with such a large object strapped to the roof rack…

The same thought occurred to them simultaneously as they looked at each other. Surely… It couldn't have… But it was. And it had. Mother-in-law had left them, in the hands of a new driver, bound for an unknown destination!

Although the alarm was raised immediately, the two men realised what had happened; too much time had elapsed for the police to trace the vehicle on the motorway. The men had no recourse other than to arrange transport home, speculating on the reactions of the thieves when they started to examine their booty.

The amusing sequel, which I picked up, was that the thieves were under the impression that the poor lady had been murdered. I felt that they deservedly received the fright of their lives, not only in opening the lid of the coffin, which would have been bad enough in itself, but they would also be extremely concerned that if caught in possession of the body, it would be assumed that they were responsible for the murder.

Continuing to use my pictures, I could see that the two men involved in the theft, after having recovered from the shock of the discovery, stole out late one night and consigned Mother-in-law to a boggy grave at the bottom of a remote disused quarry. Up to the time of writing, nothing more was ever heard concerning her disappearance; but even now when I think of it, I picture with amusement the fear and horror those thieves experienced on opening up that coffin!

Peter, who had worked a lot as a medium in the past, is often very good at locating lost objects, including bodies (for some reason he was never called in to work on the last resting place of Mother-in-law). One day a girl in her early twenties came to see me to ask if we could locate the whereabouts of her father, who had gone missing. At that particular time I was extremely committed, so I asked Peter to see her. Peter works in the same way that I do, so I will pass the story over to him.

Peter continues: The girl was about twenty-two, understandably pale and distraught; dark-haired and with dark eyes red from weeping. I brought her in and sat her down, and asked her to tell me all she knew about her father's disappearance. All she was able to say was that he had simply walked out of the house early one winter's evening, and had never been heard of since.

I sat feeling completely relaxed, and used the three keys that I always use when available. I start by asking what relationship the missing or deceased person has to the enquirer (in this case, of course, I already knew this), their age, and how much time has elapsed since he or she last had contact. I always envisage this in the same way as a programme is entered on a computer – a three-key entering code; at this point I should receive a mental image on my inner 'screen'. Sometimes the initial image is not correct, at which time I have to put my mind in 'scan' mode until the questions I put to my client result in an ongoing sequence of mental images that appear to be accurate. Very occasionally, no mental images will form – almost as if there is some form of block on this means of communication.

However, with this girl the process went very smoothly and easily. The first image I saw was of a river at night. It seemed I was standing on one bank looking across at the far bank. I could then see someone I realised was her father, standing not far from the viewpoint from which I was mentally observing. In his hand was a bottle, and I realised that he was drinking heavily from it. Without seeing him actually fall into the water, I received a strong impression that, beset by a number of personal problems, the poor chap had simply drowned his sorrows in drink, fallen into the river and been swept away.

'But they've dragged the river and looked everywhere for him,' the girl said. 'I don't think he can be there.'

I disagreed, and received a strong mental impression of a particular weir with water cascading over it. This time the scene was in daylight, set in beautiful wintry countryside. Surrounding this weir were lazy fronds of pond weed, and although I couldn't see the body, I again received a further impression of its presence under the weeds. It's difficult to describe how an 'impression' is received; the only manner in which I can describe it is to say that it seems that I am starting to talk about whatever is under discussion almost before I've had time to think about it. This impression strongly gave me the feeling that the body was trapped under these weeds, close to the weir.

'I have a definite feeling that your father's body is trapped by a weir,' I said. 'Around the weir there is a large area of weeds, and deep under these weeds is where he will be found.'

'I know where you mean,' said the girl. 'The police have searched the river with divers, including the weir area. He's definitely not there.'

I felt so certain that the body was there that I argued, 'You must convince them to search there again. There is no doubt in my mind that's where his body is.'

I could see that the girl did not believe me. 'Please listen to me!' I told her. 'Go back to the police, and tell them you yourself have a strong feeling that that's where he is.' Sadly, I felt my plea was falling on deaf ears; however, we parted on good terms, after I had made her promise to let me know of any news.

Some weeks later she rang me. 'You were right, and I'm sorry I didn't believe you,' she said. 'I had a terrible time convincing the people concerned to dive again. Eventually they did, and my father's body was found exactly where you said; close to the weir and deep under the weeds.'

I thanked her for letting me know, and was glad to experience the relief in her voice. The sorrow of parting in these circumstances is bad enough, but it is infinitely worse when the person concerned disappears without trace.

Chapter 16
Psychic Detectives

The British Airways 747 banked slightly on its approach to runway 32 of Luqa Airport, Malta, enabling us to see Valletta harbour set in the deep blue sea of the Mediterranean, with the island of Gozo in the distance. Robert Strickland, a member of the British aristocracy whose family has had interests in Malta since the days of Queen Victoria, had been asked if he could help in any way with the theft of some important jewellery from the house of a Maltese lady who had been given the jewels by an Indian Sultan. Robert, who had known both of us for some while, contacted us with the offer of a free holiday on the island in return for any assistance we could give in the recovery of the jewellery.

During the landing, I had a hunch and turned to Peter and said, 'Do you know, I think this affair is going to end in a very unusual way. Let's see what happens.'

Peter looked at me rather quizzically, and shrugged his shoulders. 'You're usually right,' he said. 'Let's go and find out.'

We stepped into the warm Malta sunshine, then across to the terminal where Robert introduced us to a charming Maltese lady and her son. We were all soon whisked away in her car through sunny streets and throngs of gaily attired islanders mixed in with tourists from everywhere. Soon we pulled up outside a nondescript building in a row of other undistinguished buildings. The front door seemed quite drab, in keeping with the rest of the street, and we were let in by our new friend to find a brilliant contrast within to the drab exterior. Immediately we were inside we found ourselves in a beautiful courtyard with flowers on every level, hibiscus, geraniums and others which I was unable to identify. A central feature was a pond with water lilies and a fountain playing; as we started to take in our surroundings we realised that the entire complex, which stretched away on either side, was composed of a number of ancient buildings at odd angles to each other that had been charmingly converted. The floors were of ancient terracotta tiles, which by their appearance had endured centuries of wear; vaulted ceilings towered above, with gnarled and twisted beams running at grotesque angles, testimony of great antiquity.

Our hostess and her young son made us quickly at home, preparing us a typically rice-based Maltese dish followed by fresh fruit. Once we had settled in, naturally the conversation turned to the theft of the jewellery. We were led to a small room off to one side of the main complex, and our hostess pointed out the top of the entry door frame. The wall was set back slightly at this point, and we were shown a recess below and behind the frame. This was not at all apparent at first glance and it was only when a chair was placed adjacent to the spot were we able to stand in turn and feel for the space behind the frame.

'That's where it was always kept hidden,' said our friend. 'It has been left there for many years. I suppose I should have bought a safe, but one always thinks of things like that after the event. One day I went to fetch my jewels to wear them to an important event on the island, only to find that they were missing.'

As she finished speaking, I received an impression in my mind's eye of a shortish, bespectacled woman, slightly plump, with mousey-coloured hair, somewhere around her mid-thirties. I relayed this description out loud, asking our friend if she knew anyone answering to that description. 'Why, that's my secretary to a T!' she exclaimed. 'But she wouldn't do anything like that.'

'This is the picture I'm getting,' I said. 'Where is she now?'

'Oh, she only works for me during the week,' said our hostess: 'She will be here on Monday.' (We had arrived on a Saturday flight.)

We agreed to let the matter rest until Peter and I could meet the lady concerned. We also promised not to arouse any suspicions in the secretary's mind; when we merely intended to draw her into light conversation to quietly sound her out when the time came. Then, as our hostess had a social commitment that day, we strolled around the historic port of Malta with our friend Robert, admiring the gaily-coloured fishing vessels busying themselves around the harbour.

We were admiring some beautiful bronze statues in a small public park by the famous Maltese sculptor Antonio Sciortino (1879–1947) when Robert mentioned that he owned a hotel on the island. In the entrance hall had apparently stood another beautiful statue of three horses with a rider by this same artist, which had been stolen from the hotel some three Christmases previously, at a time when some reparation work was being carried out. The thieves had entered through a window which was being changed, and the aperture had only been covered with a sheet overnight preparatory to the work being completed the following day. This had easily been pushed aside, and the statue removed, it was thought, by associates of the workmen involved in the repairs. In spite of intensive efforts carried out by the police, no trace of the missing statue was ever found.

Peter was the first of us to say that the theft had been the work of three men, and that the statue had been hidden under some rubbish at the back of one of the men's houses in a lean-to, which appeared to be almost a hovel. He then picked up that it had been passed on to an antique dealer's ring with Mafia-style associations, finally being sold into a wealthy family on the Italian mainland. He described the statue as now standing in the great hall entrance of a very imposing residence on a table against the right-hand wall; the floor of the hall was laid with black and white square tiles.

Unfortunately we could not bring this initial approach to a successful conclusion, for although we divined the approximate area on the Italian mainland where the residence was, it would have necessitated a lot of expensive research to match the mental impressions of the residence with pictures or a tour of the area; even then, once a successful match had been accomplished, what does one do? Go to the Italian police, saying, 'My friend has a psychic impression that a statue stolen in Malta is now in such-and-such home?' Or knock at the door – judging by the mental impression of the size of the property, it would be answered by a member of the owner's staff – and say, 'Please, mister, can we have our statue back?' This type of investigation, as will be seen, does have its drawbacks!

We continued our stroll around Valletta, surrounded by the bustle and chatter of the busy streets, admiring the attractive wares on display for sale everywhere. The evening was spent under romantic candlelight in one of the many colourful restaurants, enjoying the unusual Maltese cuisine.

There remained one more day of relaxation for us before the secretary returned to her duties on Monday. We opted for a boat trip to the island of Gozo, strolled on its beaches and swam in its delightful rocky coves. We ended our excursion by visiting the extremely beautiful Blue Grotto, only accessible by boat, with its cavern and great depths of scintillating turquoise-blue water.

Monday came, and it was decided that Peter and I would at different times approach the secretary on the basis of an informal chat rather than making a frontal approach directly relating to the robbery. When we were introduced, it surprised neither of us to see that she exactly resembled our mentally visualised pictures of her two days previously. During the introductions by our hostess, she struck us both as being very cool, having almost the psychological make-up of a poker player, but having also on the surface an extremely agreeable manner. After this introduction we went our separate ways, until an hour or so later I passed her at her work for our hostess. This consisted of correspondence relating to a carpet business with imports from India; in fact a large room in one of the buildings was given over to a storage area in the front of a small warehouse to keep a large stack of carpets.

I engaged her in casual conversation, then gradually steered her in the direction of the robbery. How did she think it had been carried out, and by whom?

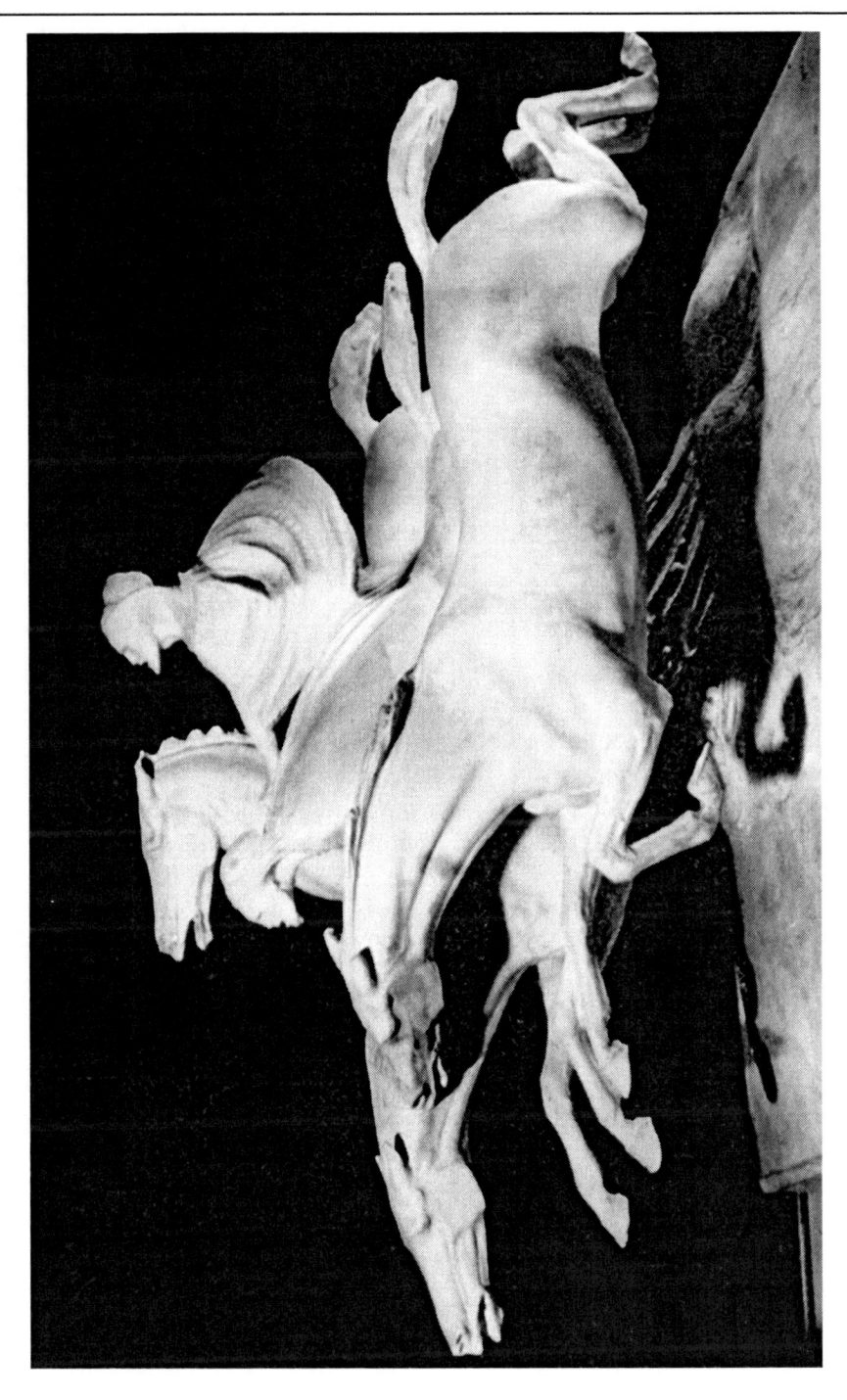

Plaster cast of the stolen bronze statue by Antonio Sciortino (1879–1947) (National Museum of Fine Arts, Valletta).

'Well,' said the secretary, 'Lena [our hostess] is very absent-minded. I think one day she put her jewellery back in a different place from the usual one, and has simply forgotten where she put it. She often mislays things, and she is always asking me to help her find where she puts them.'

At this point I realised where she was coming from; the secretary, having stolen the jewellery, had taken it and hidden it at some point elsewhere in the building. If challenged to the point by an intensive police investigation or some other means of heavy pressure, she could bring about a delay, pretend to search for it herself and 'accidentally' discover where Lena had put it. I behaved as if I could see the logic in what she was saying, made my excuses and left her to her work, so that I could confer further with Lena and Peter.

I tackled Lena first. 'Yes, I know what she is trying to say. She is saying that I have hidden the jewels in a different place from the usual one, and simply forgotten where that place is. Once or twice she has almost convinced me that this is so, and it is true that I often mislay things. However, the things that I mislay are usually far more trivial in nature; but I suppose it is possible that I have done what she says. For this reason I haven't yet gone to the police.'

To eliminate the possibility that this had happened, we decided to carry out a very comprehensive search of the entire property, consisting of the seven buildings. Myself, Peter, Robert and Lena conferred together, and commenced an exhaustive search, making sure that we only carried this out while the secretary was there. Peter and I tried hard to visualise the whereabouts of the jewels, but all we could come up with was a mental picture of them wrapped in a black velvet bag in a dark place. Neither Peter nor myself could seem to get *outside* this dark place mentally in order to see where the dark place was, so as to speak. We ferreted about in all the nooks and crannies, examined the tiled floors for any loose surfaces, and even considered the possibility that the jewels had been lowered into the deep pool in the centre of the courtyard. Nothing.

Then Peter had an idea. Lena had mentioned that she knew one of the senior members of police on the island very well on a social level. 'I would suggest,' said Peter, 'that we invite him over to dinner here, and ask him to question the secretary in such a way that she would feel under pressure, but that she would not be directly accused. I just have a feeling this could produce results.'

'That would be easy to arrange,' said Lena. 'I know that he would come; I'll give him a call.'

Fortunately (because the duration of our stay on the island was limited), the Inspector was free to come the following day. A very intelligent man, he had been educated in England and Rome, and was charming company. When he arrived we introduced him to the secretary. He spent the last two hours of the afternoon talking with her, during which time we distanced ourselves and busied ourselves elsewhere.

At the end of the afternoon, the secretary took her leave, and the Inspector stayed for dinner. After the usual exchanges, he said, 'This one is exceptionally cool. I've gone through as much as I can with her, because of course apart from the fact she is regularly in the house working at her job, there is absolutely no evidence we can proceed on. We'll just have to see what happens.'

Following this, we all went down to dinner and spent a very convivial evening in this man's fascinating company. He regaled us with many interesting anecdotes, some of them very amusing. One intriguing story he related to us was that he spent part of his early childhood as an orphan in the Vatican. He told us that a certain number of orphans, under circumstances I am unable to remember, were brought up as young children there, and were allowed to roam without hindrance throughout the buildings. He was apparently transferred elsewhere at the age of nine, but told me he remembered seeing many unusual things stored there, one of which seemed to be the preserved remains of a non-human being, a memory, which he said, would remain with him always.

The time came to say our goodbyes to this charming man and the evening ended with vows to keep in touch. Peter and I felt there was little more that we could do to find the jewels. We were quite sure that the secretary was the thief, but we could not, as before, successfully visualise where the jewels were hidden, only that they were wrapped up in a dark place; and as sometimes happens with Remote Viewing investigations of this type, for some reason we could not expand our mental pictures to encompass the location.

We were scheduled to return to the UK the following day, and made our farewells accordingly. It was with some regret that we wished our hostess goodbye and every success in recovering her jewels, as we had thoroughly enjoyed our stay on the island. We promised to keep in touch.

A week later after our return to the UK we received a telephone call from Lena. 'You'll never guess,' she said. 'The secretary called me after I had returned from a shopping expedition and showed me that my jewels were exactly where I had originally hidden them, and tried to convince me that they had always been there! I'm not going to take the matter further; thank you very much for coming over both of you, and I'm sure if you hadn't they would never have returned!'

Peter reminded me that I had said before our arrival that the affair would end in a strange way, and so it proved.

What controls certain elements in Remote Viewing I'm not sure. For example, the following incident will show the ease and clarity of solution that is sometimes achievable with particular types of problems. One day Sheila Chaudhuri, a close family friend of ours, rang me to ask if I would be able to help with regard to the theft of a Rolls-Royce by one of the directors of the company she was working for at the time, who had absconded with it. It transpired that this director, who had been responsible for plunging the company deeply into debt, had disappeared abroad, leaving the remaining directors with a tangle of commitments. They were naturally anxious to recover the Rolls-Royce, which constituted a major company asset, the sale of which would do much to alleviate the mounting financial problems. All the normal avenues, including the police, who were unable to take action as the case was a civil one, had been explored to establish the whereabouts of the car, which seemed to have disappeared without trace.

Sheila had obtained permission from the remaining two directors to approach Peter and myself to see if we would be able to help in any way. All the normal avenues of investigation having failed, the two directors were only too pleased to grasp at any straw available, as they saw it; I understood from Sheila later that this was how they viewed the situation.

Accordingly, Peter and I met Sheila at her East London home the following weekend. It happened I had arranged to see a friend of Sheila's at the same time, so when we arrived I went upstairs to see this friend on her own while Peter remained downstairs with Sheila.

Sheila continues: I gave Peter as much information as I could relating to the disappearance of the Rolls-Royce. I was sure, as were the two directors of the company, that the car had been hidden in the West London area, not far from the firm's premises. Peter then asked me if I had a map of England in the house. I was able to produce a motoring guide; Peter spent a while studying this and then said, 'The car is nowhere near London or Heathrow. It is in Exmoor in the West Country. It is stored under a sheet in a derelict building, which is adjacent to a disused church. The car is powder blue in colour.'

I was very surprised to learn that Peter felt the car was so far away; also at the time I was not aware of the colour of the car, never having seen it myself. I checked this by means of a quick phone call to one of the company directors; it was indeed powder blue, not a common colour for a Rolls-Royce.

At this point Anne came downstairs. She had not been able to hear the discussions down below, but started by saying, 'The colour of the missing car is powder blue. I can see it strongly in my mind's eye.'

Armed with this information and Anne's confirmation, I was able to invoke the help of a good friend of mine, with whom I had been at university, Rob Tiffin. On leaving university, Rob had set up a successful debt recovery business, and after I had received permission from one of the company directors, I contacted him, relaying the information Peter had given me. Armed with what most people would consider to be extremely slender evidence, Rob agreed to take the case on. I therefore gave Rob the registration number of the Rolls, and arranged for him to collect the spare set of keys to the car from the office. Shortly afterwards, he set off early one morning, and the next thing I heard was a call from Rob on his mobile, saying that he was at the wheel of the Rolls! Afterwards, he told me that he had managed to locate the car in Exmoor within a very short space of time from Peter's description of the location; one of the easiest recoveries he had ever had to make!

Anne continues: Another good example of how a case is made much simpler where there are significant landmarks around the target area of a psychic or Remote Viewing investigation is shown additionally in the following incident.

One day a client of mine, Jeeta Smith, who had been coming to me for consultations for some time on a regular basis, arrived at my office in a very distressed state. She was the owner of a luxury clothes shop in a coastal town in Kent, and the previous evening had been robbed of stock worth many thousands of pounds; could I help? Immediately an image flashed up in my mind's eye of the shop, which I had never visited. In this incident, all the details were particularly clear, and I could see straightaway the layout of the shop, how it was positioned in relation to the street, and the moveable racks on which the clothes were hung and arranged. A second image flashed up, of a small, mousey-haired woman with a pale face, looking rather down-at-heel, fingering the clothing with a slightly furtive manner.

'Jeeta, do you remember seeing a woman in your shop [and I gave Jeeta her description] shortly before the robbery?'

'Yes, I do,' she said, 'there was something furtive in her manner when she was asking about the prices that made me feel uneasy, but I couldn't put a finger on it.'

'I'm confident this woman was the thief,' I said.

'Can you suggest how we can find her and bring her to justice?' Jeeta asked. 'The stock was insured to an extent, but because of the high cost of the premises, we couldn't afford to fully cover what the stock was worth. I'm desperate to get it back if it's at all possible.'

For some reason, with startling clarity, a picture of a cobbled street came into my mind. In present-day England, such streets are rare. 'Jeeta', I said, 'I can see a cobbled street. It is rising on a hill, and at a point about halfway up, it curves to the right.' Jeeta could not place where I was describing, but I continued, 'At the point where this cobbled street curves to the right up the hill, there is another street running off to the left with a normal road surface. At the intersection of these two roads on the corner, there is a first-floor flat. This is where the woman lives, with an accomplice.'

Jeeta thanked me and said, 'But what, if I can find this place, can I do to recover my property? I can't just knock on the door and ask them to hand my stock back!'

'Go to the police,' I said. 'Tell them that you've received an anonymous phone call with the information I have given you. I'm not known in your area, and if you tell the police how you came by this information they will just humour you, look sympathetic and send you on your way!'

Jeeta did exactly what I said. The officer who made out the report instantly recognised the description of the location, saying that there were only two cobbled streets remaining in the entire town, and only one fitted the description made. The entire stock was recovered, and I had another satisfied client.

Don't think, however, that all investigations are as easy as this. If this were so, the world's problems would be over! I receive a lot of enquiries, and many end up quite fruitless for reasons I am still unable to explain. One of the most frightening challenges I was ever presented with started when a coloured lady made an appointment to see me after one of my major articles in *Woman* magazine appeared. This lady was a childminder; it seemed that one day a mother had brought a young girl around to her to look after for the day, and the minder herself had had to go out to the local shops for a short while to get some essentials, leaving her fifteen-year-old son in charge. The mother left her child with the minder on a regular basis, and both of them, the minder and the mother, had been somewhat concerned, as over the previous two days or so the child had unaccountably seemed restless and subject to peculiar moods which were not normal; whether there was any connection with this and the horrific events which were to follow is not known.

The minder, returning from her shopping, was horrified to see that smoke was billowing out of an upstairs window; there was a fire engine outside the house, with firemen running everywhere and two police cars parked with their lights flashing. Her son was outside obviously in a state of shock, and a neighbour had draped a blanket around his shoulders, as he was violently shivering. My client told me she went up to him to ask how this had all happened; the police tried to keep her away until she managed to get across to them that she was the boy's mother. The boy sobbed to her that he had been watching television in the next room, going from time to time to the room where the little girl lay sleeping. Suddenly, a short while after one of his periodic visits while he was watching a programme, he smelt smoke. Not immediately connecting this with the room where the child lay sleeping, as there was no fire or electrical appliance there, he looked first into the kitchen and then started to check two other rooms, but suddenly noticed a wisp of smoke issuing from under the closed door of the bedroom where the child was. (It had been kept shut to avoid disturbing the child's sleep by any noise from the television.)

The boy had opened the door and was horrified to find thick clouds of smoke, with a fire of such heat and intensity emanating from the child's bed that in spite of his making every effort to approach the bed (which he was hardly able to see through the smoke) he was driven back by the intensity of the flames. He had then instantly run to the telephone and called the emergency services. His mother told me her son was older than his years, very sensible and had told her that he was completely mystified as to how a fire could develop an intensity of that nature in such a short space of time, as he had looked in only a matter of a few minutes before.

If this were not enough, the horror of the police findings subsequent to their investigation, and the coroner's report, which followed, invoked many recurrent nightmares for all concerned during the months that followed. My client showed me some terrifying photographs taken by the police during their enquiries. These showed that half the head and half the body of the child had been burned away; the astounding thing was that the remaining halves were not even charred! The bed, also, had been burned in the same manner, almost as though a cosmic laser had been applied to the bed and sleeping child. Another astonishing thing was that the boy had heard no warning screams emanating from the child's bedroom, although he was only feet away in an adjoining room.

The coroner's report gave the cause of death as Spontaneous Human Combustion, a phenomenon which at the time I had never heard of. Peter and I researched some information on this, and found that a number of virtually identical cases had been recorded. A curious feature often present in each case is that only *part* of the victim's body and supporting furniture, such as a bed or chair were burned, with almost a line of demarcation, on either side of which was burnt flesh on the one hand, and completely unharmed flesh on the other, the same applying to the supporting furniture.

Again, it seems to be general in these fortunately rare cases that the victim surprisingly does not seem to cry out in any way. Interestingly, no report appeared in any of the papers or media that related to the tragic event experienced by my client. Peter and I have discussed this terrible phenomenon many times, and neither of us can come up with any answer.

The foot of Dr John Irving Bentley was all that remained following his death by spontaneous human combustion, 5 December 1966, Northern Pennsylvania, USA. Photo by permission of Fortean Picture Library.

Chapter 17
Zeebrugge – Night of Terror

A feeling of darkness and intense cold enveloped me. Water in the darkness; water of a cold that seemed to penetrate to my very bones. There was a salty, oily tang to the air; and a feeling of terrible danger and despair. I felt trapped; a man's voice, seemingly in my head, rang out loud and clear: '…for thine is the Kingdom, the Power and the Glory…' They were the final words of the Lord's Prayer. As this came to a conclusion, I heard other men's voices, accompanied by a loud banging sound. A voice said, 'Someone will hear us as long as we keep it up.' One of the others was talking about how his leg was hurting and asking for help, and a feeling of terrible urgency overwhelmed me…

During the evening, I had been sitting in the private lounge of a Folkestone hotel, looking out at the bleak winter weather in the darkness and feeling very warm and comfortable. Around me were deep velvet armchairs, the prints of Old Masters hanging from the walls, lending an air of timelessness to the scene; underfoot was a deep-pile carpet, and in the corner, a television. The owner of the hotel, a friend of mine, had invited me round to give readings to some of her clients. They had been coming to see me at intervals; I felt very 'switched on', as I always do when the atmosphere is right, and the clients warm and sympathetic. One by one they came in to see me with queries such as, 'Is my little boy going to pass his exams?' and, 'Can you see any form of job on the horizon?' – the list of questions was endless. My pictures came and went – not always in the form that my clients wanted to hear, and they would often tell me so; but I would tell them, as I always do, 'This is what I see; you will have to make up your own mind based on what I tell you.'

Although feeling particularly well tuned in as I was, a welcome break was suggested by my hostess. A nice cup of freshly made percolated coffee arrived with a prawn sandwich. I decided to relax completely, and turned the television on. The picture sharpened into focus; after only a few seconds, a printed newsflash appeared on the screen. It was announcing that a disaster had occurred on one of the cross-Channel car ferries; the picture then showed a partially sunken vessel in the darkness, surrounded by artificial lighting and rescue boats, foam creaming from their bows. As more information came through, it seemed that my mind started to pan in to the newsflashes. At the same time, linking in as I was, it seemed that I was also detaching myself objectively, asking myself why or how it was that I should happen to switch on the set at that precise moment – why should this be? In many years, I had never turned on the television in this way at a client's premises.

I had a strong feeling that, as on many other occasions, some external influence had guided me to switch on the set at that point. An overwhelming sensation of confusion and turmoil was taking place in my mind – voices crying out – a terrible sense of urgency – and the newsflashes continued. I heard a name that was to be indelibly stamped for all time on my consciousness: *Zeebrugge*. The announcer, emotion and concern showing through his normally calm and polished presentation, was visibly upset as more details of the disaster came pouring in.

'A Sealink car ferry boat has overturned and partially sunk at Zeebrugge… rescue work is continuing… helicopters are airlifting passengers to safety… rescue launches are pulling others from the sea, with many people still believed to be trapped in the upturned hull.'

My coffee break was now over. My first client after the break was shown in to me; she was not aware of the disaster at all and, poor soul, obviously had many problems of her own. My heart went out to her – it turned out that her husband was extremely ill – could I reassure her and tell her that he was going to recover? I started the reading, finding it difficult to concentrate. My mind was still with the disaster; however, I managed to direct my inner 'television screen' towards my client's problems.

Somehow, I got through the rest of my evening; with a vast sense of relief, I said goodnight to my last client. Normally I enjoy my work enormously, to the point of making close friends of many of them. However, since the first newsflashes of the disaster had been screened, my mind had been overwhelmed by the incident, and as the evening had worn on, I had been finding it increasingly difficult to focus my attention on the problems of my clients.

The feeling returned to me, that of some external influence drawing my attention to the incident. Was it the 'Hand of Fate' beloved of many novelists, or some discarnate entity? I still had the definite feeling that 'someone' had influenced me to watch that first newsflash at the split second I had turned it on.

My secretary brought me in another coffee; she had been watching the disaster on the television in the lounge next door. As she relayed to me the updated information, my mind seemed at that point in time to be linked in again to the newsflashes.

Time to go; time to go home with Peter. I always ask Peter to drive me home, because after any session when I work with clients, I frequently feel drowsy and disorientated. Tonight, however, I was wide awake. As we got into the car the night was very black; a bitterly cold wind was blowing and my mind was going out to the poor people on that stricken ferry. Any survivors in that cold sea, I thought, could not last long. The announcer had talked of people still trapped in the hull; my mind stepped back from this thought as one steps back from an abyss; a feeling of claustrophobia engulfed me as I thought of being in total darkness in that icy water while we drove home that night.

It was good to get home, to step into the light and warmth and leave the winter cold and darkness behind. We sat down to eat, and for a while my pictures faded in the warm glow of the fire; we purposely did not switch on the television. Later we relaxed together, talking of friends, things we had to do, and making plans for the future until Peter, yawning, said he would just have to go to bed (it had been a long day for both of us). I declined, sitting comfortably by the fire and gazing into the embers. As I did so, my pictures began to return. Coldness… darkness… the feeling of entombment… and despair. Although the area was in intense darkness, I could 'see' three men trapped in the hull, their sole means of existence a giant bubble of air. One of the men was praying, and the Lord's Prayer sounded in my head. One of the others was in pain; it seemed his leg was hurting, and he was clutching it and at the same time asking for help. The third man had some object in his hand and was knocking hard on the steel hull with it. 'Someone will hear us as long as we keep it up,' he was saying, bracing himself against a bulkhead in the darkness, obviously preparing for a vigil.

It was difficult to describe my emotions at that point in time. It came home to me that, apart from the men themselves, I was the sole person to be aware of their plight. Knowing that these men were trapped down there in this awful predicament, and being completely unable to help them, brought about in me a profound despair the like of which I had never before experienced. Mechanically, I detached myself from this interior viewing of mine, and while wondering what on earth I could do next, wandered over yet again to the television set and switched it on. The disaster was still at this time being broadcast from Zeebrugge. In the darkness of the night, the flares and lights illuminated the scene, the dark water emphasising the boats; highlighting the spray that curled away from their hulls.

The scene changed to a series of flashbacks as the announcer described the events leading up to the catastrophe. I learned that at about 6.30 in the evening the car ferry *Herald of Free Enterprise* had sailed from Zeebrugge with the inner and outer cargo doors still open. Just after passing the outer mole of the harbour, the boat had keeled over and capsized due to water pouring in through the still-open cargo hold doors. A dredger had been working in the harbour area and immediately went to the aid of the stricken vessel, commencing to search for survivors and alerting the port control.

A British coaster was in preparation for leaving the port at 6.30. The captain immediately ordered his boat to proceed to the wreck. She was followed by two tugs, who positioned themselves by the submerged ferry just aft of her funnels. These were followed in turn by many small boats and fishing vessels, all searching the water for survivors. Two more ferries left the harbour, one of them anchoring near the wreck and preparing a helipad on her deck, at the same time opening the stern ramp to prepare to receive casualties. The second lowered a boat to search the area, but without success. Later on she was to send two men with an intimate knowledge of the *Herald* to board her in the continued search for survivors.

The first of the divers, two of them, arrived at the scene via a barge from the port around 7 p.m. I remembered, at this point, earlier in the evening when divers had been mentioned, that the first impressions of the trapped men had filtered through to me, and this awful feeling of helplessness returned. I resolved I must help these men but who on earth would believe me? No matter, I had to make a start somewhere.

On the screen a Helpline number was flashing up. All I had to do was to phone through explaining who I was and direct help to those poor trapped men.

'Who's calling, please? Are you a relative of one of the passengers?'

My mouth went dry as I realised how it must sound to a busy switchboard operator. 'No, I don't personally know anyone on the boat. Have you heard of me? My name is Anne Owen, I am a well-known clairvoyant and have appeared on television a number of times…'

My voice started to trail off as I realised how this must be coming across to someone who did not know me. The voice at the other end of the line remained silent while the busy chatter of a large switchboard remained in the background.

'I can see three men trapped in the hull, and divers need to be urgently contacted to free them. I can describe where they are… near the…' My voice trailed off as a high-pitched giggle sounded on the line.

'I don't think we can help you here, madam; I'm sorry but I'll have to leave you now…' The inevitable click accompanied by background static followed.

I could not blame her; events of this nature always attract the unbalanced who want to draw attention to themselves, and any hint of the extrasensory in the majority of cases, even in these enlightened times, will still provoke fear and ridicule among the uninformed. I tried again, and got a different operator but the same response.

The thought of those men trapped in their grim underwater prison in total darkness gripped me in despair; I could not remember feeling so completely helpless before. But wait! A second thought occurred to me. I had in the past done a radio phone-in programme with BBC Radio Kent where the presenter, Gerry Savage, had been very supportive of the venture. Listeners would call in;

I would start by giving an accurate description over the air of the house or flat they lived in, followed by circumstances surrounding the caller at the time. Relatives, relationships, jobs, plus a description of their immediate future, had to be delivered accurately at high speed, in keeping with the tempo of the programme. As I had to constantly prove myself in the face of the sceptics, and had done so successfully, Gerry had become my champion.

I rang his home, found out from his wife that he was on duty at BBC Radio Kent, and managed to contact a member of staff there. I felt strongly that Gerry would back my story, and thanks to his media contacts would be able to relay the information through the right channels to direct divers to the spot.

At the time of the disaster, during an emergency or adverse weather conditions, the staff at BBC Radio Kent frequently stayed on duty throughout the night. This, of course, was such a time. I could not contact Gerry, as he was very involved with the transmission in connection with the disaster. I managed to speak, however, with someone at the station, explaining in detail why I needed to contact him so urgently. The woman who answered was sympathetic; fortunately I had had dealings with her on the programme previously and she knew how I worked. She promised to contact Gerry as soon as possible.

At this point I felt my fears easing, although of course I knew there was still a long way to go. It was also the only route still open to me.

I took hold of myself. There was nothing further that I could do at this point in time. I returned to the scene of the disaster, switching on the television again. Newsflashes were being almost continuously transmitted...

A Belgian Sea King helicopter was now over the wreck, bringing a Belgian diving team who were proceeding to board the stricken ferry. The whoppa, whoppa, whoppa of the helicopter's rotor blades added to the many confusing background noises, in the glare of the floodlights from surrounding vessels. Another ferry, inbound from Chatham to Zeebrugge, was launching a lifeboat, which commenced to circle round the wreck for survivors. Then, one of the crew noticed some lights on the upper car deck. The lifeboat made for the stern of the vessel, only to find they were the headlights of an overturned lorry. Unfortunately they were unable to approach further because of cars blocking the entrance.

Fighting to keep myself under control while watching all this going on and having heard nothing from BBC Radio Kent, I called back to find out if there had been any further developments. The voice at the other end of the line – a man this time – was very apologetic and concerned. 'Unfortunately Gerry is transmitting live most of the time now. We've tried several times to catch his attention but with the situation as it is things are very difficult. However, we know he's having a short break soon. I'm sure we can do something then.' Once more there was little that I could do.

It was now around nine o'clock. More and more divers were being brought in; one of our naval vessels at Ostende had dispatched her entire team by boat. Another locally-based boat moored in Zeebrugge had mustered her divers by telephone and was proceeding towards the wreck. Even as far away as Portsmouth, the Royal Navy Clearance Diving Centre was alerted. At this time, I was trying to shut out the images that were crowding my brain of the three trapped men.

I knew that if I allowed this terrible situation to fully enter my mind again, I would only break down; which would impair my thinking at this critical time.

The telephone rang; it was Gerry's wife. 'Anne, I've managed to get your message through. He's going to personally contact one of the salvage personnel in charge of the diving teams. It's going to be all right.' Tears sprang into my eyes and I could feel myself choking. 'Anne, are you OK?' she said kindly, her voice full of concern over the line.

Foolishly, I nodded, then realising of course that videophones were not generally available yet, reassured her. 'Thank you so much,' I stammered. 'I've suddenly got a good feeling about this now.' We said our goodbyes; the line went dead.

I went back to the sitting room in the darkness of the hour, threw myself into a deep armchair and relaxed again. Again, with nothing to do but wait, the television came alive again. A close-up showed that by now a lot of the windows on the uppermost side of the vessel had been broken in, and many passengers were being assisted out and helped into the waiting boats, to be ferried to the port for onward transport to rapidly created rest centres and hospitals. It was wonderful to see them being transported to safety, although of course the condition of some of them was pitiable. As my heart went out to them, the clutching hand of fear and despair gripped me as, once more, try as I might, I could no longer shut out the thoughts of those three men…

Again the darkness; again the feeling of being entombed. I became aware again that one of them had hurt his leg… they were praying for help. This continued for a while, and then they started to sing to keep their spirits up; I seemed to feel this rather than hear it, in a manner difficult to define.

At this point I lost consciousness; slipping into a light, disturbed sleep in the armchair, with troubled thoughts tumbling across a kaleidoscopic panorama of the mind that seemingly led nowhere.

I awoke with a convulsive start to the loud purr of the telephone, and snatched at the receiver in an uncoordinated daze in such a way as to almost let it slip and cut off my caller. Luckily I recovered my grip in time to hear a voice I knew so well of old! 'Hello, Gerry!' I exclaimed in delight. 'Thank you so much for calling back. I—'

His warm voice cut across mine with a depth of understanding that in the past had enabled us to work together so well on live shows, and now was to reassure me in a way that made me feel that together we could be in with a chance to save those poor men.

'How wonderful to hear your voice again. Just to let you know I've managed to contact one of the port authorities I know personally and he is putting every effort in to locate the men. My wife has explained everything. I have to go now; we're still working and monitoring everything from the studio. God bless.' And he was gone.

With a feeling of relief I sat back in my chair, my only concern being that help might arrive too late. However, I felt the matter was now out of my hands and, after yet another short prayer, continued to watch the intermittent newsflashes that were coming up, operating the hand-held scanner to monitor successive channels to find the latest information. By now, normal programmes were beginning to return to the screen; however, here and there, hopping as I was between channels and programmes, I could see that footage of the ferry was still being shown. This revealed a very confused overall situation; a lack of organised lighting seemed to dominate the scene; while the noise of the helicopters appeared to be swamping the voices of those attempting to communicate by radio between the rescue vessels and those aboard the stricken ferry who were assisting survivors to safety, and – sickening thought – organising the removal of bodies from the wreck. All this confusion was considerably hampered by gangs of reporters, who were regrettably impeding rescue workers by attempting to board, accompanied by almost continuous flash lighting.

Fortunately, under coercion from the rescue team leaders, they were eventually herded from the vessel back into the waiting tug.

It was now getting quite late in the evening. A report announced that all the available headlamps were gradually failing. Most of the survivors above water level had been rescued, and divers were being organised to begin recovering bodies while still searching for survivors.

Again, reporters were dramatically impeding the rescue operations – jumping aboard uninvited two of the rescue tugs as they were leaving the port. When they returned alongside the *Herald*, the reporters jumped back onto the wreck, severely hampering the attempts of the crews. With complete disregard for the saving of human lives, merely to obtain copy for the press and media, they continued to obstruct the operation, until the officer in charge threatened them with physical removal. Grudgingly, they returned to the tugs waiting alongside; yet again, the urge for money had been quick to stifle any feeling of human compassion.

At this late hour, reclining in my armchair, for the first time I was beginning to feel relaxed. I had a sense of anxiety being eased, of my concerns leaving me; although I continued to watch the newsflashes, a feeling almost of detachment began to enter my consciousness.

I discovered afterwards, through the wife of one of the ferry company operatives, that around 12.30 in the morning some divers had been dispatched to the wreck to hammer along the hull. It must have been these wonderful people, who of course should not be singled out in preference to those many heroic individuals who worked ceaselessly in terrible conditions of cold and darkness, who eventually found these poor trapped men. Previous to this, diving operations had been stopped apparently; the authorities, thank goodness, had listened to Gerry when he had telephoned through on my behalf.

Strangely, I could no longer tune in to the three men. Whenever I tried, nothing came up; my mind would not focus and my mental screen was a total blank. I tried focussing on various stages of the rescue operation which I knew would have had to take place; everything from the scene of the original entombment to medical care – nothing. I find this is often a function of how I operate – it almost seems to work on a need-to-know basis only; once the requirement for the extrasensory gift has passed, it seems the signals cease; only to be brought back into play when the need arises.

As is customary in these matters, a Court of Inquiry was held afterwards on the sinking of the *Herald of Free Enterprise*. This of course is not a matter for discussion here, but some years later, quite by chance, someone showed me a copy of the official findings of the Court of Inquiry, which vividly brought back to me the memories of one of the worst nights I have ever experienced.

This paragraph, almost at the end of the report, is a graphic summary of that night:

> At 0030 divers were dispatched in an inflatable craft to hammer on the bottom of the wreck because there was no obvious access to the engine room. Officers and seamen from the other Townsend ships who were familiar with the *Herald* layout arrived and more headlamps became available. Further searches were thus carried out.
>
> At 0115 three survivors were found in the forward drivers' accommodation. It must be assumed that these were the last to be found alive.

An interesting sequel occurred a little while later. A writer for *She* magazine, reading the story of the rescue, which was printed in the *News of the World* at the time, decided to follow it up. With some difficulty, she managed to locate the three lorry drivers. She wrote:

> The survivors' account of waiting in the *Herald*'s hold to be rescued matches Anne Owens' vision uncannily. Roger Bloomfield, one of the three lorry drivers, said they spent the time 'whistling and singing and trying to keep up morale'.

Brian Gibbons, the very last man to be saved from the ship, explained how they spent time talking and keeping up morale: 'We were in the drivers' cabin, about four flights below the water level. Jock (Ian Calderwood) got a blanket to cover up Roger because his foot was badly injured; he kept telling us to call out our names while I kept tapping the hatch hoping someone would hear us.'

So there it is; a terrifying experience, fortunately with a happy ending for the three concerned. A pity that those extrasensory abilities cannot be more generally harnessed, or called forth at will when required. It is my belief, however, that we, all of us, are moving forward in terms of evolution in a way that will allow us to harness these abilities to an extent that they will one day become part of our everyday life.

Her amazing powers saved three men in Zeebrugge disaster

THE WOMAN WITH X RAY EYES!

Psychic Anne saw trapped ferry men

Another News of the World Exclusive

By ROSALIE SHANN

THE woman with the X-ray Eyes paced the floor of her bedroom as the nightmare pictures flickered through her head like a horror movie.

Psychic Anne Owens "saw" three lorry drivers trapped in an air bubble inside the hull of the stricken ferry Herald Of Free Enterprise.

The 47-year-old housewife knew time was running out for the terrified men... and she knew she was the only one who could save them from the icy waters of Zeebrugge.

"I heard them praying, crying out for help," said Anne. "But all the time I knew that the rescue divers had stopped searching.

"My husband Peter kept saying 'Come to bed Anne, there's nothing you can do.'

"But I told him 'I have to help them—I must help.'"

Anne, who has used her remarkable powers to solve murders and diagnose illnesses, sat down on her bed and tried to send a telepathic message to the rescuers.

"Dive," she told them. "Go on diving. You must go on diving."

In the end Anne phoned the emergency services.

"There are three men trapped down there. You've got to get them to carry on diving," she warned.

But Anne said: "They thought me a crank and did nothing."

In desperation, she rang her local Radio Kent and spoke to producer Gerry Savage about her visions.

Gerry remembered: "Anne was very agitated as nobody would believe her.

"But I knew already how remarkable she was as she had been on my chat shows. So I passed on her message to the authorities and the three men were rescued."

Anne's X-ray Eyes have given her other visions of terror. Like...

THE CASE OF THE BLOOD-SOAKED JUMPER:

●Mother-of-two Anne, who has earned worldwide fame with her psychic skills, once helped police track down the killer of a girl student in Wiesbaden, West Germany.

She became involved when the murdered youngster's professor sent her a despairing note.

It read: "The police cannot find the guilty person. Would it be possible that you can help?"

Anne came up with so many accurate details that police sent her photos of the murdered girl... together with her blood-spattered woollen sweater.

Soon Anne began seeing grisly images of the murder—as well as a terrifyingly clear picture of the killer.

Her amazing X-ray Eyes even "saw" the fiend's name... Karl-Heinz Schaffner.

Astounded detectives confirmed that Schaffner existed and within days they had their man.

THE CASE OF THE RIPPER CLUE:

● British police were also stunned by Anne's powers during the hunt for Yorkshire Ripper Peter Sutcliffe.

Anne told them in September 1980 that the man they were looking for was a lorry driver from Bradford.

And her information was proved chillingly accurate when Sutcliffe was arrested five months later.

But Anne has also used her X-ray Eyes to help cure the sick. Like...

THE CASE OF THE DOUBTING DOCTOR:

● A sceptical woman GP heard how Anne could diagnose ailments by staring at a patient's body.

She decided to test Anne's powers and called at her cosy cottage home in Kent.

But the doctor found more than she bargained for when Anne gazed at her with her piercing grey eyes—and announced she had something wrong in her stomach and would need an operation.

Soon afterwards the woman underwent emergency surgery on an

Anne's X-ray Eyes have been giving her "mind pictures" since she was a child.

"I always knew when someone in the family had something wrong with them," she said.

"I used to look at them and then say 'Have you got a pain in your chest?' Invariably I'd be right.

"I see everything as a series of very clear, almost photographic images inside my head.

"It's like a TV screen. I get pictures of what's beneath the person's skin. It's not even necessary for them to remove their clothes."

As she grew up Anne realised she could look into people's minds and see what they were thinking.

Sometimes she saw bright colours round their heads. At other times she actually 'read' their thoughts.

"For instance, if another girl looked at me at a party and thought 'Gosh, Anne's hair looks awful tonight,' I'd pick up her thought," she said.

"I worried—not because of my hair—but because I was telepathic. I was terrified I was abnormal. I thought perhaps I was going mad.

"Then I got married and had my children. When one of them fell over and hurt his knee he would cry out 'Rub it mum, make the pain go away.'

"And I did and the pain would go away.

"I think it was then that I realised this extraordinary 'sight' could be put towards helping other people."

Like...

THE CASE OF THE HEALING HANDS:

● Housewife Brenda Dawson, 46, from Maidstone, Kent, was in agony from a slipped disc and Anne was asked to visit her.

A friend said: "She talked to Brenda soothingly, looked at her intently and then put her hands on her back.

"She hasn't had the pain since."

Mrs Susan Newman also went to Anne when she was suffering severe migraine.

Susan said: "She just looked at me and held my hands lightly and I felt relaxed. The pain in my head just went away. It was amazing."

But Anne doesn't only deal with medical ailments.

She also advises people on their personal and business problems... and even uses her X-ray Eyes to find out why clients' cars have broken down.

Anne said: "I know this sounds mad, but I can often help out by 'seeing' hidden mechanical faults."

And that is exactly what happened in...

THE CASE OF THE DUMBFOUNDED DAD:

● Anne was out driving with her father when her X-ray Eyes suddenly picked up something.

"Into my mind came a picture of a back wheel coming off," she said.

"'Daddy, Daddy,' I shrieked. 'Stop the car-a wheel's coming off its bolts!'

"Daddy stopped the car and got out to look. When he got back in, he looked pale and shaken.

"'You're right,' he said. 'How on earth did you know?'"

HORROR at Zeebrugge: Anne 'saw' trapped men

A few samples of press cuttings from some hundreds worldwide

Chapter 18
Days in the Life of...

'Hello, Anne. I'm just about to catch a plane at Gatwick for a board meeting in the Midlands. My company is thinking of having a merger with this American outfit; we are considering trading five of our shares per unit in the projected deal. Do you think they'll bite?'

'I can see that two of the directors are willing to go ahead with your deal. However, the third one could be a problem for you. He's trying to persuade the other two not to buy in, as he's worried about their accountant's forecast projection being based on rather optimistic figures. To swing this deal, would you be able to tell them at this stage that one of your subsidiaries is considering taking over Valtec Trading?'

'I'd rather not at this stage, Anne. If this gets out right now, the opposition could step in and grab them before we've got all our money together.'

'Why don't you arrange for the signing of a promissory note from your company – I don't see a risk ahead for you in doing this. In this way you can nail your deal, and present this as a fait accompli. My advice to you is to go ahead and do this; I don't feel there is any problem with the shareholders coming up with the money. This is going to swing that third man, and you won't have a problem. Contact your secretary straightaway to put this in hand.'

'Anne, I think that's an excellent idea. Having dealt with you for so many years and found your advice to be always correct, I'm going ahead along the lines you suggest. Many thanks, have to go as we are all just about to board the aircraft. Bye, speak to you next week...' Our conversation terminated with the click of disconnection.

Another of my high-flying clients, in all senses of the word. At different times, I have had many businessmen and women seeking my advice, of which the foregoing is an example. A fascinating side of my work is that I never know who is going to come on the line or phone up next for an appointment.

Naturally, the majority of my clients are not high-profile people; just average, honest persons who are in need of help either with their emotional or financial worries, or perhaps advice on concerns of health where they feel conventional medicine is unable to help them. However, a few thumbnail sketches of some of the high-fliers or more way-out clients will serve to show that boredom does not number among the problems of my calling...

For example, I had at one time a Far Eastern princess who would ring sometimes two or three times a day – when I say day, I am referring to a twenty-four hour one, as she had no desire to check international time zones before ringing me. I would often be awakened at some ungodly hour of the night before being plunged into an international intrigue or details of some torrid love affair requiring my advice. She was also extremely shrewd in business, and would often seek my opinion before going ahead with a number of deals she was involved with.

The princess was an intriguing personality. She was driven everywhere in a black limousine by an engagingly pleasant character who doubled as a chauffeur and bodyguard; he was about as broad as he was tall and a karate expert. She had great charm and generosity, often taking Peter and myself out to expensive restaurants, where we would dine among the rich and famous. Listening and advising on her governmental intrigues and love affairs was quite fascinating, but she had a sadistic side to her nature. She was always unjustifiably venting her spleen on many unfortunates with whom she had dealings, and seemed to take great delight in dismissing people and hurting them without reason as she eventually did with us. Ah well, it takes all sorts…

Then there was the man who came to see me from time to time whom I nicknamed 'the Cat with Nine Lives'. When I first met him – he had come to me for a general reading – I was struck immediately by his secretive yet sensitive and gentle manner. Though he gave nothing away to me, I was able to tell him details regarding his emotional life. The first thing that came to me was that his wife was always shouting at him, and had effectively driven him away to the point where he was finding happiness with a Japanese girlfriend. It took him aback when I told him this, and I continued with advice to help him over his domestic situation.

However, there was something about his secretive manner that was intriguing me. Suddenly I asked him: 'Why do I get this impression of explosions often happening around you? It's not making sense to me.'

He laughed and said, 'That's amazing! I trained with the Army as an explosives and bomb disposal expert, but I retired from that a few years ago.'

'But I can see that in some way you're still involved with explosives – how can that be now that you have retired from this work?'

He was now completely taken aback, and went on to tell me how he had been hired for his expertise by some wealthy Arabs, and was now involved with training some of their troops in the Middle East in the art of blowing up bridges and fortifications. In one aside he mentioned how it was possible to put something in the fuel tank of a vehicle, which would react in some way to explode hours after the attacker had departed. He then went on to tell me of several incidents during which he had escaped death by seconds during his amazing career – hence the soubriquet that I had bestowed upon him. He came to me at infrequent intervals from time to time, once telling me that he had built up quite a fortune in gold and silver as payment for his services.

Moving across the spectrum, I received a very beautiful bouquet of flowers one day from one of the Kings of Gangland, Ronnie Kray, of Kray brothers fame. This had come about with a story that began some months earlier when a young woman came to see me for a reading. She was an interesting character who had a kissogram business (for my readers abroad this consists of an attractive young girl, generally scantily attired, who is hired to arrive on an unsuspecting person's doorstep, perhaps singing or delivering a naughty message in the form of a birthday surprise or similar occasion). She drove an old Rolls-Royce everywhere. She came to me as a client, and told me that for some reason I cannot now recall, she wanted to visit the well-known criminal, Ronnie Kray, who was serving a life sentence at the time for his gangland crimes in Broadmoor prison.

She kept in touch with me, telling me she was visiting him in prison at regular intervals, and amazingly she fell in love with him and married him, after he had proposed to her! She described him to me as always being the perfect gentleman, which I found to be true, as after my client had told him of her involvement with me, over a period he wrote me several letters, one of them asking me for a reading to see if I would be able to tell him if he would ever be released from prison, or would he end his days there. I wrote back saying I could not see his release taking place, and my prediction proved to be correct, as he was never released before his passing. I will however never forget that beautiful bouquet of flowers…

The following anecdote will show that even the clairvoyant can remain in the dark sometimes! A wealthy American couple contacted me after having heard of my diagnostic skills, which had been written up in *Woman* magazine at the time, regarding a health problem that their daughter was suffering from. The three of them flew over from the States especially to see me, and I made various recommendations and treated her. It happened that my husband Peter called by at my clinic in Maidstone at the time, and he and the father took to each other straightaway as they had a lot in common. Peter has a great love of flying, and he discovered that this man in his earlier days had been a crop-spraying pilot. These individuals can be some of the wildest flyers, having to zoom at very low level between trees, radio masts and power lines to spread their pesticides. Peter was kept enthralled by this man's fascinating flying anecdotes, which included tales of way-out flying ferrying an old two-seater aircraft from the States to South America in the days before modern navigational aids.

We all got on extremely well, and one day the man telephoned us from the

States to say that a group of his friends was shortly coming over to England and would very much like to have readings with me. A little while later I received a telephone call from the owner of an engaging drawl announcing he was the friend of our friends, and that he would like to bring his group to my house for readings. This was arranged, and a few days later nine people turned up at our house in a taxi built to seat five. They all poured out in a flurry of arms and legs, and we ushered them in and sat them down. Two of them were older women, dark, very good-looking and weighed down with gold necklaces and very expensive jewellery. The men again were dark and rather Italianate in appearance, and were very expensively dressed in dark suits, with heavy gold rings and wristwatches, and the majority wore designer sunglasses.

I remember Peter passing an aside to me as they entered, saying, 'It must be their day off – they haven't brought their violin cases.' The entire party was charming, but there was a faint tinge of menace – not towards us – which I could feel lurking about somewhere. Peter made them some coffee, and I gave them all readings – they apparently had properties in the Caribbean and Florida, and owned racehorses. All in all, it was a convivial morning. We enjoyed their company, and they were extremely generous when they settled for their readings before they all piled back into the same taxi, waving their goodbyes with flashing smiles.

About six weeks later, Peter telephoned his pilot friend in the States for one of their regular chats. His daughter answered the phone, and he asked her if her father was available. The dramatic response came in a slow Southern drawl, 'Daddy's in prison,' and she rang off without further preamble.

Peter of course was dumbstruck, and didn't feel he could ring back to elicit further information. Both of us were completely mystified until we received a letter from a mutual English friend, enclosing some newspaper cuttings giving details of the greatest drug bust ever in the state of Florida, in which our friends had been key participants. We felt very sad that such charming and likeable people could be involved in bringing misery to others on such a scale, and heard afterwards that he had yielded to temptation due to financial pressures.

To me the amazing thing was that all my usual perceptive skills had been completely blind to what had been going on in the background; this was certainly a lesson in complacency for me, should this ever recur. It does seem, however, as we have experienced unwitting involvement with criminals two or three times in our life, that if there is a personal connection of any sort our psychic abilities seem to be shut off in some way.

It came home to me one day just how important it is to listen to our intuition when we are prompted by it. In this instance it was Peter who was strongly prompted to follow his feelings one Saturday morning at our

Maidstone clinic. I was finishing a particularly difficult session with a client just before one o'clock, when we were due to close and leave for a welcome meal, as I had not had time to eat earlier in the day. Peter was taking my telephone calls that morning, as my usual secretary was away on holiday. As we were leaving the clinic to eat, I was mentally looking forward to a relaxing afternoon in the garden, extremely glad to have finished work for the week. Peter then said to me, 'I know that you're not going to be happy about this, but I have booked you in one more client this afternoon immediately after lunch. This girl pleaded to see you this afternoon, and normally I would simply have given her an appointment next week in the usual way. However, and I cannot tell you why, I felt it to be really important that you see this girl as soon as possible. I realise it is going to cut into our afternoon, and I know you desperately need to relax, but as a favour to me would you see her?'

I was not overly pleased to finish lunch and open up the clinic again afterwards, particularly as I had been so looking forward to just relaxing at home in the sun; but something in Peter's manner convinced me, against my will, to do as he asked. Accordingly, after lunch we returned to the clinic just before the appointed time to find a young girl looking very distressed sitting on the steps. My heart went out to her, and I began to wonder what on earth had happened to bring her to me in this condition.

After the initial greetings, I sat her down opposite me to begin her reading, thinking to myself I could by now have been beginning to relax at home. I took her hands in mine, turning them over as I did so to look at her palms. All thoughts of relaxing at home disappeared in a flash as I looked at her disfigured wrists, which were terribly scarred. I was horrified as I instantly realised she had recently attempted to take her life, and these scars were the stark testimony of the means by which she had endeavoured to achieve this. At the same time I experienced further consternation as I started to tune in to her, suddenly realising she had the firm intention of attempting to take her life again.

As gently as possible I went into her story, unravelling the complex strands of her existence. She was deeply in love with a man who had callously cast her off as a spent plaything. Calling for help in the form of a prayer asking to be given the inspiration to divert her from her terrible purpose, I was able gradually to put this man in perspective to her from a viewpoint she had never considered before. By degrees, during the course of an hour or so I was able to bring her around to a different way of thinking; I made her promise to come and see me again if she felt in danger of being overwhelmed by despair, after I had talked her through her problems. She gave me her word she would do this; and to my enormous relief, the following week she called to thank me for seeing her through her darkest hour.

A note I received from Ronnie Kray together with some beautiful flowers while he was a guest of Her Majesty at Broadmoor

A year later she came to me for another reading as a changed person, telling me how she had managed to rebuild her life again. I felt embarrassed as she thanked me profusely; it came home to me that she would no longer have been alive if Peter's strong feeling of intuition had not persuaded me to stay on almost against my will that summer's afternoon.

On a different note, one evening a woman telephoned me to book a party at a flat in London's Knightsbridge. She spoke with an unusual accent that I had difficulty in identifying, giving directions for parking our car in a private underground car park. This immediately told me that this client, who had asked me to give readings to a group of six or seven of her friends, must be extremely wealthy, if she lived in a property in that area with these facilities.

Peter and I arrived as directed at the entrance to the underground car park, where we were stopped by a uniformed attendant who enquired after the purpose of our visit. He indicated that we should leave our car to one side, where we noticed an extraordinary collection of beautifully restored antique and classic cars. These we found out belonged to the husband of the woman who was our hostess for the evening. We were shown into a lift, from which we were decanted into probably the most sumptuous surroundings we had ever experienced. Our hostess – of Middle Eastern appearance, as were most of the guests – was dripping with the most beautiful jewellery, also being adorned with large and heavy gold ornaments; she introduced us to her friends, who were attired in like manner. The walls were hung with exquisite and priceless oriental rugs, complementing the gold and silver coffee table and rich carpeting.

The Arab women, for that is who they proved to be, were very pleasant towards me, but they were all slightly merry with drink, which they told me was absolutely forbidden to them. I was surprised to learn that they comprised the harem of an unimaginably wealthy Arab who was away travelling the world. They told me that they would be subjected to severe reprisals if he found out that they had been drinking in the way they had, and that Peter and I would never normally be allowed in, if their communal husband had been aware of our presence. Their 'corner shop' was Harrods; I could see many expensive items had been purchased which were not really appropriate to their lifestyle, and which appeared to have been purchased out of boredom rather than necessity. I gave them all readings in the usual way; their lives appeared to me to be largely made up of drunken apathy and boredom. I left that evening reflecting how these people, although surrounded by enormous wealth, all seemed to be leading such sad and purposeless lives.

For some months Peter and I had a highly interesting position with the *Evening News* newspaper, which is no longer in existence. When the paper was launched, or rather relaunched, as some years ago the same paper was printed on a daily basis over a period of many years before going into liquidation, we were approached by the new editor to run a sort of agony aunt column, where readers would write in with their problems of emotional relationships, missing persons, robberies etc., and we would publish our replies, having used extra-sensory means to arrive at solutions.

The paper would mail us a selection of readers' letters once a week; Peter and I would sift through them, and after having selected some which we felt were more interesting than the others, or perhaps we felt more in tune with certain of the readers' problems, we would receive our impressions and note them down. A reporter from the paper would make a weekly visit and write up our notes a couple of days before publication, and our weekly column would appear. We never received any feedback on our effort, and as the weeks went by we fell into a routine.

Among the letters one day was one from a girl saying that her boyfriend had disappeared after saying he would be away for a week in connection with his work and would contact her on his return. Three weeks had passed, and she was becoming frantic with worry; could we help?

We reflected deeply on the letter in our usual way, and both of us came up with the same answer. We could 'see' the man involved, wearing a green shirt and playing cards in what looked like a form of barracks. These barracks were set in a jungle-type environment, with exotic-looking trees and a feeling of heat surrounding our mental pictures. We said that he was in no danger and would contact her on his return.

This was duly written up in the paper in the usual way, and because we had simply relayed our impressions, as we always did without further consideration, we thought no more about it.

However, interestingly, the paper – presumably wondering what exactly they were paying us for – contacted the girl after our reply had been printed asking her how correct we had been. She informed them that to her knowledge he would never go to a country of the type we were describing, had always disliked playing cards and never wore green shirts because he didn't like the colour green. At the time the paper didn't mention anything to us, but about ten days later the girl rang the newspaper back very excitedly to say that everything we had said was absolutely correct. Her boyfriend had never told her too much about his work, which she knew had military associations. The Army had apparently sent him along with others on a secret training mission to Africa, where he was stationed in some barracks and had worn a borrowed green shirt, even playing cards out of boredom at times with his fellow trainees.

No enquiries on our work were conducted after that, but sadly the paper was wound up for the second time, leaving two previously extremely well salaried agony aunts unemployed in a journalistic sense; however we were well compensated by the paper for loss of contract.

The following episode I found very rewarding in terms of righting a wrong that had been done and helping someone to get back on track after a very traumatic experience. A lady client came to see me regarding, as often happens, a problem in her marriage. She and her husband were under a great deal of strain and I did my best to calm her down, analysing their problems as best I could and making several suggestions. Suddenly I said to her that I was concerned for her husband's involvement with three cars (he had a garage where he bought and sold vehicles) and named the make of one, a Mini; giving the colours correctly of the other two, as it subsequently proved. I was also picking up a strong connection with the city of Canterbury.

I asked her to tell her husband to be particularly careful in relation to these three cars regarding any transactions he might make. She agreed to pass the message on, and I heard no more for some months. Out of the blue, one day I received a call from her urgently, requesting a further appointment. She duly arrived in great distress, and as soon as she had settled in she told me that her husband had been arrested and sentenced for stealing cars to a term in Canterbury prison. She continued by saying that she knew he would never do anything like this, and he had strongly denied that he had been guilty of any theft, saying that he had been set up, and was now on hunger strike, saying that he had no desire to continue to live.

At the time I was giving lectures at the local Police College, demonstrating how to develop intuitional skills for the solving of crimes. Examine your feelings and hunches, I used to say (and still do), and don't just dismiss these in the face of what may be really convincing red herrings. Following my own philosophy, I suggested to my client that we write a letter to the Chief Constable, whom I knew well, asking him to reopen the case. Apart from lecturing, I had often worked for the police in an unpaid capacity to help them solve certain crimes, and because of my success rate with them felt that at least I could get my client's husband's case reopened, knowing myself that he was completely innocent.

I had pieced this case carefully together, and was sure that this man had been set up by one or more individuals as an act of revenge of some sort, although I was equally sure that my client's husband had not intentionally set out to harm these men in any way. It turned out that they had been rebuilding cars and selling them to their victim, thereby earning money while at the same time drawing social security benefits. Government officials had descended on them some time previously, making a thorough investigation and they had lost their social security allowances, blaming the innocent garage owner, thinking he had made a tip-off to the social services. To achieve their revenge as they saw it, they stole these vehicles (the three that I had 'seen' all that time ago) and sold them with false papers to my client's husband, informing the police at the same time by means of an anonymous tip-off, resulting in his imprisonment.

We wrote the letter out carefully, my client and I, and handed it in at the police station marked 'For the attention of the Chief Constable'. To our surprise, we were asked to wait while this was delivered to him upstairs in his office. A short while later, we were invited up to see him, and we were ushered in and comfortably seated. Knowing him well from several previous meetings, I put the case to him, explaining that I was totally sure that there had been a miscarriage of justice, and would he be able to see his way to re-examining the case. He listened intently, made one or two notes on his desk pad and promised to look into the matter. He took my hand in parting, and I felt he was totally sincere in his intention.

To our vast relief and gratitude, my client's husband was released from prison on bail in just under four days, and was later completely acquitted. Again, this incident was reported in an article in *Woman* magazine.

To end this chapter on a lighter note, I will always remember a highly successful evening I had which was held over a very old public house in Essex. It was probably the largest group of clients I have ever given readings for at one sitting, and the party lasted until 3 a.m., far later than I ever normally allow myself to work. This pub, like quite a few others, was haunted, although I didn't know this when I arrived. I worked very hard as usual, dealing with clients' emotional problems, their hopes and fears, employment situations both present and future etc until I was virtually exhausted, saying at the end to our hostess, 'I'm afraid I just can't see any more people, I'm completely drained!'
She left me to go downstairs and apologise to a group who were patiently waiting to see me, saying that unfortunately I could give no more readings during this visit.

As I was packing my things away, which normally consist of leaflets, tape recorder, tapes etc., and sipping a coffee which our hostess had thoughtfully provided, a man and a woman, dressed in the style of the late 1930s, entered the room. I looked up at them from where I was sitting, and said, 'I'm really sorry, I'm totally exhausted. I just won't be able to give any more readings tonight, but I will be coming here again soon. The lady downstairs will be able to make you an appointment.'

The couple said nothing, but put on expressions as if to say, 'We would really like to have readings from you, but quite understand you're not able to give them to us at this time.'

I remember thinking that their clothes were curiously dated in style, the man wearing a very old-fashioned suit with large lapels and flapping trouser-ends, while the woman wore a smart tweedy-looking jumper and skirt in a style not seen today, with a tightly curled and rather dated hairstyle. I then got up and turned away to call down to the hostess through the half-open door, 'I'm terribly sorry. I did say I can't see anyone else tonight.'

The hostess came to the foot of the stairs and called out, 'But no one else is coming up!'

I turned around to say something to the couple who had just entered – to find no one was there!

This was witnessed by the woman who was my driver for the evening (Peter was unable to accompany me that night); we were both incredulous and looked at each other blankly. Our hostess came up the stairs to enquire what was going on; we both told her what had taken place. 'Oh, a lot of us have seen that couple. They appear here from time to time and then vanish; they are our resident ghosts!' She laughed and added, 'You can always tell the ghosts from the real people here, because they are the ones who disappear through the wall without paying!'

Chapter 19
A Clairvoyant Overview

I am often asked what it is like to be a clairvoyant. Many people imagine that having the gifts that Peter and I have life is just plain sailing for us; any problems that may arise can be solved by extrasensory means, and what an ideal way to resolve all the day-to-day worries which beset us all. Would that it were so! Unfortunately this is not the case at all. For some reason, often those faculties just won't work when they are most needed! Another problem is that we are often very aware of people's attitudes towards us. This is fine when we are surrounded by friendly and sympathetic individuals. However, when someone is near who is hostile or jealous, this is very easy to detect. Often the person concerned doesn't realise that their transmissions can be easily picked up, and it can be upsetting to be talking to someone when on the face of it they are being quite pleasant, but their thoughts can often be totally different. On the other hand, when I have clients who are in a desperate plight of some sort or other, and I am in a position to show them the solution or a way out of their problems by using my gifts, this is highly rewarding, in a way I find difficult to express.

Another aspect of being involved, if you like, in an extrasensory way of life is that one learns fairly early on that it is essential to keep one's feet firmly on the ground. What I mean by this is that we — all of us — are living our own individual lifetimes on this our physical and very beautiful planet. We have incarnated on this earth to participate in a physical environment, to enjoy and endure what life has in store for us, and to learn and develop to the best of our abilities. It is essential to be very much a part of everyday life; if care is not taken it can become all too easy to become over-introspective and to seek an extrasensory way of life to the exclusion of ordinary day-to-day living. This is what I mean by saying it is essential to keep one's feet on the ground.

It must be wonderful, I hear you say, to have these gifts; to be able to take advantage of them and to avoid life's problems, great or small. One example I shall always remember of having clairvoyant faculties and not being able to take advantage of them took place a few years ago in the following manner. One day two friends and I decided to participate in Forward Projection. The experiment consisted of selecting a date forward in time and visualising the front page of a newspaper with the date selected printed on it. Holding that mental image, we would attempt to read the headlines by mental visualisation and see what each of us could come up with.

We asked Peter to join us as a participant, but he was rather busy at the time. However, he offered to briefly sit in with us, and quickly 'saw' the date we had selected for the experiment at the top of the front page of the newspaper. He then saw in his mind's eye a prominent photograph taken as an aerial view of a large fire with smoke billowing skywards in thick clouds. Try as he might, he could only 'see' a vague outline of the text with the word 'fire' indistinctly visualised. Peter got up and left us, briefly expressing hope that his participation had helped in some way, and went off to continue with what he had been doing.

The rest of us had just settled in to see if we could achieve any further result, when a visitor arrived which terminated our efforts. The sequel to Peter's involvement was interesting, however, and showed the definite foretelling of a sad event involving a close friend of his.

A week later on 17 October of that year, the date selected for the experiment, Peter received a phone call from this friend from a hospital where he lay being treated for burns and smoke inhalation. It appeared he had been welding an exhaust pipe on a friend's car when suddenly it caught alight. He rushed to apply a fire extinguisher, but, under pressure as he was, he was unable to locate it quickly enough; the fire swiftly consumed the car, and then spread to the building, which was a beautiful old Kentish oast house. Within minutes the fire took hold, and although the fire brigade was rapidly summoned, the place was soon filled with suffocating dense smoke.

His friend's main concern was to save one of his children and his mother-in-law who were trapped upstairs in another part of the building, unable to find their way out due to the dense smoke. He bravely fought his way upstairs, and with a superhuman effort saved them both, grabbing the child under one arm, and dragging his mother-in-law down the stairs with the other, blinded by the dense smoke and having to feel his way to safety. His dog, to whom the family was devoted, sadly ran off back into the smoke after being rescued, to perish in the flames.

Along with the buildings, he lost many irreplaceable cherished possessions; and the experience, as one would expect, has left him a changed man.

An aerial photograph appeared in the local press of the buildings on fire with dense clouds of smoke billowing up hundreds of feet into the sky. This is what Peter had 'seen' a while previously, together with the date at the top of the printed page. Is it not both sad and strange that Peter's forward viewing of this incident was insufficient, despite his great efforts to discern more detail, to identify and warn his friend of the impending disaster?

Extrasensory viewing is often like this; sufficient in detail to positively identify the coming about of an event or happening, but lacking sufficient detail to prevent it.

Again, as this book was in the throes of completion, Peter underwent two curious experiences, culminating in a precognitive dream relating to the gigantic series of waves, the dreaded tsunami that devastated vast areas of the Pacific region resulting in the loss of an untold number of lives. Some three weeks before the disaster, Peter was in consultation with a business colleague by telephone several times a week. Discussions were carried out relating to business statistics gathered over a long period, and projections were being based on these for the future. These statistics had not varied a great deal from month to month, and the business was largely dependent on a lack of fluctuation.

Peter was concerned that trading could be affected occasionally by a sudden massive fluctuation due to unforeseen circumstances, and unaccountably found himself on several occasions during the three-week period referring to these possible extremely uncharacteristic changes as a 'Pacific wave'. 'What if a Pacific wave were to occur in these statistics?' he would say. 'This could throw our figures out and seriously affect the business.'

This was a term neither I nor our partner had ever heard him use; even Peter himself was surprised at his uncharacteristic use of the words, which he had used a number of times during this same three-week period.

The night before the disaster struck, taking many thousands of people's lives, he dreamed that he was sitting in a very pleasant hotel facing onto a beautiful beach, with a tropical ocean stretching away to the horizon. Seated by a picture window looking out at the idyllic scene with a number of others, he suddenly saw a giant wave approaching over the ocean. In alarm, he leapt up from the table and warned others in the room, drawing their attention to it. Everyone immediately jumped up and tried to escape. Seconds later the wave struck, shattering the hotel windows and flooding the room, carrying away tables and chairs before it. With everyone struggling in the water, the dream abruptly faded away.

The following day he was amazed to see the havoc wrought by the tsunami everywhere on the television and in the news. As with the fire which devastated his friend's house, he was unable to make a connection beforehand with the disasters that had struck. It was a brief lifting of a corner of the veil, insufficient to be of help to anyone but sufficient to pinpoint specific incidents.

Extrasensory Viewing is often like this. There is sufficient detail to positively identify the coming about of an event or happening, but not enough detail to be able to benefit from it.

Of course, having these abilities to pick up impressions can have its lighter and highly useful side. Many of you, I am sure, have suddenly found yourselves thinking of someone you haven't seen for a long time, to find that you suddenly receive a letter or telephone call from that person,.

Many people also, during the course of an initial conversation when meeting a person for the first time, may receive a variety of impressions. Occasionally some are privileged in this situation by recognising a voice or person as someone who seems amazingly familiar to them, although they have never met before – in this lifetime! Often, when you 'take' to a person straightaway and it is mutual, you may well be renewing a centuries-old friendship. On the obverse side of the coin, we have all met people we have taken an instant dislike to for no apparent reason whatsoever – it is possible you have been enemies in previous lifetime situations. Of course, not everyone we meet as we go through life, and find we experience differing emotions on meeting them for the first time, would we have necessarily met in a former lifetime. Sometimes we just like people because we have a great deal in common, just as we feel an aversion to certain others which may be based at a deeper level of awareness, where we subconsciously know there is something devious hidden away in the individual's personality.

First impressions on meeting a person are of paramount importance. At times, all of us have met people for the first time who appear really genuine and easy to get along with, but during that initial encounter you may have experienced a feeling of mistrust which you may have instantly dismissed. *Don't dismiss it!* First impressions are extremely important; look back on the many situations where you have dismissed this initial mistrust – to your own cost later. Always go by your feelings, which stem from your Higher Self, and use them as a guide through life. I have never known anyone who has always listened to that Silent Voice within to do other than avoid in most cases the many pitfalls which lie in our way. Prayer also never fails, although we may perceive it as having done so. What we sometimes pray for could, without our knowledge at the time, be to our detriment. Only later may this become apparent.

It is becoming evident, and it is certainly Peter's and my own experience, that people who have been involved with UFOs seem to develop heightened extrasensory awareness. With evidence going back many centuries, as discussed earlier, of extraterrestrial visitors visiting and influencing inhabitants of this planet, are we the subjects of gradual development by these visitors from space? I like to think so, bearing in mind that we do, I feel, have certain extraterrestrial visitors from time to time who do not have our best interests at heart, but who are being kept in check by those who have.

Another perspective I like to consider is how great technical innovations seem to be introduced mysteriously and simultaneously in different countries. These often appear many years prior to the event in fictional form at a time when they are not technically achievable. Science fiction is a good example of this; space rockets and interplanetary probes were written up in this form some seventy or eighty years ago in the 1930s to become reality only in recent decades. The origin of computer technology is another interesting mystery: a quantum leap forward in technology came about, seemingly without prior development in this field, not long after the Second World War almost out of nowhere; were they introduced to our civilisation by some extraterrestrial source via so-called inspiration?

Correspondingly, the science fiction of today will become the science fact of tomorrow. I sometimes receive the impression that a space race or races in some way inspire certain concepts in writers which are written up as science fiction. In this way concepts are conceived, and over an extended period brought into reality as technology evolves. The many concepts conceived by Leonardo da Vinci, too well known to repeat here in detail, such as flight, the submarine etc., eventually have become realities as technology has evolved. Where we find ourselves now, at the beginning of the twenty-first century, we are able to look forward to possible concepts such as interplanetary travel and teleportation becoming reality ahead in time. Let us not forget that flight by man was deemed to be an impossible dream, going back to periods in our history now lost in the mists of time.

Meditation should play an important part in our everyday life. By this means an inner peace and tranquillity of mind can be arrived at, and many of life's problems solved in this way. To meditate, first find as quiet and comfortable a place as you are able, and experiment a little at first to mentally picture a scene that to you is the most restful. For some people, to picture themselves standing in a peaceful garden surrounded by flowers, or sitting beside a beautiful clear pool watching fish drifting lazily beneath pads of water lilies will enable them temporarily to relax in a mental world where thoughts and solutions to problems can often seemingly arrive from nowhere.

A friend of ours likes to picture himself seated in a Buddhist temple in the East, gazing at a large impassive gold Buddha surrounded by a mass of candles, while outside the temple the mountains stretch away into the infinite distance… Whatever situation you decide to visualise in your mind, crystallise the mental image in as full a range of colour as you are able to achieve. Mentally move about in this inner scene, and you will often find new details appear unexpectedly. During this period, which should range according to the time you have available from ten to thirty minutes (whatever you are comfortable with), you should feel completely relaxed. New thoughts and perspectives should come to you, often giving solutions to problems in a way you had previously not thought possible. Ideally, do this at your quietest time of day; many people find it suits them better very early in the morning before the chores of the day begin to intrude; others find it more beneficial to meditate at a quiet time in the evening. Over a period, I can guarantee that you will achieve a much greater peace of mind than you previously thought possible; many problems that you thought insurmountable will often resolve themselves in a surprising way.

As an example, let me cite Peter. In his early twenties, for some reason he suffered terribly from sciatica. Over a period of some months, this affliction caused him more and more pain, to the point where it was agony even to walk a short distance, and he was becoming extremely concerned that he would be crippled for life. In desperation, on the recommendation of a friend, he meditated for a few days, at times attempting to picture what had taken place within his body to cause this condition.

One day, without quite knowing why, he lay on his back, and wriggled around for some time trying to twist his body into different positions. After some experimentation, over a period of time it occurred to him to put all his weight onto one particular point in his back, then raise his knee, clasping it between his hands, then straightening his leg and body together. He felt a slight snapping sensation low down in his back, and the intense pain he had been suffering for months suddenly ceased. At first not quite believing this, he stood up and took a few steps. Amazingly, the sharp pain was now gone, although as might be expected the general area on that side of the lower back was quite sore. However, in a few days the soreness disappeared, and Peter was restored to full health again.

Over the next few months, once or twice the sciatica returned. Fortunately it was easy for Peter to repeat the procedure he had learned and developed, and the condition henceforth was easily remedied.

Some months later a friend of his developed the same condition. Peter showed his friend how he had cured himself of the problem, and was delighted to find that the series of exercises worked for his friend as well. Over the years, Peter has shown this exercise to many people with whom he has come into contact with this problem, and in virtually all cases the sciatica has disappeared. The only proviso is that the patient has to be sufficiently fit to carry out the exercise.

As so many people suffer from this problem, we have written out the exercise sequence for our readers. To the rest of you who do not suffer from this, I can only say that one day you may, and if you don't we are fairly sure that you will know someone who does, and it will also serve to illustrate what it is possible to achieve with some meditation.

Sciatica is caused by *inflammation of the sciatic nerve*, the longest nerve in the human body, generally due to pressure exerted upon it by a slipped disc or displaced ligament. To rectify the problem via these remedial exercises, the patient should begin by lying flat on a hard, level wooden surface covered by a thin carpet. Depending on which side the sciatica occurs, the points of the two bones in the lower back – known as the sacroiliac/pelvic bone – should be identified by the patient and one of them used as a pivotal point on the side where the pain occurs.

This then is the exercise: Place the weight of the body on this pivotal point on the side where the pain is; the upper half of the body should then be slowly raised from the floor while at the same time the leg on the same afflicted side is also slowly raised and slowly bent at the same time so that the knee may be clasped between the patient's hands. At this point the patient should pull the clasped knee as far as possible towards them and endeavour to touch the knee to the chin or as close as possible, aided of course by the bending of the top of the body from the floor as mentioned above.

The body is now curved in a bow-like attitude and kept upright in this position by the elbow and the whole weight of the body is centred and rolled around on the apex of the pivotal point – the sacroiliac or pelvic bone – in the back, while the patient continues to grasp the knee. This exercise should be continued for thirty seconds or more.

Then, with the patient's back in its bowed position off the floor and maintaining the body weight on the point of the bone (the elbow still maintaining the body in the upright position), the knee is slowly unclasped and the leg slowly straightened, keeping it as high as possible maintaining the arc of the back in the 'bow' position. The back remains in the 'bow' position as high as possible off the floor while the leg is lowered, slowly straightening it as much as possible during the lowering, while equally slowly at the same time the back is also lowered and straightened so that eventually the patient ends up by lying completely flat again in the same way that the exercise was begun, taking care to relax completely at this point.

During this time a light snapping sensation is often, but not always, felt just below the sacroiliac/pelvic bone as the knee is straightened and lowered. This is the sensation of the displaced ligament or slipped disc returning to its normal position. The patient should remain in this position for a few moments, making sure that he/she is completely mentally and physically relaxed. The exercise should then be repeated immediately afterwards in its entirety twice more, thus completing the treatment for the first day; then the entire cycle is repeated again on day two and day three. To prevent the problem from recurring, the patient should ensure that he/she always makes certain that the back is kept straight in a seated position, and also when retiring to sleep, lies as straight as possible where practical. Should the problem recur at a later date, the exercises should be repeated.

(Copyright, Peter Valentine)

Do of course check with your doctor beforehand that you are fit enough to undertake this series of exercises before you commence them.

In an earlier chapter, I mentioned how it is possible to mentally travel backwards and forwards in time, to experience for yourself incidents in previous lifetimes. Of course, as I have explained previously, there will be those among you who may not be able to achieve this if you have some form of mental block caused by a bad former life experience. However, for those interested, the method that Peter and I employ, which does not use hypnosis, is first of all to ensure that the session is conducted in quiet, relaxing surroundings, preferably in a room with a soft light, i.e. with no harsh glare to distract those holding the session. The person conducting the session should initially relax the subject by having a good conversation along the lines of establishing if he or she has an interest in a particular period in history or in a place or country that they may never have visited.

During this initial relaxing talk, the subject may unexpectedly volunteer that they have always had a fascination with flying or a particular period in history, for instance, but have never for some reason explored the possibility of becoming involved with those interests. Having discussed these interest areas for a while, while continuing to ensure that the person is completely relaxed and free from any external distraction, the subject should be asked to mentally visualise in their mind's eye looking down at their feet. Just after this has been said, with a snap of the fingers, you should ask the question, 'What do you see on your feet?' If you have not previously undergone this experience, you may often be surprised, for the subject in nearly all cases will reply by telling you that they are seeing anything from military-style boots to Roman sandals, wooden sabots or even tell you that they don't wear anything at all on their feet!

Ask them to really focus on their feet and tell you in fine detail the material of the footwear; if for instance there are brass eyelets on the boots, or other such features. Ask them to hold this image and then say, again with a snap of the fingers, 'What do you see above your shoes; what are you wearing, such as trousers, or a robe perhaps?'

Your subject will normally respond with something that you had perhaps not anticipated, such as a kilt or a dress – if a man starts with a description like this, remember that sometimes we change sexes in some lifetimes!

Continue – onwards and upwards! – asking them to complete the description of what they are wearing, how their hair is styled etc., and then ask the subject to mentally crystallise this picture. The next question should be: 'Where do you find yourself; what in the mental picture are you standing on – a tiled floor in a building, or are you standing in a field or wood somewhere?'

Gently ask your subject to describe in detail the type and pattern of the tiles, for example, or perhaps a garden in which he or she finds themselves. Ask them then to look around. Is there a house nearby, or are they standing near a river? Ask them also to describe how they feel. Do they feel happy, uncertain, fearful? Continue by asking why they feel this way. Ask them to mentally go to where they live, and if they have a family with which they are connected.

Continue by asking your subject to again mentally crystallise all these details, and then ask who they are in that time. Often, but not always, they will volunteer a name. Then you can ask them if they can tell you where they are, perhaps the name of a town, village or country for example. Keep a notepad handy and note any details that your subject is able to tell you. It will be found quite fascinating to ask them to, for example, describe the front door of somewhere where they once lived, and ask them to enter the house and describe its interior room by room.

It is important not to conduct these sessions for too long at a time, or to continue if the subjects find themselves in a distressing situation. If this occurs, return them to present time by saying, 'I want you now to leave this time and return to present time.' Any problems of this nature that may arise can then be discussed in normal conversations in the here and now and resolved. Allow your subject time to mentally readjust to their current surroundings – after all, he or she has just returned from a long journey!

If progress during the session doesn't seem to be fruitful, ask your subject to leave that period and go forwards or backwards in time. Continue by saying, 'I want you to go forward in time [or backwards, according to how you feel the situation is developing] by one hour. [Or a day, a week, a hundred years or more even.] What do you see now?' Your subject will then, depending on the time span, be viewing a different scenario and describe it accordingly. So much will depend on the situation; and as experience is acquired gradually it will come to you. Sometimes your subject will respond by saying, 'I am not getting anything' in terms of mental images. This can be because your subject may be at a time period between lives, and it does not seem normally possible to access these periods for some reason. You can then ask them to return to their last life or go forward to the next lifetime, say to the age of ten or twenty years, for example. Having stepped off the mental time machine, your subject will normally just continue to see mental images as before; if they need a nudge they can be asked again to look down at their feet in their immediate surroundings.

In the same way as I have just mentioned, when bringing any session of mental time travel of this nature to a conclusion, always gently say, 'I want you now to leave this time and return to present time,' allowing time for the person to readjust to their present surroundings.

Often the subjects will recover further knowledge from their experiences by a later process of simple reflection; however, it is often possible to trace details of the former lives you have noted down on your pad from existing current records relating to the period visited. The new knowledge acquired by the subject, if they didn't already know it before, will enable them to realise, if any doubt existed, that life always goes on!

In this summary or overview, let us now return to the subject of UFOs and their apparently increasing role in our general awareness in recent times. In my view it seems that a growing proportion of the inhabitants of this planet are undergoing psychic development in the various forms of extrasensory perception and awareness due to the influence of extraterrestrial visitors. Is it the purpose of a space race to gradually raise our awareness to new levels of spirituality – to enable us to overcome the basic instincts of power and greed of a minority which repeatedly crushes and oppresses the majority of peoples on this our planet, to their great cost? It seems logically possible to me that these visitors themselves, with their obviously incredibly advanced technology, could themselves be tools of a Creator at infinitely higher levels.

The majority of the great religions have their belief systems and writings based on a Master, who long ago came on Earth to teach and establish written principles which are still being taught today. Of these religions, an examination of most of them will reveal a common thread which, bearing in mind the problem that their concepts are set in an earlier, centuries-old time frame involving translation from ancient languages, reveal remarkable similarities. Stripping aside many of the embroideries, quite a few of which were added in to the original writings by unscrupulous priests in order to gain power in later times, the main underlying principles are *love one another* and *help others where help is sought*.

Of course, most of us are far from perfect, but the secret appears to me as with many others is simply to do your best where you can, and try to forgive others for the harm they may do. By just following these simple precepts, and also by using meditation and their own intuition as it develops, people will often find that seemingly by chance their lives will change for the better, giving them a far greater sense of purpose and fulfilment to life.

Prayer is also, as I have mentioned and demonstrated earlier, in my view fundamental to life; without it we run the risk of spiritual atrophy, as it keeps us in touch with our Creator; however we may personally view Him. When meditating on this, I was privileged to receive an impression of a beautiful flower. It came to me that the flower would never be able to flourish and grow without water; if we are to learn and grow, prayer and meditation represent to us what water is to the flower. For those who do not believe in prayer, I have heard it said among yachtsmen that there are no atheists in a storm!

Another thought that has occurred to me is that from the overall viewpoint of our varied lives in each successive lifetime, as we take up a different belief system (or not!) with each life, does it not make a mockery of holding rigid religious views from any perspective?

Changing themes once more, as mentioned earlier, I was fascinated to read of peoples' accounts of being abducted by certain space visitors. Information recovered under hypnosis revealed that many of them had been subjected to medical intervention, and even operated upon, inside the spacecraft itself. There are many incidents of this type on record, and anyone interested will find a wealth of information on this subject available today in book form and on the Internet. What particularly interested me however, is that there are quite a few accounts of young women on record who have mysteriously become pregnant having never associated with any man. Some of these, in an endeavour to resolve the mystery, have submitted to an investigation under hypnotic regression, to discover that they had been abducted in the same manner as outlined above in a spacecraft in some case histories, and impregnated by a form of artificial insemination; others by extraterrestrials themselves. In other cases, males have been abducted and induced to impregnate alien females. The resulting children – in some cases it has been possible to maintain contact for evaluation – often develop remarkable psychic abilities. For those interested in this subject, one of the best books I have read on this theme is *Abduction – Human Encounters With Aliens*, by John E Mack MD (Simon & Schuster, 1994).

I found these accounts highly intriguing, and they stayed in my mind for quite some time. Later I meditated upon them deeply, and the thought that came to me in the form of the silent voice that I have learned to revere and respect over a very long time span arrived in the following words. It relates to the story in the Bible of the Virgin Birth, and I write it down here in the exact form in which I received it: *Joseph/Mary. Mary impregnated by person aboard space vessel. Messages received by Joseph and Mary from space vessel occupants. Jesus mixture of space race and terrestrial planted on earth to promote spiritual awareness of Earth people – suffering pre-programmed to establish the growth of a spiritual belief system. The 'Star' was the space vessel.*

The Christian religion is the one in which I was raised, and because of my upbringing I had meditated on the origins of it and received this response. This is not in any way intended to promote the Christian religion as the 'one and only'; this is a purely personal experience which I feel I was extremely privileged to undergo. For me as an individual it throws light on a momentous event in our Earth's history, and I leave the reader to draw his or her own conclusions. In no way is this intended to compete with or detract from the works of the other great Masters' teachings such as those of Gautama Buddha or Muhammad's Koran for example.

Life is a continuous learning curve for all of us. Peter and I have always considered it to be an exciting adventure, often with its hardships and challenges, but we always view it as a temporary stay each time around to learn and grow.

Today, in the early part of a new century, where the chains of dogma in religion are gradually being freed by the keys of enlightenment, the one message that comes across to us via the concept of reincarnation more than any other is that we never die: *We Live Forever*!

If readers would like to share any experiences they may have had, they may care to contact us via the book website
www.we-live-forever.com
or write c/o the publishers.

Lightning Source UK Ltd.
Milton Keynes UK
UKOW02f0134260915

259314UK00002B/48/P